T0306167

The Global Property Investor's Toolkit

The Global Property Investor's Toolkit

A sourcebook for successful decision making

By Colin Barrow

CAPSTONE
be inspired!™

John Wiley & Sons, Ltd

Copyright © 2008 by Colin Barrow

First published in 2008 by Capstone Publishing Ltd. (a Wiley Company)
The Atrium, Southern Gate, Chichester, PO19 8SQ, UK.
www.wileyeurope.com

Email (for orders and customer service enquires): cs-books@wiley.co.uk

The right of Colin Barrow to be identified as the author of this book has been asserted in accordance with the Copyright, Designs and Patents Act 1988

All Rights Reserved. No part of this publication may be reproduced, stored in a retrieval system or transmitted in any form or by any means, electronic, mechanical, photocopying, recording, scanning or otherwise, except under the terms of the Copyright, Designs and Patents Act 1988 or under the terms of a licence issued by the Copyright Licensing Agency Ltd, 90 Tottenham Court Road, London W1T 4LP, UK, without the permission in writing of the Publisher. Requests to the Publisher should be addressed to the Permissions Department, John Wiley & Sons Ltd, The Atrium, Southern Gate, Chichester, West Sussex PO19 8SQ, England, or emailed to permreq@wiley.co.uk, or faxed to (+44) 1243 770571.

Designations used by companies to distinguish their products are often claimed as trademarks. All brand names and product names used in this book are trade names, service marks, trademarks or registered trademarks of their respective owners. The Publisher is not associated with any product or vendor mentioned in this book.

This publication is designed to provide accurate and authoritative information in regard to the subject matter covered. It is sold on the understanding that the Publisher is not engaged in rendering professional services. If professional advice or other expert assistance is required, the services of a competent professional should be sought.

Other Wiley Editorial Offices

John Wiley & Sons Inc., 111 River Street, Hoboken, NJ 07030, USA
Jossey-Bass, 989 Market Street, San Francisco, CA 94103-1741, USA
Wiley-VCH Verlag GmbH, Boschstr. 12, D-69469 Weinheim, Germany
John Wiley & Sons Australia Ltd, 42 McDougall Street, Milton, Queensland 4064, Australia
John Wiley & Sons (Asia) Pte Ltd, 2 Clementi Loop #02-01, Jin Xing Distripark, Singapore 129809
John Wiley & Sons Canada Ltd, 6045 Freemont Blvd. Mississauga, Ontario, L5R 4J3

Wiley also publishes its books in a variety of electronic formats. Some content that appears in print may not be available in electronic books.

A catalogue record for this book is available from the British Library and the Library of Congress.
p. cm.
Includes index.
ISBN 978-1-84112-763-7 (pbk. : alk. paper)
1. Real estate investment. 2. Real property–Foreign ownership. I. Title.
HD1382.5.B377 2008
332.63'24–dc22 2007050366

ISBN 13: 978-1-84112-763-7

Typeset in 11/15.5 Berkeley by Thomson Digital, India

Substantial discounts on bulk quantities of Capstone Books are available to corporations, professional associations and other organizations. For details telephone John Wiley & Sons on (+44) 1243-770441, fax (+44) 1243 770571 or email corporatedevelopment@ wiley.co.uk

Contents

Introduction

More than 2 million British citizens now either own or are actively looking for homes abroad: a number that is expected to rise to more than 3 million within 5 years, according to figures from Saga. By 2025, according to a study published recently by Grant Thornton, the accountants, over 2 million British homeowners – around a tenth of the total homeowners in the country, could own a property overseas. Mintel, the respected research company, conducted a study found that over 800,000 British people now own a home abroad, and double that number would like to buy one. The viewing figures for TV programmes such as 'No Going Back' would support the belief that the potential overseas property buyer population is substantially higher than that. If you add the populations of the other rich overseas property buyers – the Dutch, the Germans, the Irish, the Americans and, to a lesser extent, the French and the Italians (who are more inclined to buy additional property in their own country) – it is not too difficult to believe the word-of-mouth statistic that over 15 million people are looking for homes overseas.

Why buy property overseas?

The reasons are myriad: some consider the possibility of buying a second home either as a place to which to retire or as an investment (either by way of a 'buy-to-let' or in the anticipation of capital gain).

The investment imperative for buying international property, particularly in less developed parts of the globe, is coming from factors such as the diminishing value of conventional pensions and annuities, increasing life expectancy and the need to diversify property investments, all of which are growing in importance and apply to a greater or lesser extent to all the countries whose citizens are casting their eyes across continents and oceans searching out new areas of property value.

Who should read this book?

Here are a few observations culled from various studies about people buying properties abroad that have a ring of truth about them. If you identify with any of these descriptions, then this is a subject you might want to explore with some zeal.

- **Retirees:** around one in five people plans to retire abroad, citing climate and cost of living as the main reasons for doing so.
- **First-time buyers:** close to half of 18- to 29-year-olds are planning to buy a property abroad, stating that that's the only way they can see of ever getting on the property ladder.
- **'Fly-to-let':** the average overseas property costs around £100,000 (that figure includes more costly countries such as France, Spain and the United States), while the average British property costs around £200,000. With the average rental yields abroad being nearly double those in the United Kingdom, 'jet-to-let', the international equivalent of 'buy-to-let', produces the same income in pounds for half the outlay.
- **Low-income entrants:** theoretically, about a million people earn enough money comfortably to afford a home in Spain, Portugal or France. About 6 million people can afford to buy further afield, in areas such as Eastern Europe, Thailand, Cape Verde, Brazil and New Zealand.
- **Investors:** according to a Grant Thornton study, the value of foreign homes owned by British citizens has surged to £71 billion, up from £29 billion 8 years earlier. Adding in the owners from other counties, this could well be a £1,000 billion marketplace. As such, the competitive pressures must inevitably increase, requiring higher

standards of information from everyone hoping to achieve superior returns on their investment.

About this book

Once upon a time, as the story goes, almost everyone buying a house abroad went to Spain or France and there was little for the prospective house buyer to decide about. 'Foodies' went to France and 'sun worshippers' went to Spain, usually electing for regions in which they had experienced satisfactory holidays. But now there are not only more choices as to destination but more factors to consider. In the first instance, *The Economist*, among other sources, considers Spain to be about 60% overvalued. The smart money is now heading for more exotic locations such as Thailand, China, New Zealand, Croatia, Bulgaria and Estonia, where not only is the amount of money needed to buy a house often a fraction of that in the mainstream markets but there is a decent prospect of good increases in values as these 'emerging' markets mature.

The factors that a potential buyer has to consider in selecting which of the 50 or so countries now being 'touted' by real estate brokers and developers is the one for them are what form the backbone of this book. These factors include:

- Tax regime for income and capital gains as well inheritance and wealth tax.
- Healthcare services, both for emergencies and for long-term care.
- The extent to which a range of long-term air routes to the country exists and can be sustained.
- The rate at which inward investment and tourism are growing: both vital factors that underpin property rental prospects and so influence valuations.
- Economic growth, inflation, the availability of mortgage finance and growth in local salaries: factors which influence the 'affordability' of property to the population at large. Unless the locals can

afford property in the market, the potential pool for onward sale or letting will be limited to other international buyers, which is typically less than 3% of any market.

- House-building rates, historic property price inflation, planning and property buying regulations, restrictions on foreign ownership, the potential for land title disputes and tenancy law in terms of security of tenure and rent controls.
- Rate of rise of cost of living, fuel, food, water, local property taxes and so forth.

Buyers either ignore this vital information, concentrating instead on climate and current affordability (that buyers 'leave their brains at the airport' is a frequent comment made by brokers); or they get less than impartial information from brokers' websites and property exhibitions where they are fed 'knowledge' from regurgitated favourable newspaper articles, themselves often little more than 'stories' circulated by the brokers themselves.

Books also play a valuable role by informing readers, but even the best of these have an important weakness. They only cover a few dozen of the hundred countries that have property markets worthy of at least some consideration as a home for investors' money

The key difference with this book is embedded in the sub-title 'A Sourcebook for Successful Decision Making'. The fundamental sources of information required to make informed decisions about property investment have been identified after extensive research into international property markets; first-hand experience of building, buying and selling properties in overseas markets; and interviews and discussions with over 200 successful property investors, brokers, lawyers and other property professionals. From these studies the key sources of all the relevant data for all the facts required to evaluate any and every property market in the world have been identified. That data is usually available online (almost invariably free) and always comprises the latest available facts.

Often a single website will suffice. For example, Climate Zone (www.climate-zone.com) gives the weather history for every country and major city in every country in the world, with detail such as average hours of daily sunshine over the past decade, maximum and minimum temperatures, snowfall and rainfall. (Climate is a vital property investment topic, but not just because it could affect an owner's enjoyment. The period of sunshine or snowfall that occurs each year can profoundly affect rental yields.) The World Wide Tax Guide (www.worldwide-tax.com) covers tax methods, income tax, capital gains tax and property taxes in every country. The CIA World Fact Book (www.cia.gov/cia/publications/factbook/index.html) gives data on inflation, economic growth, political system and environmental issues.

When it comes to other subjects, sometimes information is only available on a continent-by-continent basis. In rather fewer cases, such as, say, finding an accredited estate agent, a search needs to start with the International Consortium of Real Estate Associations (www.worldproperties.com/CountryHome.aspx) where you can find the national real estate associations or regional associations covering most major countries. From there you can link to, say, the Hellenic Association of Realtors (www.sek.gr) on which site you will find both a directory of members and the basics of buying property in that country.

How the book is structured

The book has four parts, each of which drills down deeper into the factors governing choice. Part 1 starts by giving the overview for property as an investment and the factors that affect global property cycles and bubbles. Part 2 moves on to examine country-specific factors such as visa restrictions; healthcare; education; economic growth; the quality of life; tax; property law; and the prospects for capital appreciation and income generation. It also covers business-related taxes, including information on what is required to set up in business; what procedures need to be gone through; how complicated the process is; how long it will take; and what costs are involved. This information will be valuable for those considering setting up in any type of business, including property rental. By the end of Part 2 the reader should be able to narrow down their choice of overseas countries worthy of consideration, both by their own criteria and by objective investment yardsticks.

In Part 3 the tools required for rigorous investigation of individual countries are introduced. This includes methods for researching a particular town or area within a country; examining internal transport infrastructure; the climate month by month, covering hours of sunshine and rain and also snowfall (if appropriate); and information on the leisure, cultural and tourism appeal of the country. Here you will also see how to find a bonded estate agent who won't run off with your deposit; an impartial local surveyor to advise on structure and local planning issues; and a lawyer who speaks your language and is on your side.

Part 4 looks at issues related to getting settled into a country. These include language issues; moving effects; and, most importantly, all the issues that relate to fitting out and renting, in both the long and the short term.

How the chapters are structured

Each chapter includes the following elements:

- A description of the **subject area**: for example, the chapter on tax identifies and explains the key taxes to look out for (income tax, capital gains tax, 'stamp duty', inheritance tax and wealth tax). Each one is described alongside the effect that they will have on property-related decisions. For example, if tax reduction, or even elimination, is a primary goal, you will need to consider how to go about changing your tax residence; the implications of that decision; what double taxation agreements apply; what will happen if you change your mind and decide to return to your home country; and how to find a reliable tax adviser.

- At the end of each chapter section, the sources of the key data are provided together with the simplest way of accessing the data. In some cases this will be a brief description of website menus, showing how to find the appropriate locations. Where the web address is relatively straightforward, a direct link is given.
- When it comes to more overarching topics, such as evaluating economies or the legal environment, for example, the subject is broken down into its constituent elements, each is examined and key sources of information are explained and listed.

Research does pay off

The Duke of Wellington, one of the most successful overseas campaigners, believed strongly in the value of research. He called the subject 'the art of knowing what is on the other side of the hill'. He invested in a substantial core of intelligence gatherers who roamed the area around where he planned a battle and kept him fully informed as to what was happening there. There is considerable anecdotal evidence that those buying property overseas could benefit greatly from taking a similar approach to gathering current data.

Taking just the most mundane of matters – currency: industry experts reckon that over 80% of those buying currency make poor decisions. On average they make just over 5% on their transactions, compared with what they could have achieved by taking no additional risks whatsoever. Around 1 in 10 buyers loses out by an amount in excess of 10%.

There are dozens of other areas where superior and timely knowledge pays off. This book describes exactly how to acquire that. Budget airlines come and go; tax rates go up and down; property ownership regulations change; countries' corruption levels, economic performance and tourist appeal all fluctuate, often dramatically. To give two recent examples: Bulgaria halved its tax rate to just 10% virtually overnight on succession to the EU in 2007. This decision will have a significant impact on the inward investment climate and in due course on rental yields on new-build properties in the capital, Sofia. There is also the uncertain outcome of a court case rumbling through the judicial systems of Cyprus, the EU and the UK concerning a house built by a British couple in 2002, on land owned by a Greek Cypriot now living in the south, prior to the 1974 partitioning of the island. Locals estimate that property values in Northern Cyprus will be affected positively – by as much as 20% – on the favourable outcome of this single court case. An unfavourable outcome may send prices into freefall. Neither of these events attracted much attention in the international press, but they and other facts relevant to sound decision-making are easy to find, as the contents of this book explain.

PART 1

The World Property Market – A Beginner's Guide

There is no shortage of 'experts' when it comes to investing in property. Nearly everyone, everywhere, who bought property a decade ago is sitting on a unprecedented pile of 'dough'. Nominally, that is, of course, because property profit is notional until we cash in our chips. This 'success' has gone to our heads, while few of us did anything very clever to achieve this paper wealth. For the most part, we just rode the wave that swept us further and further up the profit curve. While not many people remember the last property collapse, though 2007–8 may refresh some memories many more are still nursing losses from the stock market collapse that followed the 'Dot Com' bubble burst. The 'expert' investors who rode that wave up have discovered two important facts: what goes up a long way fast can come down just as dramatically; and that they had either forgotten or never really knew the fundamentals that underpin long-term share prices.

Now, there are no absolute guarantees with any investment, except that your chances of success are improved exponentially if you understand something of the forces at work in the market – in this case, the property market. If you really are an expert and your property investments have outperformed the general trend, then skip this chapter. If not, read on.

Property – the backbone of wealth creation

Property has been a worthwhile source of wealth for generations. More private individuals have become millionaires in this way than by any other route to wealth. Property has the added attraction that financial institutions will actually back your investment as a matter of course, rather than having to be persuaded as is necessary in order to attract funds for other wealth-creation activities. With that borrowed money, through the miracle of 'gearing', it is possible to acquire an asset 10 or even 20 times the value of the ready cash you have to hand. The property investor can then enjoy the growth in value of the whole asset for just a fractional downpayment. Research shows that most people who achieve a comfortable retirement have a large element of property, both in their home country and overseas, in their portfolio. But for most of these property millionaires their home country was the boundary of their domain. Indeed, for some, the Duke of Westminster perhaps being a prime example, their riches were the happy result of owning a few dozen acres of land in an area that became immensely desirable for reasons that had little to do with their own efforts; though it must be said that they have proved adept at enhancing the value of what serendipity provided.

The world *is* enough

The spur to the next wave of property millionaires is undoubtedly the opening up of vast new tracts of the world to the adventurous investor as brought about by the extension of capitalism, or at the very least capitalist-driven economic thinking, and its corresponding policies. Countries that until recently placed restrictions on their own citizens owning private assets (China, Vietnam and Russia, to name but a few) are now opening up their markets so that 'even' foreigners are welcomed both to own property and stay for extended periods, or indeed take up permanent residence should they so wish. For the countries of the former Eastern Europe, removing restrictions on the ownership of property and creating 'functioning market economies' has been part of the price for gaining EU membership. For countries such as Turkey, Ukraine and Albania, the mere prospect, however distant, of EU membership has knocked down barriers that hitherto restricted property ownership. For Vietnam, membership of the World Trade Organization was the prize; for Russia, it was membership of the G8; for China, the Olympic Games; and for Thailand, the need for funds to fuel its tourism-dependent economy.

In a nutshell, the globalisation of financial instruments such as mortgage finance, foreign exchange and international banks, alongside cheap air fares and the richness and 'reach' in communications brought about by the Internet have created for the first time in history a world market in properties open to all. Of course, there have always been individuals and companies who owned property assets overseas, but this has until now been the domain of a very small minority of relatively sophisticated buyers. Spain, France and Portugal for the British and, to a lesser extent, the Germans; Mexico for the Americans; and the Black Sea Coast for the Russians were the first signs that a world market in private property assets was beginning to emerge.

As a consequence, for the first time ever, it is now possible for citizens of almost any country to buy property in another. Not only can they buy property, but that property is very likely to be available at prices a fraction of those currently available in their home market. Those who until now have found either getting a foot on the property ladder or building a property portfolio near impossible will now find an escalator in front of them.

CHAPTER 1

Why Buy More Property?

In this chapter:

- Understanding why property is such an attractive investment proposition.
- Seeing how demographic changes are forcing the pace of change.
- Working out how much you can ratchet up your cash.
- Monitoring enthusiasm for the market.

If you are reading this book then you probably already own a property and you may even already own a second one, either as a holiday home or as a 'buy-to-let' investment. There is nothing new in second home ownership. Wealthy Romans took up residence in spacious country villas on the borders of Lake Como or the River Tiber; in the 17th and 18th centuries wealthy Amsterdam merchants huddled in the city in winter time but spent the summers in their second homes on the border of the River Vecht or in the countryside of the Gooi area. For Swedes, the second home tradition dates back to the 1930s and more than one-fifth of the population owns a second home. What is new is the rapid growth in second home ownership combined with an appetite to buy properties further from the home shores.

Around three-quarters of a million British citizens own a second home in the UK or abroad: a number that has doubled in a decade and looks set to double again over a similar future period. Three million French citizens own holiday or investment properties, putting British ownership statistics in the shade According to the National

Association of Realtors (NAR), Americans bought a record 2.82 million second homes in 2004, and by 2006/7 nearly 10 million US citizens owned another property. Until recently, buyers from the North-East of America looked for second homes in the South, while San Franciscans retreated to Lake Tahoe and Bostonians headed out of town to Cape Cod. Now they are increasingly buying in neighbouring countries such as Mexico and Brazil, and further afield in more exotic locations such as Thailand and Europe.

If you bought your property 3 or more years ago, there is every chance that you are already sitting on a sizeable profit. That in itself might be enough of a spur to look carefully at buying to one or two more. But not only is property a good investment; potentially, it is the best investment, pound for pound, that you could make. If you add in the 'fun factor', the chance to see pastures new and the fact that more people become millionaires in this way than any other, there is every reason to look carefully at adding more properties to your portfolio.

Keeping track of world interest in property

You can see to what extent other people share your excitement in buying a property overseas at any particular point by checking out these websites. Too much exuberance may be a warning sign that a bubble is building up. That may not in itself be a reason not to buy property; rather, a signal to be more careful about where and what to buy.

Office for National Statistics (ONS)

(www.statistics.gov.uk/socialtrends36/)

Social Trends, published annually by the ONS, draws together social and economic data from a wide range of government departments and other organisations to provide a comprehensive snapshot of British society today, and how it has been changing. You can download the full report or select 'Housing' where you can find statistics on the numbers of people buying overseas properties.

Survey of English Housing (SEH) carried out by Communities and Local Government (www.communities.gov.guk)

Launched in April 1993, SEH provides a wide range of information on the housing circumstances of households in England, including detailed information on those households with a second home and the numbers of people either owning or planning to buy a property overseas. The survey now comes under the umbrella of a new government department: the Department of Communities and Local Government was created on 5 May 2006. Type 'Survey of English Housging' into the search pane in the top right of the screen to access the latest data.

The Global Market Information Database (GMID) (www.euromonitor.com/GMID.aspx) **(fee payable)**

GMID, published by Euromonitor, provides key business intelligence on countries, companies, markets and consumers. Subscriptions start from £500 a year, but it is freely available for use in business libraries around the world. It includes: country-specific statistics on demographic, economic and marketing data for 205 countries from 1977 to date; market data (6-year historic market-size data for more than 330 consumer products in 52 countries); as well as 5-year forecasts; and lifestyle indicators – information and models of lifestyle indicators such as eating and drinking habits and of particular benefit data on home ownership trends and crime patterns for 71 countries worldwide. In effect, it draws on over 4,500 market reports for consumer, industrial and service sectors around the world.

Second Homes in Germany and the Netherlands (http://igitur-archive.library.uu.nl/geo/2006-0801-205705/Dijst _ 05 _ SecondhomesinGermanyandtheNetherlands.pdf)

This paper is based on two empirical studies carried out in the Netherlands and in Germany, examining why the scale of second home ownership increased enormously in the last decades and focusing on two issues that arise from this trend: first, the impact of the residential environment of the primary dwelling on second home ownership; and, second, the impact of second homes on travel. This link is to a pdf download of a thought-provoking article by Martin Dijst, Martin Lanzendorf, Angela Barendregt and Leo Smit of the Urban and Regional Research Centre Utrecht (URU), Faculty of Geosciences, Utrecht University.

Mortgage Daily News (www.mortgagenewsdaily.com/10252006_Homebuying_Second_Homes.asp)

This is a publication by Brown House Media, Inc, with a broad range of articles and research studies on patterns of second home ownership. This link is to a review of a longitudinal research by the US Census Bureau Projections, entitled the Health and Retirement Study (HRS). This showed that slightly more than half of older American second home owners spend 2 weeks or less in their second homes and two-thirds spend fewer than 4 weeks. This, the study claims, perhaps indicates that most of these second homes are held for investment rather than recreation. Only 12.9% plan to make their second home their main residence in the future. The study is longitudinal, so the authors were able to conclude that, of those second home owners identified in the study in 1998, 45% owned only one home by 2004; to extrapolate from that, the typical second home belonging to older households is owned for 15 years before being sold. For the typical second home owner, equity in that home represented 13% of the household wealth.

Increased life expectancy and the demise of guaranteed pensions

The world is reeling from an astounding discovery: 'We're all living longer'. This in turn means that we have to make a better and different financial provision in order to accommodate increased longevity, which makes it all the more important that we include and extend the role of property in our investment portfolio.

The average American citizen, just as those from Britain, France and Germany alive today, can expect to live 10 years longer than their less fortunate compatriots born 50 years ago. The really astonishing statistic is that half that gain in life expectancy came about in the past couple of decades and was 'discovered' not by the medical profession or by the drug companies who could reasonably have expected to bask in a glow of favourable publicity. Rather, it was one of the dullest professions – the actuaries – who first shed light on the growth in longevity.

Actuaries: life expectancy's bean counters

One of an actuary's responsibilities is to advise employers on how much money has to be set aside to ensure that pension liabilities can be honoured. Today, consultants at the Mortality Investigations Bureau, a working party at the UK's Worshipful Company of Actuaries, say that the average assumption for a man retiring at 60 should be that he will live until 87. In 1950, the expectation was that those retiring at 65 would be dead before their 66th birthday.

Changes in life expectancy are not confined to the UK, or even to wealthier countries: Global life expectancy at birth in 2006 was 65, and is expected to keep on rising, to reach 75 by 2050. In the more developed countries, the projected increase is from 76 today to 82 by mid-century. In the less developed countries that are nevertheless making progress, life expectancy is projected to rise to be closer to that of developed countries, from just under 66 today to 76 by mid-century.

The news is not universally good. Overall figures on life expectancy in developed countries conceal some remarkable regional differences: life expectancy in Eastern Europe since the late 1980s, particularly in the Russian Federation and the Ukraine, has actually dropped and in 2006 was 2 to 4 years lower, at 66.6 years, than it was in 1955. That fact has had some dramatic effects on local property markets as depopulation depresses demand and prices.

The impact of this increase in longevity is having a profound impact on strategies for pension provision. Few can rely on their employers to provide an adequate pension and many are closing down final salary schemes, curtailing benefits and requiring increased contributions. In 2006/7 the FTSE 100 companies – those organisations who, next to governments, are most likely to have the resources to pay pensions – are underfunded to the tune of £60 billion. The state provision of pensions, while looking generous in some countries, is also probably unsustainable. Only in Italy and the Netherlands are state pensions and benefits three-quarters or more of average earnings. In the UK, the USA and most less-developed countries, including Mexico, pensioners can expect to have their income slashed to little more than a third when they retire.

Most of us will have to invest our way to a satisfactory retirement, and property has an important part to play in that process.

Tracking life expectancy

You can check out life expectancy changes and so establish just how long you will need to finance your retirement. You can also monitor changes by country. Increases in life expectancy are usually the end result of better living conditions and improved healthcare provisions, which in themselves also make a country potentially more attractive to buy into. Look out for countries where life expectancy is declining (Zimbabwe's life expectancy has halved to around 35 years in little over a decade); this could signal serious dangers for local property markets.

More ways to convince yourself to buy property

Government Actuaries Department (GAD) (www.gad.gov.uk)
GAD provides advice that affects the pension entitlements of over 3 million public-sector workers in the UK and, in addition, advises the governments of many other countries on similar topics. It is not just governments that rely on their data; the pensions advisers in private

companies often use this service as a default source of information upon which to base their own calculations. Select 'Life tables' from 'Demography'. There you will be able to extract an Excel spreadsheet and a chart showing the life expectancy for males and females over the period from 1981 to 2051. The statistics show that life expectancy increased by an average of around 5 years for the period to 2006 and is expected to increase by 10 years by 2051.

United Nations Population Fund (UNFPA) (`www.unfpa.org`)

UNFPA is an international development agency that promotes the right of everyone to enjoy a life of health and equal opportunity. Their research studies help countries in using population data for policies and programmes to reduce poverty. Their latest study 'The State of World Population' can be down loaded in PDF form by selecting the icon with that heading from the top of the home page. The data makes for startling reading. From the report you can find the life expectancy statistics for all countries individually and by continent and state of development.

Organisation for Economic Co-operation and Development (OECD) (`www.oecd.org`)

The OECD was founded in 1961 as the successor to the Marshall Plan-inspired Organisation for European Economic Co-operation (OEEC). Today, it has moved beyond a focus on its own 30 member countries and is setting its analytical sights on a further 70 or so countries, between them accounting for over 90% of the world's market economies. The Organisation is, for example, putting the benefit of its accumulated experience to the service of emerging market economies, particularly in the countries making their transition from centrally planned to capitalist systems. It is also working increasingly with dynamic economies in Asia and Latin America.

Select 'Browse by topic' from the left-hand vertical menu, followed by 'Aging society' from the central menu. Once in that area, click on 'Pension systems' in the left-hand vertical menu box. From here, you can search statistics, publications and documents and information by country.

Property as an investment

A sound investment should meet four criteria. It should:

- have the capacity for being profitable
- be reasonably secure
- have a ready re-sale market
- produce cash flow during its life.

Capacity for being profitable

This doesn't mean that the investment has to be profitable – anything to do with making money involves a risk that events won't pan out as expected – just that it could be. Perhaps the most vivid example of this is what happens to your money when you buy a new car. The day it leaves the showroom, its value drop by up to 20% and within a year it could be worth as little as half its cost. That fact doesn't seem to deter nearly 2.5 million people a year from buying new cars in the UK.

Reasonably secure

In other words, money should be put into assets that generate value for customers and markets. Pyramid sales schemes are a good example of 'investments' that fail this test, as most of the money potentially to be made comes from recruiting more salespeople rather than selling any real product.

Ready re-sale market

You need to be able to get out of as well as get into investments, as you may need your money for some other purpose or have spotted an even better investment.

Produce cash flow during its life

Wine, art and jewellery don't meet the last of my tests, but that's not to say that you shouldn't buy them, just as it isn't 'wrong' to buy a new car, if that is what you want. Stocks and shares, bonds (loans to companies and governments), bank deposits and property meet all these criteria.

Property around the developed world has appreciated in value by an average of 85% in the 8 years to 2007, according to *The Economist* magazine's Global House Price Index. Since records began in 1973, UK property prices have risen 16-fold while returning an average of around 6% in rent to landlords. (See Part 2 on evaluating economies for more on tracking property prices.) Over 2.2 million people buy a property each year in the UK, taking 10 weeks on average to find a property and have an offer accepted. It takes a further 20 weeks to complete the legal processes, according to statistics from the Office of the Deputy Prime Minister (www.odpm.gov.uk).

> So, from this information you can see that, by any standards, property looks like a sound investment proposition and one that Senior People Enjoying Affluent Retirements (so-called 'SPEARS') have latched onto. According to research carried out by Brewin Dolphin Securities (www.brewindolphin.co.uk), the largest independent private client portfolio manager and stockbroker in the UK, property at home and abroad is where they keep the bulk of their investments (over £80 billion is held in property, compared with just £70 billion in shares, bonds and unit trusts) and so they can fund that affluent retirement.

Understanding the gearing effect

Gears ratchet a small wheel to a larger one to make something (a car, usually) go faster. The larger the relative difference between the size of the wheels, the faster the speed. Financial gearing used to buy assets such as property has much the same effect. In this case the small wheel is analogous to your cash and the large wheel to any money you borrow. The more you borrow, the faster you can make your money work.

If you were a high-flying sales executive who had pocketed a £20,000 bonus in 2004 and put it in the stock market across a spread of shares to track the market average, you would have made a whopping 74.5% return over the 3 years to 2005. Realising your investment would see you with a cash pile of £34,900.

According to the Nationwide Building Society, over the same period, had our executive invested in property he would have made just 36.92%. Looks like the stock market would have been a better investment, at least over that period. In fact, if you go back as far as 1973, stock market returns averaged 11% while property delivered 9%. No contest: stocks and shares deliver better returns.True: if you had picked Wales or Latvia to buy your property in, you could have made a 56% return, but then you might have gone for London where prices have risen by just 18% over that period.

But before you toss this book aside and back out of the property market, let's see how the deals work out in reality. In 2004 there were no properties on the market for £20,000 and the average house price was around £180,000. What would have happened had we bought a bargain property costing £150,000, using the £20,000 as a deposit and getting a loan or mortgage for the balance of £130,000? Incidentally, property is the only type of investment that you can borrow to buy without offering any other collateral. According to the Nationwide records, our house costing £150,000 in 2004 would be worth £205,380 in 2007. We would have paid out £7,800 a year in interest at 6% to whoever lent you the £130,000: a total of £23,400. So, you are a net £181,984 (£205,380 minus £23,400) better off than back in 2004. You are also more than 5 times better off in buying a property (£181,984 divided by £34,900) than you would have been had you gone into the stock market.

The magic that has turned a seemingly lower total return over 3 years (properties at 36.92% versus the stockmarkets at 74.5%) into a much higher return of 108.77 % per year is known as 'gearing'. When you buy a property using borrowed money, you enjoy all the increase in value but only have to put a fraction of the cost down at the outset. Simply put, over this period the property investor has got a return of 36.92% on money thatcost only 6% (the average mortgage rate over the 3 years). This works in much the same way as the gears on a car. Changing up gears enables you to go faster for any given amount of power.

Checking out gearing and profit returns

The following websites will explain the thinking behind financial gearing and provide tools to measure the profit returns you can expect for various levels of personal investment compared with amounts borrowed.

1278 Software Systems (`www.1728.com/compint.htm`)

On this site you will find a range of calculators. This link is to the compound interest calculators where you can work out the return for any other property value, time period or interest rate.

Business Balls (`www.businessballs.com/finance.htm`)

Businessballs (launched as Businessballs.com at the end of 1999) is a free, slightly quirky learning and development resource for people and organisations: on it, you will find a fuller explanation of financial gearing.

Standard Chartered (`www.standardchartered.com.sg/cb/pb/financialtools.html`)

Standard Chartered first opened for business in Singapore in 1859 and today operates the largest branch network (20) among international banks in the Republic. This link is to a number of financial calculators including the Standard Chartered Gearing Calculator that provides a framework to measure how much financial risk and exposure your current, as well as future, borrowings are against your current assets and reserves.

FIDO (www.asic.gov.au/fido/fido.nsf/byheadline/Reverse+mortgage+calculator?openDocument)

This calculator lets you test how your choices about borrowing money to finance an investment in property will affect the returns you can expect to make over the longer term. The key word here is 'expect': the calculator cannot predict how your personal situation will actually work out – it will just show you what will happen if your assumptions pan out. But by trying out a range of assumptions, you can spot danger points. For example if your investment decision only delivers the profit returns you want if the interest rate on borrowings doesn't exceed 6%, then you have to assess what the chances are of that event occurring are.

The FIDO reverse mortgage calculator on this website shows the effect of decisions you may make about:

- how much you borrow
- whether you take an initial lump sum, or arrange regular income payments or a combination of both
- how long you borrow for
- interest rates and various fees.

It also shows how your home equity may be affected by future changes in the value of your home. You can:

- select a low, medium or high rate of increase in value (these rates are based on advice from actuaries), or
- choose your own rate.

Of course, you must consider your own circumstances carefully when using this calculator, and you may need expert advice.

CHAPTER 2

Why Buy Abroad?

In this chapter:

- Recognising the value in overseas property markets.
- Appreciating the attractions of diversifying your investments.
- Tracking the dangers in foreign markets.

The two most compelling arguments are diversification and reward. Many foreign markets are without a doubt more risky than investing in property in the UK market or your home country. I would go further and say that they are definitely not 'widows' and orphans' investments'. (Financial advisers' phrase to describe extremely safe investments: ones that they would be happy to recommend to someone totally dependent on their performance).

But while risk is not in itself a guarantor of profits, it is one of the conditions that help create the climate in which profits can be made. You will find no one prepared to take your bet on a horse race once the race is started. Beforehand, what the going conditions are; whether all the horses will show up; how well trained the horses are; and who will the jockey be are all factors that contribute to uncertainty and hence risk. It is only when all these risks are in play that you can get good odds and so, if your horse wins, make a good profit.

Having all your eggs in one basket is never a good idea. Even if you decide, after reading this book, to keep your property investments all in your home country, you will be safer if you spread your bets by having property in different parts of the UK and perhaps even different types of property such as a shop, office or warehouse. Those are all governed by different factors to those driving residential property, so while one may be having a tough time, another can be in good shape.

Higher potential rewards

According to *The Economist* magazine's Global House Price Index, the UK property market has given the world a good run for its money. Over the decade to 2007, it stacked up 178% gain, more than all bar 3 of the 20 countries in the index and much better than the average of 85% clocked up by the whole of the market it studied.

Those facts sound like a compelling reason for staying at home, until you look a little more closely at the figures. If you take the latest year's figures, growth in property prices in the UK are the fifth slowest in the developed world and the average growth rate is 4 times that achieved by UK properties. In fact, the fastest-growing markets have been those overseas markets into which the Brits have been buying strongly.

Now, as all good investments have on their labels: 'the past is not always a guide to future performance'. It does seem highly unlikely that mature property markets such as the UK, France and Spain, that have already been researched and bought into by foreigners for decades, can deliver the growth in value that the hidden gems on offer in under-explored regions have to offer. Property looks like a case where history is likely to be 'bunkum'.

You can track house price movements abroad and for comparison purposes in the UK at the following websites. They are mostly concerned with UK property prices and are illustrative of the dynamics in the market. See also 'Property performance and appraisal: narrowing down your choice of country', where a more extended range of sources for monitoring overseas house prices is given and you can find further information on sources of information on overseas property price historic trends.

Websites for tracking property price movements

Research Worldwide (www.researchworldwide.com)

This is a colossal site, providing a consolidation of real estate information with knowledge and advice sourced from local experts covering 1,400 cities and towns in 240 countries worldwide. The site has links to 16,450 research reports, 783 property-related trade associations and 113 benchmark indices covering property prices and other related information. To find house price indices worldwide, select 'Benchmarks' from the top right of the horizontal menu bar. That will take you to a page showing links to both commercial and residential property price indices. Select 'Worldwide House Price Indices' and you are taken to the latest quarter's house price movement, country by country. The data is consolidated from various sources, including The *Economist*'s Global House Price Index.

House Price Crash (www.housepricecrash.co.uk)

The aim of the site is to act as a counterbalance to the huge amounts of positive spin the housing market receives in the main media and to provide anyone involved in the market with up-to-date data and commentary. The forum has proved the most popular part of the site, attracting over 10,000 users a day.

In April 2006 the site set about developing more content, with a view to it being the definitive independent source for house price information and discussion on the web.

***Financial Times* House Price Index** (www.ft.com/cms/s/1d089640-fb60-11d8-8ad5-00000e2511c8.html)

The FT House Price Index series is updated with the most recent monthly data available from the Land Registry, smoothed and seasonally and mix adjusted then combined with an 'Index of Indices' model in order to account for transactions not yet reported to the Land Registry. The Index uniquely uses all of the Land Registry data, including cash purchases. It is designed to provide the most factual record available of domestic property prices in England and Wales and a true guide to house price inflation. The FT Index weights the information from the Halifax, the Nationwide and the Office of the Deputy Prime Minister.

Halifax Bank of Scotland
(`www.hbosplc.com/economy/housingresearch.asp`)

The Halifax House Price Index has been in operation since 1984 and claims to be based on the largest sample of housing data available in the UK, providing the longest unbroken series of any similar UK index. Select 'Historic data' from the horizontal menu across the top of the page, where you will find five Excel spreadsheets showing historic house prices nationally, regionally, by county, by postcode and by age of property.

Land Registry (`www.landreg.gov.uk`)

This is the government department responsible for registering title to land in England and Wales and recording dealings (for example, sales and mortgages) with registered land. Select 'House Prices' from the left-hand vertical menu, where you will find what is claimed to be the most accurate independent house price index available. It uses the Land Registry's data set of completed sales, making it the only index to be based on actual price paid. The index gives not only the national average house price figure but also regionally and right down to local authority level.

Nationwide House Price Index (`www.nationwide.co.uk/hpi`)

House price information is derived from Nationwide lending data for properties at the post-survey approval stage ands is based on a representative house price over time rather than the simple average price. Unlike the Land Registry, Nationwide does not use the simple average price as it believes that that figure is too easily influenced by a change in the mix (i.e. proportion of different property types, locations etc).

Like BBOS, the Nationwide also claims to have the longest unbroken run of house price data – it stretches back to 1952 on a yearly basis, with some indices going back to 1946.

Although similar to the Halifax method, the Nationwide substantially updated its system in 1993 following the publication of the 1991 census data; and by using mix-adjusted prices it believes its system is more robust to lower sample sizes because it better identifies and tracks our representative house price. Select 'Data download' from the left-hand vertical menu.

But higher and different risks

If one side of the coin is the potential for higher profits, which does seem to be what is on offer in the countries of, say, Eastern and central Europe, Asia and South America and other more far-flung places, the other should have a hazard sign warning of dangers ahead. Overseas property markets carry all the usual risks, the adverse effects that rises in interest rates, growth in unemployment and a decline in economic wellbeing of the population bring.

They also carry a few more. None of the countries reviewed here uses Sterling as its currency. That means changes in exchange rate can reduce, eliminate or even enhance your profit in terms of pounds returned. These changes can be violent and are rarely predictable with great certainty. (See 'Money matters' for a more detailed explanation of exchange rate risks and how to reduce or even eliminate them.)

Many overseas countries have only the most limited experience of being 'functioning market economies', to use the EU's term for using market forces as an economic star rather than the 'centralised command' system favoured by the Soviets. Few of these countries have had more than a handful of elected governments in their entire history and in many cases ownership of the land on which property is built is at best in dispute and at worst is still mined after a conflict barely a decade in the past. Even in countries where the land title is reasonably certain, there are often pressures to declare an essentially illegally low purchase price, with all the inherent dangers in adopting such a strategy (See 'Researching the legal environment'.)

These are very real additional risks which are covered comprehensively in the chapters in Parts 2 and 3, where some idea of the size and scope of the risk and, where possible, how it might be countered are covered.

Websites that help track overseas property risks include:

Pensions Management (www.pensions-management.co.uk)

Published by Financial Times Pensions Management, this is the magazine read and respected by professional advisers in the pensions management business. Its articles provide expertise from all angles, to give you the whole picture. Each month, it reports on the latest developments, interviews experts and highlights the key statistics. The online article database is free once you have registered on the site (also free). Typing 'Overseas property' into the search pane yields over 70 articles. At the time of writing, the latest of these published in the preceding 6 months included: 'Property: a positive outlook but it's time to invest further afield'; 'Property's become a global game' and 'The pros and cons of investing in a place in the sun'.

About Property (www.aboutproperty.co.uk)

This is a consumer site for everyone interested in homes and property. Its aim is to report the latest property news in the most objective and factual way possible, drawing on daily news content provided by Adfero Ltd who have a range of similar sites including a network of Adfero news sites some of which are www.politics.co.uk, www.myfinances.co.uk, www.inthenews.co.uk and www.travelbite.co.uk.

For current news on risks and rewards in overseas property markets, go to: home>news >overseas-property.

This is Money (www.thisismoney.co.uk)

This is produced by Associated Northcliffe, the publishers of the *Daily Mail*, the *Evening Standard* and the *Metro*. It is one of the leading personal finance websites written in jargon-free language, as witnessed by its is Plain English campaign accreditation. It carries data and statistics provided by Digital Look, Moneyfacts, Moneysupermarket, Moneyexpert, SimplySwitch, Baronworth Investment Services and The Annuity Bureau, among others. Select 'Homes Abroad' from the left-hand menu to access dozens of current articles including: 'The Pitfalls of Homes Abroad', 'When is it Time to Sell Overseas?' and 'Warning on Foreign Homes Risk'.

CHAPTER 3

The World Property Markets – Segments and Drivers

In this chapter:

- Grasping the essentials of property cycles.
- Exploring beyond the residential market.
- Recognising factors driving prices.
- Spotting trends.

Property cycles

The property market moves in a different way from the stock market. In the last couple of major stock-market busts, property prices hardly moved. In 2007–8 for example, world stock markets moved up and down by a many percentage points in a single day as property prices moved in a year. The reasons for property's solidity include negatives (such as the fact that a property is harder to sell than a share) and positives (such as people's greater confidence in physical assets).

The reasons for property being less volatile than shares don't matter half as much as whether you understand how the property market itself works. The property market is certainly cyclical, and it provides a few clear warning signs for peaks and troughs. The chapter helps you identify these signs, hopefully well in advance of any downfalls.

Over the next decade or so, the factors driving up property prices and rental incomes in many overseas economies look strong.

Generally, the property market is split into two main sub-groups: residential property (self-explanatory) and commercial property (including retail outlets, factories, warehouses, offices and the like). Economic theory has it that these two markets behave differently, as they are driven by different factors. Residential property is largely owner-occupied. Even in the UK, after a decade of buy-to-let activity, only 10% of the housing stock is in the hands of landlords whose prime interest is renting out their properties and hoping for capital growth. Of the remainder, 20% are in the hands of councils and 70% with owner-occupiers. The factors that cause house prices to rise in this market include the usual suspects:

- **Supply**: Too few new properties being built, perhaps because of planning constraints, means that prices tend to go up.
- **Demand**: Provided that there is reasonably full employment, wages are rising, interest rates are low and the population is expanding (because of an increase in the birth rate, more immigrants arriving or households fragmenting through divorce), property prices will tend to rise. The key ratio here is affordability. Where mortgage repayments exceed 5 times salary, house prices may be constrained; where they are below 3 times salary, people feel that they can afford to splash out a bit more.

The commercial property market matters too

This is something of a simplification but it is sufficient to paint the general picture.

The ownership of commercial property is the mirror image of that for residential. Only 10% of commercial property is in family ownership: a boss or his or her family owning their shop, factory or office, for example. The remaining 90% is owned by institutional investors whose primary goals are to diversify their portfolios so they are not over dependent on the stock market and to achieve a satisfactory and rising rental yield. Institutional investors have deep pockets and hold their property portfolios for decades.

What drives up property prices in this sector is rental yield, and that is more to do with the general health of the economy: strong economic growth, plenty of inward investment from overseas companies eager to set up in the country and a healthy balance of trade. (See the various chapters in Part 2 where all these elements are examined in detail.) When the rental yield, expressed as a percentage of the value of the property (e.g. £5,000 rent for a property that cost £100,000 is a 5% yield) starts to rise, it is often triggered by an overheating economy.

Overseas property, such as apartments and houses, is a hybrid. It is a residential product bought for, at least in part, a commercial purpose; to rent and eventually sell for a profit. As a buyer of overseas property for your own use, you are mostly concerned with the first set of factors. But if your interest is primarily in achieving a good rental yield while your property's value steadily rises over the long term, then the second set of factors matter most. The drivers for the commercial property sector include:

- **Supply**: Prices tend to go up when too few new offices, shops and warehouses are being built, perhaps because of planning constraints.
- **Demand**: Prices tend to rise when the economy is expanding, consumers are spending rather than saving and new businesses are being set up at a faster rate than previously. The key factor for businesses is to get their facilities set up as quickly as possible, in order to take advantage of an expanding market. Rather than be left behind or leave room for a competitor to expand, a business is likely to pay a bit more in order to land a property *now*, rather than wait for prices to stabilise or decline.

While all these factors do affect property markets, they are not easily distilled into anything you can use yourself. Set out below are some sources of information that will help you to begin to get a handle on these market(s). (See also the preceeding section for information on UK domestic markets.)

Tracking commercial property markets: useful websites

HBOS (www.hbosplc.com/abouthbos/group _ company _ websites.asp)

At the time of writing, HBOS, Britain's biggest mortgage lender, was working on plans to draw up a new index to chart the buy-to-let market, as the bank had become concerned at the huge discrepancies emerging in the property market generally. Some sections of the market were rising at 2–3%, while others, such as Kensington and Chelsea in London, were rising at 25% plus. There was also a worrying statistic in that auctioneers claimed that more than half the properties coming up for auction were previously owned by buy-to-let investors, with many being distress sales. The bank originally considered splitting its monthly house price index into three sub-divisions, based on price. Instead, it has decided to set up a new index charting the buy-to-let market, which would allow potential property investors to chart the fortunes of their potential investments more accurately.

Worldwide (www.researchworldwide.com/benchmarksearch.jsp)

A consolidation of commercial real estate information, knowledge and advice sourced from local experts, covering 1,400 cities and towns in 240 countries worldwide. This link is to a country-by-country list of organisations providing commercial property indices. At www.researchworldwide.com/info/comrankings.jsp you can see the latest country rankings, showing the total return on commercial property for the last year.

Investment Property Databank (IPD) (www.ipdindex.co.uk)

IPD has been in property information services since 1985 and is an acknowledged market leader. Its international network employs one of the world's largest team of specialists in the collection and analysis of property performance records. At this link you can see commercial property price movements across 21 countries for periods of 1, 3 and 5 years.

European Public Real Estate Association (EPRA) (www.epra.com)

Since February 2005, EPRA has been responsible for producing the 'FTSE EPRA/NAREIT Global Real Estate Index Series'. The index is designed to track the performance of listed real estate companies and REITS(Real Estate Investment Trusts) worldwide. The series acts as a performance measure of the overall market and can also be used as the basis for measuring movements in average commercial property values, much as the Halifax price index of domestic property is. The index series is broken down into three index families and 37 indices in Asia Pacific, Europe and North America, including 12 real-time property indices covering the world's largest markets.

INREV (www.inrev.org)

This is the European Association for Investors in Non-listed Real Estate Vehicles: in other words, all the private companies investing in property markets, mostly commercial but some in the domestic market. The only accessible part of the website of much value to non-members is the membership list. You can get to this by first going to the site map and from there selecting 'List of Members'. There are 210 members listed, with the country in which they operate. Selecting members in any country you are interested in will yield rewarding facts on the strength or otherwise of the commercial property market there.

Watching the cycles

Any economy follows a cyclical pattern that moves from *boom* (when demand is strong) to *slump* (economists' shorthand for a downturn). Figure 3.1 shows an elegant curve which depicts the theoretical *textbook cycle*.

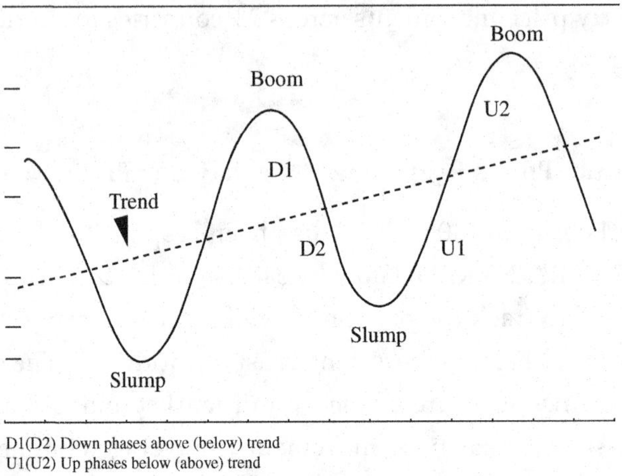

Figure: 3.1 The Text Book economic cycle

Four phases typically occur in each textbook cycle:

U1: where demand is picking up and toeing the line of the long-term trend.
U2: where demand exceeds the long-term trend.
D1: where demand dips down to hit the long-term trend.
D2: where demand slumps below the long-term trend.

The long-term trend is a line that best fits the data rising when volume is increasing or declining when demand is falling away. Look on the Nationwide Building Society website (www.nationwide.co.uk/hpi/historical.htm) where you can see a chart of UK house prices showing 'slumps' in 1971, 1979, 1984 and 1997, followed by 'booms' in 1975, 1981, 1991 and 2002.

Cycles are most evident in areas that experience a delay in balancing supply and demand. House building is a classic sector in which delays can be years, and even decades, long. The actions that need to be taken between deciding that too few properties exist and increasing the supply are extensive (buying land, getting planning permission, buying raw materials, finding builders, and only then building the property).

In between, while demand exceeds supply, the only slack in the system lies in prices, which go up to balance out the 'supply and demand' equation.

Thousands of property developers across the world watch for signs that a particular market needs more properties, and then they start building. Almost inevitably, they build more properties than the market needs, and prices start to drop, once again balancing out supply and demand.

The Nationwide figures show the movement in *real* house prices; that is, after stripping out inflation. (If actual house prices rose by 10% while inflation in the economy was 3%, the real price rise is 7%, the difference between the two figures.)

While the cycle revealed in the Nationwide chart is nothing like the perfect textbook version in Figure 3.1, you can see three clear major upswings in the past 35 years and only two dramatic slumps. Had you bought a property in 1974, you would have had to wait 12 years until 1986 to see it return to its original price, after a long slump in prices. You would, however, have had to wait only 3 to 4 years to have your property valued at its original price, as inflation drove up prices sharply.

In the 1970s and early 1980s, inflation, that is the overall general upward price movement of goods and services in an economy, was much higher than today. Double figure rates of inflation were not uncommon then, while today a rate of 2% is more usual. But when prices rise greatly across the board, as they do in periods of high inflation, no one gets any richer. Sure, you may earn more money if your pay goes up, but as you have to pay more for food, fuel, clothes and so forth, your higher income doesn't make you any better off. It is only when the price of one asset (in this case, property) rises at a rate faster than general price rises in the economy that you actually become wealthier in real terms as a result of owning that asset. Inflation, as they say, makes fools of everyone. It certainly doesn't make you richer.

Today, the major economies of the world are more closely synchronised into a single business cycle than ever before, and so are property prices. For many countries, particularly those tied in an economic manner (such as the EU and those gearing up for entry), the synchronisation is particularly strong. So, while each country may not replicate this cycle exactly, with similar interest rates, economic strategies, employment policies, and an increasingly powerful political direction, large tracts of the world look increasingly like a collaborative 'sink-or-swim' endeavour.

Spotting a turning point

To make sound property investments, avoid buying in at the top of a cycle. Of course, this advice is easier said than done. No economic models exist that can work out the *exact* turning point for a market.

While property markets as a whole experience cycles, parts of the market lead and lag in the cycle, often by many years. For example, between December 2004 and December 2005, house prices in the north of England fell back by 2.07%, while those in Northern Ireland powered ahead by 13.22%, a difference of more than 15% in the behaviour of one market compared with the other. For individual postcodes within the United Kingdom, the differences were more marked still.

In the final analysis, all property markets are local. It doesn't matter a jot where you buy a share in a public company – in Wales or Belfast or wherever – but in terms of *property*, where you buy is nearly everything: location, location, location!

Still, you can get a feel for when a local property market is becoming overheated. If prices rise in a particular area by 20% a year for several years, it is hard to see how they can go on rising at that rate for several more years and still represent good value. Buyers are more likely to search out better value elsewhere, causing price rises in the area to slow down or even drop back.

The 'dinner party test', also known as the 'taxi driver test', is another pointer to excessive euphoria. Back in 1999, all anyone talked about was shares in Internet companies: dinner party guests and taxi drivers alike. Then the Internet share-price bubble burst.

Greed and unrealistic expectations are what cloud people's judgement, encouraging them to enter markets too late or stay too long.

A couple of centuries earlier, Isaac Newton and Jonathan Swift, the author of *Gulliver's Travels*, were busy losing their shirts on a sure-fire investment that had risen several thousand per cent between 1719 and 1722. The South Sea Bubble, as it became known, pulled in thousands of investors, from royal dukes to hotel porters, before collapsing totally. Isaac Newton, who lost more than £20,000 – a fortune then – reputedly complained: 'I can calculate the motions of heavenly bodies but not the madness of people.'

Sources of help and advice with understanding and anticipating economic cycles and their impact on world property markets follow.

Understanding economic cycles

Tutor2u (`www.tutor2u.net/economics/content/topics/econgrowth/cycles.htm`)

This is the link to the publishers of e-learning resources tutorials on economic cycles. Using the UK economy as their example, the tutorial shows the cycles and GDP performance since 1955. (If you are a bit hazy on the meaning of GDP, you can look it up in the A–Z Glossary, listed in the horizontal menu at the top of this page).

Economic Research Cycle Research Institute
(`www.businesscycle.com`) **(fee payable)**

Founded by Geoffrey H. Moore, the 'father of leading indicators', ECRI, as the institute is known, monitors over 100 proprietary cyclical indices for major economies, covering more than 85% of world GDP. It regularly interprets this data to form a sophisticated cyclical forecast which is available by subscription.

ECRI is perhaps the only organisation to give warning of each of the past three recessions; equally impressively, it has not yet issued a false alarm.

ECRI works closely with business, government and academic communities.

It provides cyclical forecasts of house prices, economic growth and inflation through its online 'ECRI Light' service, which includes the weekly 'Recession-Recovery Watch Dashboard'. Its historical data going back to 1967 is used to produce its 'Leading House Price Indicator'. From the right-hand vertical menu headed ' Solutions for', select 'Individuals' for full details on the 'ECRI Light' service which costs from $149.99 a year.

Investor Words
(www.investorwords.com/1641/economic _ cycle.html)

Launched in 1999 by WebFinance Inc., a financial Internet company headquartered in Annandale, Virginia, *Investor Words* is a financial glossary on the web whose goal is to help individuals understand and keep up to date with the terms that they need to know in order to succeed in today's financial world. Currently there are 6,000 definitions in the glossary, including that of economic cycles, found at this link, and new terms are added frequently. Also, the links between related words and term listings by subject can help you obtain an appreciation of topics even when you do not have a clear focus of what you need to know.

While the glossary is free, the company offers a wide range of paid-for services (www.wiseradvisor.com, www.investorguide.com, www.webfinanceconsulting.com) to help individuals with their finances and investments.

International Monetary Fund (IMF)
(www.imf.org/Pubs/FT/weo/2006/02/index.htm)

This link is directly to the IMF's World Economic Outlook and Economic Cycles report, which presents its analysis and projections of economic developments at the global level, in major country groups (classified by region, stage of development, etc.), and by individual countries. It focuses on major economic policy issues as well as on the analysis of economic developments and prospects. It is usually prepared twice a year, as documentation for meetings of the International

Monetary and Financial Committee, and forms the main instrument of the IMF's global surveillance activities. Scroll down this page to the contents page of the report, where you can download either the whole report, selected chapters or any or all of the 100 charts and tables. (Change the year in the web address to see any other report.)

European Central Bank (ECB) (`www.ecb.int`)

The ECB is the central bank for Europe's single currency – the euro – whose main task is to maintain the euro's purchasing power and price stability in the euro area.

In the horizontal menu bar at the top of the page, select 'Search' and, once the search pane opens, type in 'economic cycles'. There you will find information on the Bank's ideas on this subject.

Federal Reserve Board (`www.federalreserve.gov`)

The Federal Reserve System, known simply as 'the Fed', is the central bank of the United States. It was founded by Congress in 1913 to provide the nation with a safer, more flexible and more stable monetary and financial system. From the left-hand vertical menu, select 'Economic Research and Data', where you will find the Fed's take on the economic cycle, among other related subjects. Selecting 'Consumer Information' from the same vertical menu take you to the Bank's research on mortgages, personal finance, banking and occasional topics such as identity theft.

***Extraordinary Popular Delusions and the Madness of Crowds*, by Charles MacKay (Three Rivers Press, 1841:reprint edition, 1995), price £7.00** (`www.litrix.com/madraven/madne001.htm`)

MacKay takes his readers through every economic bubble, from the Mississippi Scheme, to Tulip Mania, the South Sea Bubble and a hundred other schemes, swindles and delusions. He shows how manias take hold, encouraging even the most intelligent to become reckless, fixing their mind on a single subject (property or Internet shares, for example) and pursuing it with insane zeal. At this link you can read enough text on each section to get a good feel for the subject. It goes a long way to explaining why markets over shoot into booms and, just as inexplicably, go into reverse.

Irrational Exuberance, by Robert Schiller (Princeton University Press, 2000), price £17.50
(www.irrationalexuberance.com/index.htm)

The definition of 'irrational exuberance' has its origin in a speech Alan Greenspan, then chairman of the Federal Reserve Board, gave on 5 December 1996, where he expressed his concerns in a 14-page televised speech around the theme 'How do we know when irrational exuberance has unduly escalated asset values, which then become subject to unexpected and prolonged contractions?'. Schiller, an economics professor, explains the psychological factors that caused the Dow Jones Industrial Average (share price index) to triple between 1994 and 1999 and led to its rapid decline thereafter. The book has valuable lessons for those trying to understand and predict economic cycles. This link is to updated information relating to the book and contact details for the author.

CHAPTER 4

It's a Global World – The Coming of Capitalism

In this chapter:

- Understanding why capitalism has become such an appealing philosophy.
- Realising how the spread of capitalist economic principles has driven property prices up, almost everywhere.
- Appreciating the impact of the EU's brand of capitalism.
- Seeing the impact of improving economics on two examples: Bulgaria and Ireland.

Marco Polo, Christoper Columbus and Sir Walter Raleigh all had one thing in common with Captain Kirk of *Starship Enterprise* fame: they all boldly went to parts of the globe where no one had been before. The first three, however, went to make their fortunes and, to varying degrees, were successful in that respect.

Those going early into a market have the potential to make the greatest profits. Once a market becomes mature and there are thousands of competitors (others in search of bargain properties) and as many suppliers (property developers and brokers with property to sell), prices tend to stabilise. Prices that once grew at between 20 and 50% a year settle back to a less stratospheric level.

Don't worry too much about not having been first to recognise the global property opportunity. Early entrants to a market only have the opportunity – not the certainty – of making higher rewards than those coming later. In fact, research into the subject of market-entry timing suggests that the second wave in does best, having learned from the mistakes and successes of the real pioneers. Ever heard of the Geniac? The name was short for 'Genius Almost-Automatic Computer'; designed by Edmund C. Berkeley in 1955, it was the first PC on the market but that didn't deter Apple, IBM and other late entrants to the market to make all the serious money.

During the Cold War years, the world was divided into three. The 'First World' was used to describe the North Atlantic Treaty Organisation (NATO) members, including the USA, the UK and their allies. The 'Second World' decribed those countries under the Soviet Union's sphere of influence who were members of the Warsaw Pact (the equivalent military alliance to NATO) or the Council for Mutual Economic Assistance (COMECON); an Eastern Bloc equivalent to the European Economic Community. The 'Third World' described those countries, such as Switzerland, Ireland, India and Sweden, who stayed aloof from the competing ideologies.

In 1991, when the Cold War ended and the Berlin Wall came down, the term 'Second World' died and the 'Third World' became a term used to describe relatively poor countries in the process of developing and becoming industrialised.

What this means, in a nutshell, is that large tracts of the world have been under the now largely defunct Communist cultural, economic and social influence. Under that system, the state planned and controlled the economy and a single authoritarian party ran the show, with the aim of achieving a higher social order in which all goods were to be shared by people equally. Even in countries such as India and large parts of Asia and the Far East, where Communism did not take hold, capitalism was not always in much favour either.

Capitalism: the ascending economic philosophy

Capitalism can be considered to have become a mainstream economic belief with the publication of Adam Smith's treatise, *The Wealth of Nations* (1776). Based around the concept of free enterprise, capitalism rules that market forces should govern, with supply and demand setting the agenda rather than governments. The Industrial Revolution of the 18th century, was the period when bankers, merchants and industrialists really began to displace the feudal system fostered until then by landowners. But, initially at least, while capitalism made people other than the nobility rich, the mass of workers were little better off. In 1848, Germans Karl Marx and Friedrich Engels published *The Communist Manifesto*, setting out an alternative vision in which everyone shared everything equally, but in practice the system, though great on the drawing board, failed to deliver either equality or wealth to the those adopting it.

Capitalism needed some fine tuning, with government action needed to curb its abuses, which have ranged from slavery to cartels, monopolies and financial frauds such as those still being uncovered at companies such as Enron and Worldcom. But the evidence so far shows that, coupled with strong democracy, capitalism delivers wealth and spreads it around. For example, in the UK 20 years ago, two-thirds of the country's richest people inherited their wealth and only a third made it themselves. Today, the proportion is reversed: see *Sunday Times* Rich List (www.timesonline.co.uk/sundaytimes).

Measuring the effects of introducing capitalism: is the EU a role model?

For half a century, some of the most enterprising and talented nations on earth had been held in check by an iron grip. Communism, the guiding philosphy for much of the countries of Eastern Europe, marched millions of people in the wrong direction, stiffled their aspitations and misused their abilities and resources. Many of those countries in Europe not inclined to Communism were pursuing economic strategies that were equally ineffective. Spain and Portugal for decades continued under dictators who used their own style of command economic principles, suppressing or ignoring the wishes of their citizens.

The EU, with its twin requirements that countries should have fully democratic styles of government and functioning market economies, is a force for change whose effects can be measured to some extent. If being brought into the EU has had a positive effect on new partipants and their property markets, that is an encouraging signal for the those countries around the globe who are now adapting the same global capitalist ideas.

Estimating the benefits of EU membership

One way of seeing how being in the EU might benefit both the new members and those aspiring to join is to see how it has worked out for the others. No disrespect to Ireland but, back in the 1970s, it was an economic 'basket case', with a stagnant economy, and its biggest export was young university graduates running for the exit to make a life abroad. Its biggest trading partner was the neighbouring UK whose population was among the wealthiest in the world, while it barely scratched a living. Yet, by 2005, in terms of wealth per head, the 'Celtic Tiger', as its economy had become known, was alongside that of the UK and by some measures was perhaps even ahead.

The transformation had come about in good measure as a result of the country joining the EU which, as well as pumping billions in what are known in EU parlance as 'transitional funds' (money to help its ecomony become more efficient), opened up a market of millions more customers to their goods. Now, the EU was not the only thing Ireland had going for it but it was the trigger that set the economy on its new and more prosperous direction.

Another country had been shrinking fast as young people began to realise that they had few opportunities in their homeland. Bugaria saw its population dip by a million between 1989 and 2003. Like Ireland, it had been, and to some extent still is, economically backward. But therein

Table: 4.1 Ireland and Bulgaria compared: the EU effect revealed

	1990	2005
Ireland		
National income per head	$13, 329	$34, 280
Unemployment	16%	5%
Average inflation over period	4%	
Foreign direct investment over period	$139 billion	
Proportion of population in secondary education	87.5%	
Increase in house prices, 1997–2005	196%	
Bulgaria		
National income per head	$2, 360	$2, 740
Unemployment	25%	18%
Average inflation over period	68%	
Foreign direct investment over period	$6 billion	
Proportion of population in secondary education	92.5%	
Increase in house prices, 2001–2005	62%	

lies the opportunity for the property investor. Look below to Table 4.1, Ireland and Bulgaria compared, where you can see the two economies contrasted. For Ireland, you can see serious economic progress. Income per head has nearly trebled over the past 15 years, foreign companies have piled in, jobs have been created and nationals have returned. At the same time, property prices have soared by 196% between 1997 and 2005, the highest growth rate in the developed world. Bulgaria, in contrast, is only just beginning to get a whiff of the benefits of joining the EU. It has received only a fraction of the inward investment that Ireland has had, but it is early days yet. Wages are low and unemployment high but falling, but the economy is now growing fast. If Bulgaria were to approach mirroring Ireland's transformation, the coming decade will see a transformation in its fortunes. Look at the percent of population in secondary education and you will see that Bulgaria's workforce is in good shape, which bodes well as we move more to an era where intellectual capital rather than physical muscle is what creates wealth. Were Ireland the only country in which the EU's magic wand had worked miracles, this argument would be less convincing. But for Portugal, Spain and Greece, the benefits have been equally convincing. And all three have acquired thriving property markets driven forward by enterprising foreign buyers, most of whom have come from the UK and Ireland.

Monitoring macro factors affecting property markets: democracy, capitalism and world trade

These are some organisations that can help you monitor the spread of democracy, capitalism and global trade, all essential factors in a healthy thriving property sector.

World Trade Organization (WTO) (www.wto.org)

The past 50 years have seen an exceptional growth in world trade. Merchandise exports grew on average by 6% annually and the total trade in 2006 was 25 times the level of 1956. The WTO, as the only global international organization dealing with the rules of trade between nations, played a major part in this globalisation. At its heart are the WTO agreements, negotiated and signed by the organisation's 150 members, accounting for over 97% of world trade, and ratified in their parliaments. The goal is to help producers of goods and services, exporters, and importers conduct their business.

Over three-quarters of WTO members are developing or least-developed countries and around 30 other countries around the world are negotiating membership. Getting into the 'club' is often difficult and can be time consuming. The shortest accession negotiation was that of the Kyrgyz Republic, lasting 2 years and 10 months. The longest was that of China, lasting 15 years and 5 months. You can check on which countries are awaiting membership and how they are progressing by selecting 'The WTO's members' from the left-hand vertical menu headed 'In the WTO'. Once there, scroll down the screen to the section headed 'Observer governments'. This is, in effect, the 'current applicants' list. Select a country to see how its application is progressing. At the time of writing, Cape Verde (application made in 1999), the Republic of Montenegro (2004) and the Lebanese Republic (1999) are among the property hot spots awaiting membership.

European Union (`http://ec.europa.eu/index _ en.htm`)

This link takes you direct to the English-language version of the EU Commission's website home page. The European Commission's principal purpose is to support the general interest of the Union and be the motivator of its institutional system. Its four main roles are: to propose legislation to Parliament and the Council; to administer and implement Community policies; to enforce Community law (jointly with the Court of Justice); and to negotiate international agreements, mainly those relating to trade and co-operation.

The main information on the Commission's website are:

- the latest official press releases, photos and live TV coverage of EU affairs
- details of forthcoming events
- links to the policies administered and implemented by the Commission
- the possibility of influencing the decision-making process
- easy access to its organisation (meetings, work programme, contacts etc.)
- direct links to its key information services.

In the horizontal menu across the top of this page, headed 'Key Issues', select 'Enlargement'. (It is possible that this topic may cease to be a key issue, in which case this link will take you to that area of the website: `http://ec.europa.eu/enlargement/index _ en.htm`).

On the left-hand horizontal menu, headed 'Enlargement process', there are three sections: 'Acceding countries', dealing with countries who have been given a final date for entry to the EU; 'Candidate countries', including countries such as Croatia, the former Yugoslav Republic of Macedonia and Turkey who are officially on track for membership at some often unspecified time in the future; and 'Potential countries' including Albania, Bosnia and Herzegovina, Serbia and Montenegro and Kosovo. There is very detailed information on the development towards every facet of EU membership including particular details on progress towards becoming a functioning market economy. For each country there is a detailed report on the political and economic profile, the current state of EU relations with that country and the 'Enlargement Package'. This last item is the key to understanding how much money and other assistance are being put into a particular country to help it advance towards the state of development required for EU membership. Also in these reports are valuable insights given in the commentary. For Albania, the statement 'Legislative progress has been made in reinforcing property rights, but implementation must be greatly accelerated' would be of some encouragement to a would-be property buyer.

Association of Southeast Asian Nations (ASEAN)
(www.aseansec.org)

ASEAN is the economic association comprising 10 countries: Brunei Darussalam, Cambodia, Indonesia, Laos, Malaysia, Myanmar, Philippines, Singapore, Thailand and Vietnam. The countries have little in common in terms of economic performance: Brunei Darussalam is growing at 1.7%, while Cambodia and Vietnam are growing at 7.7%; GDP per capita is just $166 per annum in Myanmar and $25,207 in Singapore. After more than 35 year of ASEAN's operation, it has become a key regional organisation, fostering and encouraging development and harmonisation of legal processes. While a long way from being an EU structure, it plays an important role in making parts of the region safer and more profitable for property investors. For example, since 1994, they have inspired and promoted no less than 25 regional tourism initiatives, 30 transportation projects and 20 banking and finance-sector action programmes that will favourably impact on the property market over time. From the vertical menu on the left of the home page, you can select links to statistics on the region and member countries. In the menu in the centre, towards the bottom of the page, you can find links to 'Areas of ASEAN co-operation', covering topics such as crime, finance, health, law and tourism, all of concern to would-be property investors.

Organisation for Black Sea Economic Co-operation
(www.bsec-organization.org)

On 25 June 1992,the Heads of State and Government of 11 countries (Albania, Armenia, Azerbaijan, Bulgaria, Georgia, Greece, Moldova, Romania, Russia, Turkey and Ukraine) signed in Istanbul the Summit Declaration and the Bosphorus Statement giving birth to the Black Sea Economic Co-operation (BSEC). The initiative is aimed at fostering interaction and harmony among the member states, as well as ensuring peace, stability and prosperity in the Black Sea region.

BSEC covers an area of nearly 20 million square kilometres, generating over $300 billion in foreign trade each year and with 350 million citizens spread across two continents. After the Persian Gulf region, it is the second-largest source of oil and natural gas, along with a rich proven reserves of minerals and metals; it is also becoming Europe's major transport and energy transfer corridor. The prospects for those investing in property can only be enhanced by the regions' determination to work together to encourage 'the development of effective rule of law, respect for property rights and administrative processes and procedures'.

From the vertical menu to the left of the home page, headed 'About BSEC', hover over 'Areas of co-operation'. That will open a new menu of options, ranging from 'Banking and finance', through 'Healthcare', 'Tourism' and 'Transport' – all of importance to a healthy property market.

South American Community of Nations (www.mercosur.int)

The new South American Community of Nations was launched at a summit in the Peruvian city of Cuzco in December 2004. The community consists of members of the Andean Community (CAN) (Bolivia, Colombia, Ecuador and Peru); and members of Mercosur (Argentina, Brazil, Paraguay, Uruguay and Venezuela); Chile, Guyana and Suriname have also indicated the intention to join this community. Modelled on the European Union, the goal is to have a common currency, parliament and passport by 2019. The region certainly has some economic clout, with a population of 361 million, GDP of $973 billion, exports of $181 billion and a territory of nearly 18 million square kilometres.

The new communities' plans of integration started out with the construction of the Interoceanic Highway, a road that intends to unite Peru with Brazil by extending a highway through Bolivia, giving that country a path to the sea, while Brazil would obtain access to the Pacific Ocean and Peru to the Atlantic Ocean. Construction started in September 2005, financed 60% by Brazil and 40% by Peru. It is estimated to be completed by 2009. This project will have an inevitable knock-on effect on property prices. There are few roads anywhere in the world, from the M25 around London, Paris's Boulevard Périphérique to the Pan-European Transport Corridors built to implement EU policy on infrastructural development (e.g. the 1,500-mile Corridor No 4 covering the route Dresden/Nurnberg–Prague–Vienna/Bratislava–Budapest–Kraiova–Constanta/Sofia–Thessaloniki/Plovdiv–Istanbul) that have not had a positive effect on property prices in their immediate environs.

There is no separate website for the organisation at the time of writing, but information can be found on the Merosur site (unfortunately only in Spanish and Portuguese at present).

Organization of American States (www.oas.org)

The OAS brings together the nations of the Western Hemisphere to strengthen co-operation on democratic values, defend common interests and debate the major issues facing the region and the world. The member states include: Antigua and Barbuda, Argentina, The Bahamas, Barbados, Belize, Bolivia, Brazil, Canada, Chile, Colombia, Costa Rica, Cuba (a member but its government has been excluded from participation in the OAS since 1962), Dominica, the Dominican Republic, Ecuador, El Salvador, Grenada, Guatemala, Guyana, Haiti, Honduras, Jamaica, Mexico, Nicaragua, Panama, Paraguay, Peru, St Kitts and Nevis, St Lucia, St Vincent and the Grenadines, Suriname, Trinidad and Tobago, United States of America, Uruguay and Venezuela. With an organisation made up of 35 countries with very different agendas, there are only a limited number of points to which they are all signed up and those include an intention to 'deliver on equal rights, social inclusion and well-being for the majority, through democratic principles'. The OAS Electoral Observation Mission is one body used to good effect to validate the electoral process in countries where both elections and democracy are still relatively new. (See also 'Foreign Trade Information System'.)

Foreign Trade Information System (SICE) (`www.sice.oas.org`)

SICE, the acronym stemming from its Spanish title 'Sistema de Información al Comercio Exterior', is the information technology arm of the Trade Unit of the OAS. Its goal is to provide the most complete information source on trade in the Western Hemisphere as possible. SICE centralises the location of public, but often difficult to locate or obtain, documents on their website in the four official languages of the OAS (English, Spanish, Portuguese and French). Knowing more about the flow of trade gives some pointers as to the prospects for renting to executives on secondment, an important factor in determining local property values.

Wikpedia (`www.reference.com/browse/wiki/Trade _ bloc`)

This link is to a summary table showing the size in terms of population and economic performance of the world's 20 most substantial economic blocs, together with links to the websites of their organising bodies.

It also provides an overview of, country membership and website links for all major economic groupings, including: the African Economic Community (AEC); the Central American Common Market (CACM); the Common Market for Eastern and Southern Africa (COMESA); the Southern African Customs Union (SACU); the Gulf Co-operation Council (GCC); the Caribbean Community (CARICOM); the Economic Community of West African States (ECOWAS); the Economic and Monetary Community of Central Africa (CEMAC); and the South Asian Association for Regional Cooperation (SAARC).

CHAPTER 5

Factors that Drive Property Yields and Returns

In this chapter:

- Understanding how political stability improves the prospects for private property.
- Appreciating the effect of inward investment on rental yields.
- Seeing the impact of tourism.
- Considering how changes in local populations and demographics enhance property price growth.
- Recognising factors with a negative impact on property.

As an investor, two factors will be high in your mind, aside from the sheer appeal of a country, an area or a particular property: These are the potential for capital gain over the time horizon you have in mind; and the prospects for renting out the property to one or more of the market segments (particularly the tourist and incoming business executive markets, though, it has to be said, you cannot totally exclude the local residents and even the student market. For example, whole apartment blocks are on sale in student areas of Berlin, fully let with double-digit rental yields and a near-guaranteed 100% occupancy for years to come).

There are a number of *special factors* that affect property markets from time to time. You could have considered the prospect of European Union membership as a special factor in favour of investing in, say, Bulgaria or Romania prior to January 2007. You might take the same view of the Croatian, Albanian and Montenegran property markets post-2007. Moneycorp, a foreign exchange company, has done some research into the impact of budget airline routes on local housing prices. Its research indicates that the presence of budget airlines can lead to a huge increase in property prices; up to 60% in some cases. They can slide just as quickly if an airline pulls out from a route, as Ryanair has done on a number of occasions.

Special factors can be specific to a country, but they can also relate to a single area within a country. For example, Bansko in Bulgaria has come to prominence as a ski resort, for a number of special reasons, including a major investment in ski infrastructure, a new highway and a major airport. Even very local factors can have a strong positive effect on property prices in a particular area. For example, a new metro station, international school, or five-star hotel can give a spur to the property prices because these additions all increase the desirability of a location. You will need to hunt out these special factors from the trail of information sources provided in each section of this book, including those provided in this chapter.

Aside from special factors, the following are the key *rational factors* that affect the performance of an investment in property.

Improvers of property prospects

While it is certainly a bonus to have special factors working in your favour, it is encouraging to know that there are some enduring forces at work, putting upward pressure on the property market.

- **A growing and functioning economy**: Over the long term, the rate of growth in the economy is a measure of a country's wealth-creating ability and eventually of the wealth of the local people. The economy needs to be able to provide jobs, increased wages and an effective banking and mortgage market in order to allow the local population to buy property. Locals buy more than 90% of the residential property in almost any market, so they ultimately underpin the real prices rather than the 'froth'. If locals can't afford their own market, that might well be a signal that prices may be getting too high.

- **Inward investment:** A country with cheap resources such as labour, land and materials is attractive to companies based in high-cost economies, often leading these companies to relocate part of their operations. Inward investment, in turn, helps to make the economy prosper and provides a pool of executives from the parent company, in need of good-quality accommodation.
- **Tourism:** Tourists, like inward-investing companies, bring piles of money into a country and create jobs in restaurants and hotels, among other trades. But a country must have something worth seeing or doing in order to draw in the crowds. Whatever that is, it needs to be have uniqueness of some sort, because the world tourism market is highly competitive. The cost of living and availability of amenities such as theatres, museums, cinemas, golf courses and the like are all factors to consider, as is the ability to get to and from the country easily by air, land or sea.
- **Political stability:** There needs to be a democratically elected government and an independent and effective judiciary. Without the rule of law, property ownership is insecure and values are held in check.
- **Taxes:** When taxes are too high overall, the economy ends up moving away from being market driven to being run by bureaucrats. Property taxes in particular need to be simple to understand and aimed at making entry to and exit from the market easy.
- **Population and demographics:** When the number of people requiring a property changes radically upwards (or downwards), it will affect property markets. For example, the influx of over 1 million immigrants into the UK in a 5-year period, combined with an equally impressive increase in the divorce rate, are factors credited with underpinning the unprecedented continuation of the property boom that was expected to fizzle out in 2005, but that continued gathering pace throughout 2006 and only appeared to stall in the second half of 2007.

Events that limit property prospects

While investors are undoubtably making fortunes in some overseas property markets, a number of factors may make future success less certain. Some of the following factors are common to every property market, but they are all more in evidence in the countries covered in this book.

- **Lack of liquidity:** By its very nature, property is not easily turned into cash, unlike shares in a public company that you can trade in seconds. In most of the markets I cover in this book, the only buyers for the types of properties that foreigners buy are other foreigners. That is because many of the developments on the market are in holiday areas rather than major centres of employment. In addition, very few of the locals have sufficient income to finance properties that are often greatly superior to those generally available in the market. You may wait months, even years, to find a suitable buyer. Also, in many cases first-time buyers prefer to go for new properties because often these properties are marketed with a mortgage thrown in, making them easier to buy.
- **Shortage of professional advice:** In any new investment area, a number of rogues operate until sound information and professional firms come into the market. The overseas property market has its fair share of rogues, and in Parts 2 to 4 are given proven methods to find contact details for relevant professional bodies in every country, who can help you find experts. Before you even reach the airport, one breed of rogues may tempt you: property investment seminars and clubs. Organisations offering seminars and clubs have sprung up, claiming in their literature that they can show people how to get rich by investing in properties. These schemes often offer the near-certainty of building a £1 million property portfolio by signing up for a seminar that costs between £2,500 and £6,000. (Don't confuse these seminars with the wholly worthwhile property exhibitions, seminars and brokers whose contact details are provide in Parts 2

and 3 and who can provide a valuable role in linking buyers and sellers.) What you get for your money from the rogue seminars, according to one industry professional, is less than what you can glean in an hour on the Internet yourself by visiting a few competent estate agents' websites. The Department of Industry took High Court action recently, to close down six such schemes following an avalanche of complaints from dissatisfied clients who felt that they had been duped. The more reputable players have called on the Financial Services Authority to regulate the sector. 'Wait until they do' is certainly the best advice here.

- **Depressed yields:** The rental and holiday let markets in many overseas markets are still in their infancy. The more successful brokers are at selling property in an area, the less likely you are to see the forecasted rental yields. In fact, take any brokers' forecast of likely rental yields for properties that they are selling with a big pinch of salt. Check out a dozen properties in the area, with a view to renting them yourself, and see exactly which rents seem realistic. A lot of new property is coming onto these markets; finding good tenants and maintaining high occupancy rates is a tough task. Many developers have absolutely no idea how to advise their clients to go about renting out their properties. If you can't survive with no rent coming in from an investment property abroad for the first 12 months, then you are probably paying too much for it in the first place.
- **Rising cost of living:** Mature economies are typically growing at between 2 and 3% a year. The emerging overseas economies that constitute the bulk of the potential foreign property market is growing at 6%. That would indicate that it will require between 15 and 30 years for the standards and costs of living to equal out. So, theoretically at least, anyone aged between 50 and 60 coming from a prosperous economy can expect to enjoy a lower cost of living on average more or less anywhere else in the world for the rest of their lives. Additionally, these countries often have the benefit of low tax strategies.

- However there are a couple of problems with these averages: First, if lots of foreigners move into a country, prices of certain goods and services tend to rise very quickly. Hotels, cleaners, babysitters and restaurants are among the first sectors to see price hikes. Second, international commodities such as oil and gas are priced independently of the cost structure of the country. Few of the countries covered in this book have such natural resources, so the vagaries of world markets hit hard and fast, as the Ukraine felt when the Russians imposed a 400% price rise on gas in 2005.Having said all that, it is hard to see how many countries in the developing world could become *more* expensive a place to live than the United Kingdom, or most other of the prosperous developed world.

Websites providing an ongoing appreciation of the factors that profoundly influence property prices

What Drives Property Prices (www.norges-bank.no/english/publications/economic _ bulletin/2005-01/jacobsen.pdf)

This paper makes interesting reading, as house prices in Norway have more than tripled since 1992. After a dip during the last part of 2002 and the beginning of 2003, house prices rose by more than 20% from May 2003 to November 2004.

Developments in the housing market have contributed to a 10–11% increase in household debt in Norway each year since 2000. So the Bank's experts have taken a look at the factors driving the property market during a period of rapid growth; and in the process have provided some important general observations. Struggle through the equations to Section 4 on page 9 where you will find their ideas on 'What drives house prices?', with some interesting pointers that apply the world over. The authors are Dag Henning Jacobsen, economist in the Securities Markets Department, and Bjørn E. Naug, senior economist in the Economics Department of the Norges Bank, the Central Bank of Norway.

BIS Quarterly Review, March 2004
(www.bis.org/publ/qtrpdf/r _ qt0403f.pdf)

This study looks at the experiences of 17 industrialised countries over two full cycles of the property market, covering a period of 33 years. Its observation is that house prices generally depend on inflation, the yield curve and bank credit, but national differences in the mortgage markets also matter, an important factor as a forward indicator in markets such as those in Eastern Europe where housing credit finance is in its infancy. The authors are Kostas Tsatsaronis and Haibin Zhu, two economists from the Bank for International Settlements, an international organisation which fosters co-operation among countries' central banks. The counties covered in the study are: Australia, Belgium, Canada, Denmark, Finland, France, Germany, Ireland, Italy, Japan, the Netherlands, Norway, Spain, Sweden, Switzerland, the United Kingdom and the United States.

Hong Kong Monetary Authority Quarterly Review: What drives property prices in Hong Kong? (www.info.gov.hk/hkma/eng/public/qb200208/fa2.pdf)

This paper presents an empirical model of property prices that combines fundamental variables with speculative bubbles. The estimates suggest that about half of the swings in property prices since the early 1990s can be attributed to changes in the fundamental variables. The remainder is explained by the build-up of a bubble and its subsequent collapse. Although this paper, prepared by Wensheng Peng of the Authorities Research Department, draws on the local market for its data, the observations have application in any property market experience growth rates outside of its normal parameters.

Institute of Economic Affairs (IEA) (www.iea.org.uk)

The IEA claims to be the UK's original free-market think-tank. Founded in 1955, its goal is to explain free-market ideas to the public, including politicians, students, journalists, businessmen, academics and anyone interested in public policy. The website has links to a range of articles, speeches, books and journals. A typical example is the text of a recent speech by Kate Barker, a member of the Monetary Policy Committee of the Bank of England, at the IEA State of the Economy Conference, entitled 'The Housing Market and the Wider Economy' (www.iea.org.uk/record.jsp?type5news&ID5237)

Centre for Economic Policy Research (CEPR) (www.cepr.net)

CEPR was established in 1999 to 'promote democratic debate on the most important economic and social issues that affect people's lives'. This Washington-based economic research instate aims in much the same way as the UK's Institute for Economic Affairs (see above) to present everyday economic issues, including factors that affect house prices, in an accurate and understandable manner, so that the public is better prepared to choose from the various policy options. CEPR's Advisory Board of Economists includes Nobel Laureate economists. Typical of articles that can be found is 'Will a Bursting Bubble Trouble Bernanke? The Evidence for a Housing Bubble', written by Dean Baker and David Rosnick. Among other issues, this article projects property prices forward to 2020, on a number of differing economic assumptions (www.cepr.net/publications/housing _ bubble _ 2005 _ 11.pdf). See also 'The Housing Bubble Fact Sheet' by Dean Baker (www.cepr.net/documents/publications/housing_fact_2005_07.pdf) in which the author explains the basic facts about the housing market, lays out the evidence that the rise in housing prices constitutes a housing bubble and explains what can be expected when it inevitably collapses.

Central Bank (www.centralbank.ie)

This organisation has responsibility for Ireland's monetary policy functions, financial stability, currency and economic analysis. It produces an Annual Financial Stability Report, which contains a comprehensive review of the factors that affect the property market at that time. Ireland has seen among the fastest house price rises in the world and the latest report (www.centralbank.ie/data/FinStaRepFiles/Summary%202006.pdf) makes for interesting reading for anyone, anywhere wanting an informed opinion on the drivers affecting the market.

University of Oxford Department of Economics
(www.economics.ox.ac.uk)

Alongside a number of other great universities, Oxford's smartest brains are worried about house prices. After all, most of the lecturers, alongside academic tenure (jobs for life), own property in one of the UK's most expensive regions. The article 'UK house prices, consumption and GDP, in a global context', by Andrew Farlow of the Department of Economics and Oriel College (www.economics.ox.ac.uk/members/andrew.farlow/Farlow%20Housing%20and%20Consumption.pdf), in around 70 pages examines almost every aspect of economic life that impinges on property prices. The article also references many of the articles of serious merit on the subject of economic factors that drive world property prices.

See also Chapter 6, where country sources of information on these drivers are examined in detail.

PART 2

Pick a Country, Any Country

There are 194 countries in the world. Of these, 192 are members of the United Nations, with the Vatican City being an independent state which has chosen not to be recognised by the UN. Taiwan meets most, but not all, of the criteria of statehood but is not recognised as such by the United States and many other countries and so is not a member of the United Nations.

Now, there is no way that all, or even most, of these 194 countries could be considered as aspiring candidates for the prudent property tycoon's hard-won cash. Only the foolhardy, or those with a particularly long time horizon, would buy property in Afghanistan, Uzbekistan, Kyrgyzstan or, for that matter, almost anywhere ending in 'stan'. Iraq, Iran, the Côte d'Ivoire, the Democratic Republic of the Congo, Gambia, North Korea, Somalia, Liberia and a score more countries are definitely too hot to handle. Even countries which appear to have returned to some semblance of normality – Lebanon being a prime example – can collapse into near-anarchy at a moment's notice.

Damac's Properties, a Dubai-based property developer, with the help of the design skills of Ivana Trump, ex-wife of the American billionaire Donald Trump, had barely unveiled a US$150 million project, La Residence, a 35-storey tower of two- and three-bedroom apartments and penthouses with private pools on the roof, in front of the Phoenicia Hotel at the prime intersection of Omar Daouk and Fakhreddine streets in the capital, when the bombs started to fall.

Not all countries that sound risky may in fact be as dangerous as that. Political stability, the growth in personal wealth and improvements in education, healthcare and infrastructure, for example, make countries such as Vietnam and China nearly as attractive as, say, Thailand, for a property investor, if perhaps not as pleasurable.

Factors to consider in narrowing down your choice of country include economic prospects, crime and corruption, political stability, healthcare, accessibility and travel infrastructure, the tax regime and so forth.

This Part identifies the key factors that are likely to impact on property prices in any country.

CHAPTER 6

Evaluating Economies

In this chapter:

- Finding out about countries you may never want to live in.
- Checking out the potential for natural disasters.
- Seeing how safe a country is to live in.
- Establishing the relative expensiveness of a country.
- Tracking business and investment friendliness.

Money, as they say, makes the world go round: it also drives house prices. The central problem in many of the world's property markets, particularly in the less-developed countries, is that the locals either don't own their own homes or can't afford to buy into the fancy new developments that have either swimming pools or easy access to the ski lifts as standard. In poorer countries, people need to live near to their work and can rarely afford a luxurious first home, or indeed any kind of second home. What changes that equation is when wealth trickles down and corruption declines to the point where legal processes are less susceptible to bribery and corruption. (Corruption in the legal process matters, as it contributes to uncertainty when it comes to ownership title, and having a degree of certainty as to what can happen to land in the immediate neighbourhood.)

The paradox is that most people are looking to buy a property where the cost of living is significantly lower than in their home country. But that in turn limits the exit route (where they can sell on to) for the property market in their chosen country to other relatively wealthy foreigners. But, usually, overseas buyers prefer to own a new property, which in turn is often easier to attract mortgage finance and to rent out.

This means that you need to evaluate the economy of the country in which you are considering buying property, in order to be confident that the essential drivers of progress are working well, but not so well as to disturb the time horizon you have in mind for your investment. For example, if you were buying a property in a country such as Bulgaria, Romania or the Ukraine, planning to rent it out for around 10 years and then retire there, you could be reasonably certain that the local cost of living would take at least a further 10 to 20 years to have caught up with that in Western Europe generally. (The maths for this calculation is based on average annual rates of economic growth in the countries mentioned being around 5–6%, while in the advanced economies it is more likely to be around 2–3%. Then take the relative starting point of the country concerned. If its income per head, at €5,000 per annum, is a quarter of that in your home country, which is €20,000, then the faster 3% or so economic growth rate, which is compounded, means the country should catch up the required three-quarters' difference in around 25 years or so. This a rough and ready rule, but is sufficient for a guide.)

Eliminating unacceptable risk

Some countries are more risky than others, either in terms of the prospects of having a secure title to the property you are buying, or because the provision of healthcare is well below the standard you would expect and require in a more developed country. But risk to life and limb is quite another matter. South Africa, for example, has, according to the United Nations, the highest rate of gun-related crime in the world except for Columbia. A recent shoot-out after a failed robbery in Johannesburg left 4 policemen and 11 would-be robbers dead. But most violent crimes, such as murder, rape and armed robbery, are committed by people known to the victims. In addition, South Africa is spending 3 times as much as the world average on criminal justice, so perhaps that defect can be remedied over time.

A low cost of living, cheap houses, benign climate and the fact that English is the local language has tempted property buyers into the market in South Africa but some countries are simply too risky to consider at any price. Buying property in an area of very high personal risk will eliminate any serious likelihood of capital gain and, while you may consider that the country has attractions worth risking life and limb for, it is unlikely that many people will be happy to rent property for holidays and leisure purposes in such countries. The chances of re-sale at any price may be difficult and indeed a prudent buyer in such markets would look on their money as effectively lost as soon as it was spent.

For Brits, some countries appear to be significantly more risky than others, though it has to be said that the actual risk of an incident serious enough to warrant contacting a British Embassy is very low in absolute terms The data published by the Foreign and Commonwealth Office (see listing below for website) gives Spain as the country where the largest number of Brits need Embassy assistance and New Zealand the one where the fewest appear to get into trouble of one sort or another. However, when the 'incident per visitor' sum is done (as done by the author and not listed in the Foreign Office table in the report), a quite different picture is revealed. France is by far and away the safest country and in Mexico you are about a hundred times more likely to need Embassy assistance.

The unruly behaviour of tourists is not the only peril in overseas markets. The very presence of a healthy market for visitors is a magnet for other hazards. In Turkey, the local Kurdish separatist movement targets tourist hot spots for a series of strategically placed bombings designed to unstabilise the market and create uncertainty. In 2006 alone, some 20 bomb attacks, liberally dotted around the coastal and tourist regions, killed 4 people and injured over 150. Were this to continue, it could well have a detrimental effect on the overseas buyer segment of the property market, as well as making life seriously unpleasant for those who have already bought property.

The following organisations will help you to track down and eliminate the most dangerous destinations from your search.

Forbes (www.forbes.com/lifestyle/travel)

This is the online US business magazine covering a wide range of business issues. In its Lifestyle–Travel section it publishes an annual list of the most dangerous countries in the world. Just type the word 'danger' into the search pane and read articles on such diverse topics as 'The most decadent and delightful spas in the world' and 'The thirteen most dangerous races in the world' (including the Big Pardubice, run each year just east of Prague in the Czech Republic, during the second week of October. In that steeplechase, riders and mounts are crushed in roughly equal proportions). The main article to look out for is their annual survey of the world's most dangerous countries. On this website you can sit back, watch the slide show and see the list of countries where body armour is more in vogue than sun cream and the advertisements are for firms offering self-defence, survival and firearms training.

US State Department (www.travel.state.gov)

This is the US Government's website for all travel issues both in and out of the United States. Select the 'International Travel' icon near the top left of the screen, on the horizontal menu bar, then select 'Travel Warnings' near the top of the vertical menu bar on the left of the screen. There you will find a list of 30 or so countries, from Algeria to Zimbabwe, where you will find terse warnings such as 'Dangers posed by landmines and unexploded ordnance throughout south Lebanon are significant and also exist in other areas where civil war fighting was intense' mingled with statements explaining that Zimbabwe's economy is in a protracted state of decline which has led to a significant increase in crime, including violent crime.

Foreign and Commonwealth Office (FCO) (`www.fco.uk.gov`).

Select 'Travel Advice by Country' from the top of the left-hand menu bar, then you will find four sections above the menu list from which you can choose individual countries. The sections are labelled:

- Countries to which the FCO advises against all travel. Here you will find a small list including the Ivory Coast, Lebanon and Somalia.
- Countries to parts of which the FCO advises against all travel. This is a list of about 26 countries, including Afghanistan, Albania, India and the Russian Federation.
- Countries to which the FCO advises against all but essential travel, including East Timor and Haiti.
- Countries to parts of which the FCO advises against all but essential travel, including Israel, Libya, Nigeria and Thailand.

Aneki.com

Aneki is an independent, privately operated website based in Montreal, dedicated to promoting wider knowledge of the world's countries and regions. Its website provides an extensive source of world rankings in a growing number of categories such as the most expensive, most populated, richest, poorest and so forth. The operators don't create the information themselves; rather, they trawl information from other organisations such as the United Nations agencies and the United States' Central Intelligence Agency's *World Fact Book.* Select 'More Lists' from the right of the horizontal menu bar at the top of the screen and you will find lists of the most dangerous countries and cities in the world, where Baghdad, Jerusalem and Brazzaville all vie for top slot.

Gallup Europe (www.gallup-europe.be)

Together with its consortium partners, including the Max Planck Institut, and with financial support from the European Commission, Gallup Europe launched in August 2006 a pan-European Crime and Safety Survey with the aim of collecting a range of measures of personal safety, along with rates of victimisation, in the most important crime categories. Among the findings of this study are that Britain is the continent's second most crime-ridden country and that while levels of crime have been declining in the United Kingdom since 1995, they are not falling as quickly as in some other EU countries. The study, based on interviews with 28,000 people in 18 countries from both Western and Eastern Europe (including 3,600 from Britain) concluded that the UK remains a 'high crime' country.

***The J Curve: A New Way to Understand Why Nations Rise and Fall*, by Ian Bremmer (Simon & Schuster, 2006)** (www.jcurvebook.com)

Bremmer's 'J Curve' aims to 'describe the political and economic forces that revitalize some states and push others toward collapse'. His premise is that if one were to graph a nation's stability as a function of its openness, the result would be a curve looking something like the Nike 'swoosh' logo. Stability is measured on the vertical axis and openness along the horizontal axis. At the top left of the curve are countries such as North Korea and Cuba, both closed and stable societies, while top right are countries such as the UK and USA – extremely open societies which are also extremely stable. In between, along the continuum, are countries such as Saudi Arabia, Russia, China and India, with varying degrees of stability and openness. The J Curve tool is intended to help determine a country's likelihood of tipping into chaos: an event that would inevitably damage property values and rental prospects by reducing tourism, inward investment and the wealth and freedoms of the local population. From the author's website you can find out more about how to apply the concept and recognise the warning signs that precede collapse. From the top horizontal menu bar, select 'Links' to be taken to a list of blog sites covering the topic generally and some countries in particular.

National Earthquake Information Center (NEIC)
(http://earthquake.usgs.gov/regional/neic/)

It may be something of a shock to learn that there are around 200 earthquakes taking place each week somewhere in the world, most of which measure more than 4 on the Richter Scale. Croatia, Slovenia, Ukraine, Turkey and India are among countries popular with overseas property buyers but which have seen recent earthquake activity. You can relax, however, as 6.5 is the point at which an earthquake is of serious concern, and those are much less frequent. Turkey's disastrous quake in 1999 measured 7.2, resulting in over 17,000 people killed, 50,000 injured, 500,000 made homeless and some €5 billion damage to property. The same year, an earthquake measuring 5.6 occurred in Cyprus where just 15 people were injured and around 80 buildings were damaged or destroyed.

The mission of the NEIC is to determine rapidly the location and size of all destructive earthquakes worldwide and immediately to distribute this information to national and international agencies, scientists and the general public.

The death penalty and other serious sentences

Around 68 countries retain the death penalty for a range of crimes, some of which would perhaps not be considered particularly serious in your home country. Carrying a relatively small amount of certain drugs that would merit little more than a slap on the wrist in the UK could warrant the death penalty in Thailand. In Vietnam, 29 offences attract capital penalties, including economic offences such as tax fraud. According to local media reports, 21 people were executed in Vietnam last year; and according to Amnesty International in 2005, a not exceptional year, at least 2,148 people were executed in 22 countries and at least 5.186 people were sentenced to death in 53 countries. These were only minimum figures; the true figures were certainly higher.

Whatever the economic or holiday attractions of a particular country, if it is a liberal user of the death penalty, and especially if its views on what constitutes a capital crime stray far from the more generally accepted norm, then you may decide to eliminate it from your prospects list.

It is not just the prospect of a death penalty that might make a country unattractive from an outsider's perspective. Penalties for many crimes, even relatively minor ones, can be severe and include massive fines and long prison sentences in harsh conditions. A crime that might attract a 1-year sentence in Canada, for example, could merit 48 years in Romania and a daunting 137 years in Columbia.

The following websites will help you find out about the prevalence of death and long-term jail sentences:

Amnesty International (`www.amnesty.ie`)

While the chances of your personally being involved in any crime sufficiently serious as to warrant the death penalty might be exceedingly remote, it is a rough guide to how a country views crime if that country retains the ultimate penalty. In its latest annual analysis on the use of the death penalty worldwide, Amnesty International revealed that there are over 20,000 people on death row across the world, waiting to be executed by their own governments. They also disclosed that at least 2,148 people were executed during 2005 in 22 countries, 94% of whom were in just 4 countries (China, Iran, Saudi Arabia and the USA), while 5,186 people were sentenced to death in 53 countries. Type 'death penalty' into the search pane in the top left of the screen and you will find these statistics and other facts, including the sobering revelation that just 75 countries have abolished the death penalty for all crimes.

United Nations Survey on Crime Trends and the Operations of Criminal Justice Systems (www.unodc.org/unodc/index.htm)

Select 'Research and Analysis' from the left-hand vertical menu, then 'Crime Surveys'. There you can find one of the UN's periodic surveys on all aspects of crime, including sentencing and fines, as well as the main components of the criminal justice system- police, prosecution, courts and prisons.

World Justice Information Network (WJIN) (www.wjin.net)

As an information, news and research network covering international crime and other related topics, WJIN is primarily a system of interconnected web-logs (blogs) and supporting tools where WJIN members can create, search and share research on crime and justice. For the most part, the reports on the site are academic in nature, but a few reports, such as 'The Worst of the Worst: The World's Most Repressive Societies', 'World Prison Population List' and 'The World Factbook of Criminal Justice', throw up a some interesting insights into life in some of the counties (such as the USA, Ukraine, China and Russia) currently being marketed as desirable places in which to buy property.

Country overviews

Before delving into the finer detail of how economies perform across countries, it is useful to have a general 'thumbnail sketch', which may provide enough information to rule a particular country or region in or out of your more exhaustive study. For example, knowing that Qatar, as well as being a useful word to use in Scrabble, as one of the few not requiring a 'u' after the 'q', has all-year sunshine and no personal income tax may be enough to attract further attention. Perhaps discovering that the presence of landmines still cripples Croatia's recovery, restricts mobility and impedes development may wipe the shine off the view from the wonderful Adriatic coastline. Thirteen of Croatia's 21 counties are affected by landmines, covering 1,700 square kilometres.

The following websites provide information across a wide range of matters relevant to property buyers:

Expat-Focus Country Guides
(www.expatfocus.com/expatriate-country-guides)

Expat Focus provides a free service (access to which requires only registration), based loosely on the Wikipedia model: that is, expatriates themselves provide much of the information. The purpose of the service is to make life easier for anyone moving or living abroad, by providing a comprehensive expatriate information and support resource. In addition to providing information, it also seeks to establish some form of support network in each country. Expat Focus hosts forums, blogs and newsletters, as well as providing book reviews and technical articles on various aspects of living in a particular country as seen from the eyes of foreigners actually living there now. Its website also carries property listings covering sale and both short- and long-term rental. Real estate brokers, lawyers and other professional advisers advertise here too.

The services provided are clustered under the following headings:

- Overview
- Climate and Weather
- Getting There
- Speaking the Language
- Visas, Residency, Immigration and Documentation
- Currency and Cost of Living
- Foreign Currency – how to secure a favourable exchange rate
- Banking
- Taxation
- Insurance

- Healthcare and Medical Treatment
- Social Security
- Employment
- Renting Property
- Buying Property
- Education and Schools
- Utilities (Electricity, Gas, Water)
- Communications (Telephone, Post, Internet, TV)
- Driving and Public Transport
- Leisure, Entertainment and Sports
- Retirement and Pension Issues
- Taking Your Pets.

Don't expect more than a few lines, or at most a page, on each section, but it is sufficient to either whet the appetite or induce caution.

Expat Focus covers only around 60 countries, a list of which you will find on Page 80, but they are the ones currently most in favour with buyers of overseas property.

Landmine Monitor (ICBL) (www.icbl.org/lm)

In June 1998, the International Campaign to Ban Landmines (ICBL) established Landmine Monitor to monitor and report on implementation of and compliance with the 1997 Mine Ban Treaty and, more generally, to assess the international community's response to the humanitarian crisis caused by landmines. On its website, in the 'Quick Links' box on the right-hand side of the page, you can search the world for signs of danger from this hazard that still claim hundreds of lives each year. In 1999, seven Austrian tourists were killed by a landmine in Croatia. In 2004, 5 people were killed in a landmine explosion while crossing the Greek–Turkish border and 2 people were injured in Cyprus in the buffer zone between Turkish and Greek zones. In 2005, over 350 mines and items of unexploded ordnance were discovered and marked in Morocco.

Table 6.1 Countries covered by Expat Focus

Andorra	Malta
Australia	Mexico
Belgium	Morocco
Bulgaria	The Netherlands (Holland)
Canada	New Zealand
Cayman Islands	Norway
China	Panama
Costa Rica	Philippines
Croatia	Poland
Cyprus	Portugal
Czech Republic	Qatar
Dominican Republic	Romania
Egypt	Russia
Estonia	Saudi Arabia
France	Singapore
Germany	Slovakia
Greece and the Greek Islands	South Africa
Hong Kong	Spain
Hungary	Sweden
India	Switzerland
Ireland	Thailand
Italy	Turkey
Japan	United Arab Emirates (UAE)
Malaysia	United Kingdom (UK)
	United States of America (USA)
	Vietnam

Source: Expat Focus (`www.expatfocus.com`)

World Travel Guides (`www.worldtravelguide.net/country`)

Columbus Travel Publishing Ltd. has been producing the *World Travel Guide* book for over a quarter of a century and has published the basic data online since 1996. It has a team of 20 researchers and a worldwide network of freelance journalists and travel writers who between them produce 4 publications of value to overseas property buyers, though they are primarily written with tourists in mind: a Country Guide; an in-depth World City Guide (providing information on over 100 culturally important cities); a World Events and Attractions Guide; and a unique World Airport Guide.

- The Country Guides cover every country in the world. For larger countries, such as America and Australia, or countries (such as France and Spain) with far-flung dependencies, each separate area is covered. The guides are rarely more than an A4 page long and provide a potted history, the prevailing economic and political situation and the country's main tourist and sporting appeal as well as some information on geography and climate.
- The City Guides provide a snippet of information (barely a couple of paragraphs long in many cases) saying something about the architecture, attractions, food and cultural environment in each city.
- The World Events Guides provide information on thousands of activities such as trade fairs, festivals, exhibitions, competitions, concerts and the like, throughout the world. The database can be searched by country; by major city or region within each country; or by theme (such as Art, Entertainment, Business, History and so forth). You can restrict the search to events happening today, tomorrow, in the next 7 or 28 days, or at any time. A quick search yielded details as varied as the Naval Academy Regatta (an international sailing competition which has taken place since the 1940s, held in Rio de Janeiro's Baia de Guanabara, with the Sugarloaf Mountain as a backdrop); the Znojmo Wine Harvest Festival (vinobrani), held in the Czech Republic, throughout southern Moravia, to celebrate the arrival of 'Burcak', the new, semi-fermented wine, in late August and early September; and the Red Bull BWA (Big Wave Africa) which, since 1999, has offered top local and international surfers the opportunity to compete at the unpredictable, deep-water reef break known as 'Dungeons', near Cape Town in South Africa. This information could be useful in choosing the time of your visit to a country and in assessing its potential for tourism that,

in turn, will affect how much rental income you might be able to generate.

- The Airport Guides give details of each country's main airports: where they are, how to reach them by public transport, links to nearby hotels, information on where you can park and how much it will cost, and what type of food and drink you can expect to find, plus information on facilities for disabled travellers. This certainly is a unique assembly of information, but at present only 65 countries are covered, so don't expect to find airports in Lithuania, Latvia, Bulgaria, Romania or, for that matter, Croatia covered, yet.

Property blogs

Overseas Properties Online is one of a growing number of websites hosting blogs where overseas property buyers, both those actually having a property and those still at the research stage, can share experiences and knowledge. As with any blog, the information is largely unedited, unverified and inevitably partisan. But a recurring theme – such as 'this developer is useless' or buying a property in this or that country is more difficult or expensive than most others – would be at least a signal as to where to do some additional checking.

There are plenty of blogs competing with Overseas Property Online:

Property Blog
(http://blog.overseaspropertyonline.com/blog/)

This is a blog on the Overseas Property Online website. The main function of the site is to act as a shop window for estate agents and property developers in around 40 countries worldwide. Rather a lot of the postings are listed as having been put on by their own blog administrator rather than by 'real' people, that is property buyers or those living in the country. So check for the telltale 'OPO admin' signature in the blog.

British Blog Directory (`www.britblog.com`)

This is a directory of blogs aimed primarily at Brits, either at home or abroad, but not primarily at overseas property buyers; rather, it covers a multitude of topics. The directory can be searched in two main ways: by location of 'blogger' or by category. However, the most useful way to search is by typing in your area of interest in the search panel at the top left of the home page screen. Entering 'overseas property', for example, came up with ongoing blogs covering varied topics such as currency conversion, life in Bermuda and the pitfalls of buying property in Turkey. The site claims to have around 6,000 themes running at any one time. Typing 'Russia' into the search box reveals that 9 blogs are running and 7 members have a specific interest in Russia, while entering 'South Africa' shows 30 blog themes running on that topic.

Newbricks.com (`www.nubricks.com`)

This site is attempting to build a global property-savvy spotter network, to help investors identify the 'Next Big Thing' in property development. The hallmarks of 'Newbricks' development are: Alternative Living; Inspired Design; Prime Location; Innovative Construction; Value for Money; and Strong Investment Potential. Newbricks invites anyone and everyone with a healthy fascination with all things propertyeither to send in information on a development or country they are researching or to join in a blog related to that topic. Currently there are over 60 country blogs running, including some more esoteric destinations in the Dominican Republic and India. Many of the blogs seem to be 'inspired' by advertisers flogging property, but the blog threads seem real enough. There are also some helpful links to additional research data. For example, you can learn that the World Bank has agreed to lend Bulgaria 240 million a year until 2009, to help it to boost its presence as a tourist and investment hot spot, then click on a link to the relevant World Bank website where you can verify that fact, rather than, say, just take a real estate broker's word for it.

Globe of Blogs (www.globeofblogs.com)

Launched in 2002, this claimed to be the first comprehensive world weblog directory. Links up to over 46,000 blogs, searchable by country, topic and about any other criteria you care to name.

Online newspaper articles

Many newspapers and journals make available at no cost articles published on property-related matters. Among the most useful are:

Times Online (www.timesonline.co.uk)

This provides articles from *The Times* and *The Sunday Times*. Currently, there are over 8,000 articles listed under the heading 'International Property'. A search within those articles for those covering the Ukraine, by way of example, narrowed that down to 13 articles. On this site you will find articles offering pointers as to where the latest property hot spots are; which countries to avoid like the plague; and how to exploit a tax loophole and put your overseas property into a pension fund. The online article database covers the past 2 years.

Google News (www.google.com)

You can tap into this by selecting 'News' on the horizontal menu at the top of the page, under the Google banner. Here you will find links to any newspaper article anywhere in the world covering a particular topic. Asking for information on real estate reveals, for example, that ING, the Dutch bank, according to the *Bucharest Daily News*, opened a branch of their real estate investment division in September 2006 and that the *Daily Telegraph* has warned about the dangers of going on broker-sponsored inspection trips. While the search database is very wide, at present Google keeps only 30 days of articles on file.

Telegraph.Co (`www.telegraph.co.uk`)

This carries articles from the *Sunday Telegraph* and *Daily Telegraph* online. There is an extensive property section (`www.telegraph.co.uk/property/index.jhtml`) carrying over 1,500 articles on varied aspects of the international property market. There is an 'Expat' section (select 'Expat' from the left-hand menu bar) containing articles on life in countries ranging from the Dordogne in France through to St Kitts in the Caribbean and on to Rio de Janeiro. The *Daily Telegraph* produces periodic surveys on the state of the overseas property market.

Find Articles.com (`www.findarticles.com`)

This aims to provide credible, freely available information you can trust. It has over 10 million articles from thousands of resources, archived and dating back to 1984. You can see a summary of all articles and most are free, though in some cases you may need a modest subscription rarely more than a few pounds. You can restrict your search to those articles which are free by selecting 'Free articles only' from the right-hand pull-down menu.

Economic performance and political stability

Confidence in the future is an important factor in determining the likely future value of assets such as property. Countries with a relatively shaky hold on democracy make for unattractive places to invest in the long term. Thailand seemed to many a safe place in which to buy property, until the coup in 2006. While that was its first in 15 years, it has had 18 coups since 1932 and 15 re-writes of its constitution. Dictatorships often re-write the rules with little concern for world public opinion and with at best a limited grasp of the economic consequences of their actions. Witness the plunge in value of assets of every class, including property, when Thailand's new leaders announced new controls on foreign investments in January 2007.

If an economy is growing steadily year on year, rather than in sharp spurts only to be followed by abrupt declines, potential buyers will have the confidence to put a toe, perhaps even a whole foot, into the market. The reasons that property buyers prefer steadiness to meteoric economic burst is that it implies that a country has a strategy and an underlying residual value proposition that will endure. High economic growth creates wealth that in turn provides a country's residents with the wherewithal to buy more or better properties, which then leads in turn to increases in price. High inflation means that property owners and investors have less money left in their pocket to put into housing and tenants have less money left over to pay the rent. During periods of high inflation, while the nominal price of properties may appear to be rising, usually the country's currency is depreciating at a faster rate, making the real value of property lower. Also, high inflation erodes confidence in an economy and in the assets that money can buy, including property. In periods of high inflation, economic activity slows down and generally people become less wealthy and investment levels decline: neither of these factors is helpful to property markets.

Ireland is a prime example where a shift in economic strategy led to economic prosperity and to one of the fastest and most sustained rise in property prices anywhere in the world.

In 1987, Ireland underperformed against the EU average GDP (Gross Domestic Product) per person by a third, yet by 2006 it was comfortably overperforming against that average by a similar proportion. At the same time, inflation was brought down by two-thirds. The much-quoted reason for the 'Celtic Tiger's' miracle performance was Ireland's membership of the EU. But economists have pored over the entrails of the EU effect and concluded that, while helpful, it was not the major factor contributing to economic growth. The real reasons were, in descending order of importance:

- In the 1960s and 1970s, Ireland had high income-tax rates which discouraged growth, but from the early 1990s taxes started to come down rapidly.
- The Fianna Fail Government, supported by the Opposition party Fine Gael in a clear demonstration of political maturity, started to cut government spending, and borrowing which, combined with falling interest rates, gave the economy a much-needed boost.
- Ireland's Industrial Development Authority (IDA), aided by zero rates of corporate tax, attracted hundreds of international companies to its shores by winning big FDI (Foreign Direct Investment) projects in such businesses as software, semiconductors, personal computers, pharmaceuticals and medical devices.

Housing markets are finely balanced by supply and demand. If there are too many buyers and too few properties, prices rise. If a market is suddenly flooded by properties, prices can stall or even fall. Usually, developers building new properties keep a careful watch and try to keep the equation in balance. But what if tens of thousands – perhaps even millions – of a country's citizens head for the exit? Fanciful? It has happened several times in Eastern and Central Europe. Bulgaria's population shrank by 1 million over the period between 1991 and 2002, leaving over 300,000 homes empty and for the most part unsold. Could it happen again? Well, if Russia's President Putin has his way: yes. In February 2006, Mr Putin commissioned a study to explore ways to repatriate 'compatriots' who were left abroad in 1991 when the Iron Curtain fell. His goal is to stem the decline in population which has shrunk by 6 million since 1992. If the incentives on offer to return to Russia pull in many of the 675,000 Russians in Latvia, the 330,000 in Estonia, the 278,000 in Lithuania or the 8.2 million living in Ukraine, the effect on local property prices could be significant. The CIA website listed below gives details on populations and trends.

> Gross Domestic Product is the total value of goods and services produced in a country over a period of time, measuring all of a country's economic activity irrespective of whos owns the productive assets in that country. For example, the output of a Japanese-owned motor manufacture in the United Kingdom is counted as part of the UK's GDP rather than part of Japan's. GDP is a measure of the standard of living in a country; by dividing a country's GDP by its population, we can deduce the GDP per head. When GDP grows at a faster rate than the population, standards of living are said to be rising, and vice versa.

The following websites provide valuable current information on economic performance and stability, listed by country and by region.

The Central Intelligence Agency (CIA) World Factbook
`(www.cia.gov/cia/publications/factbook)`

The CIA website itself is worthy of closer inspection, as, here, you can find a host of fascinating information in the Library and Reference section, listed on the left-hand menu bar. Selecting 'World Factbook' from this menu will allow access to previous editions and so offer a perspective on changing events. The above link will take you straight to the latest edition of the Factbook. The CIA keeps the Factbook up to date on a regular basis throughout the year, so you can be reasonably confident of having the most current information to hand.

- **Country Data:** Once in the Factbook, you are offered a pull-down bar in the top left of the screen, which allows you to select any one of the 233 countries or regions afforded separate status for analytical purposes by the CIA.(For example, while the Gaza Strip is not a recognised country, it is included in the CIA data.) For each country there are around half a dozen A4 pages of basic economic, political and demographic information, as well as information on political disputes that may cause problems in the future. For example, looking at 'Brazil' will reveal that at the convergence of that country's borders with Argentina and Paraguay, money laundering, smuggling, arms and illegal narcotics trafficking are rife, as is fundraising for extremist organisations. The country is also in dispute with Uruguay over certain islands; with Argentina over land; and with everyone else over its claim to the United Nations Convention on the Law of the Sea (UNCLOS) to extend its maritime continental margin. Alongside information on the age, sex, life expectancy and general health of the population are the basic economic facts on GDP growth and GDP per head, inflation rates and the country's level of international indebtedness. You can also see information on the main political parties; when the last election was; who won and by what margin; and what problems may loom on the horizon. For example, the facts that Thailand is currently facing armed violence in its three Muslim-majority southernmost provinces; that land subsidence in the Bangkok area, resulting from the depletion of the water table, is a serious problem; that a snap government election held on 2 April 2006 was invalidated by the Constitutional Court; and that HIV/AIDs affects 1.5% of the population (around 8 times the rate prevailing in the UK, for example) may temper the enthusiasm of the more risk-averse property buyer.

- **Rank Order Pages:** These allow you to follow a number of analytical threads which let you compare and contrast countries with one another. Select 'Guide to Rank Order Pages' from the left-hand menu bar. These are lists of data from 47 of the Factbook data fields, given in descending order – from highest to lowest – with two exceptions (the Unemployment Rate and the Inflation Rate, which are in ascending – from lowest to highest – order). Using these pages, you will find that Bermuda has the highest GDP per capita and the Gaza Strip the lowest and that Slovenia, Cyprus and Greenland are all ahead of Portugal, Argentina and Russia in this respect. When it come in inflation, Zimbabwe leads the pack (with 200%) and Venezuela, Ukraine, Russia, Jamaica, Kenya and Turkey all have double-figure inflation rates. Using unemployment as a criterion for ranking shows countries such as Poland, Croatia and South Africa, for example, among a list of 100-plus countries, with around a fifth of their workforces unemployed, which in turn would indicate that few of the locals will be in the property market in any serious way.

World Economic Forum (www.weforum.org/en)

Select 'Initiatives' on the left of the horizontal menu bar, near the top of the screen. Once there, select 'Global Competitiveness' from the vertical menu bar on the right of the screen. There you will find the Growth Competitiveness Index (GCI), first published in 1979, with its coverage expanded each year since, now extending to 117 major and emerging economies. Factors covered by the GCI include access to highly skilled people; efficiency of government processes; quality of infrastructure and research institutions; and the competitive pressures faced by companies. The overall GCI aims to measure the capacity of the national economy to achieve sustained economic growth over the medium and long term, taking into account the current level of development. The Index is tested each year to confirm that it does indeed correlate with rates of economic growth from the recent past.

The report itself costs £65, but it is covered extensively in a series of press releases appearing on the Forum's site and elsewhere, around mid-September when it is published. Korea, Estonia, Chile, Slovenia, Cyprus, Malta, Thailand, the Czech Republic and Hungary are countries which have started to make a strong showing in this study, indicating that their medium- to long-term economic performance should be beneficial to those investing in property among other activities.

World Bank (www.worldbank.org/)

Among the myriad of studies and reports published by the World Bank are these less well-known ones on governance. One, on 'Political Stability' (by Kaufmann *et al.*) draws 194 different measures from 17 different sources of subjective governance data constructed by 15 different organisations, to arrive at a single score for each country. The scores range from around –2.5 to around 2.5, where higher or positive values indicate greater political stability. Afghanistan, at −2.21, is close to the bottom of the league; Lebanon scores −0.59; Thailand 0.55; and Switzerland 1.64.

The Economist (www.economist.com) **(fee payable)**

While the *CIA Factbook* provides unrivalled historic economic and political data, free of charge, if you want an authoritative opinion of what the future holds, you will have to pay for it. *The Economist* provides the most cost-effective and reliable way to have a crystal ball in your hand, and a 3-year subscription to receive the hard copy mailed to your address and to have access to the Internet database will cost £50 a year. Some information on this site requires an additional payment, but the vast majority is covered in the annual subscription cost. These are some of the ways you can access 10 years' worth of data on *The Economist's* website, using the 'Research Tools' pull-down menu at the top left of the screen.

- **Economics A–Z:** provides an explanation of the most commonly used terms in economics, including 'inflation', 'GDP', 'inward investment' and so forth.
- **Backgrounders:** give a paragraph or two of information on an industry, country or business sector, together with pointers to further data.
- **Surveys:** lists recent studies on countries or topics such as EU enlargement or progress in Portugal over the past 15 years, which provide a comprehensive perspective.

- **Forecasts:** which can be found by selecting the country in question from the pull-down menu on the left of the screen, named 'Country Briefing'. Once in the country area, you will find a choice of sections including; forecasts (of GDP, inflation and the like); factsheets (showing average GDP growth over the past 5 years, inflation rates and the proportion of Foreign Direct Investment); economic data; and political forces, as well as a list of all *Economist* articles on the country.

NationMaster.com (www.nationmaster.com)

A few years back, when Luke Metcalfe was surfing around the *CIA Factbook*, he came to the conclusion that while the individual figures didn't mean much on their own, they'd be more illuminating if they were placed alongside those of other countries and shown relative to population. NationMaster is a vast compilation of data from such sources as the *CIA World Factbook*, the UN and the OECD. Using the tools on the website, you can generate maps and graphs on all kinds of statistics with ease. Their aim is to be the web's one-stop resource for country statistics on everything. Using NationMaster, you can see the ranking at a glance for all of a country's key economic data, among other factors. So, for example, at a glance you can see that the Czech Republic has the 100th-fastest growing economy, while its GDP per head puts it in 41st place.

Alexander's Gas & Oil Connections (www.gasandoil.com)

Why overseas property buyers will benefit from tracking the oil and gas sector is because the industry is fast proving a reliable indicator of property price movements. Trinidad and Tobago, for example, on the back of discoveries that have made it the biggest supplier of liquefied natural gas after its larger neighbour, the United States, has seen its economy grow at near-Chinese rates. Foreign direct investment is growing rapidly; unemployment has dropped from 22% down to 7% in a decade; and prices of top-quality houses have tripled in just 3 years.

Alexander's Gas and Oil Connections is a portal site for largely free information on the global gas, oil, power and affiliated industry, read largely by professionals in the oil and gas and industry (upstream, mid-stream and downstream); the service and supply industry; the power industry; major banks, governments and universities, as well as by many analysts, consultants and other experts around the world. It provides news on exploration and production discoveries, as well information on international developments that could have a bearing on oil or gas supply and demand.

CountryWatch (www.countrywatch.com) **(fee payable)**

This is an information provider for corporations, government agencies, universities, schools, libraries and individuals needing up-to-date news and information on each of the recognised countries of the world. CountryWatch provides country-specific intelligence in an up-to-date series of publications for each of 192 countries, including demographic, political, economic, business, cultural and environmental information, as well as daily news coverage and a significant news archive. A 5-year macroeconomic forecast and a 20-year forecast of energy demand, supply, and pricing is provided for each country. One-year online-access to information on all countries costs from $99.

Cost and standard of living

One factor high on the list of desirable features for most people buying properties abroad is that the country they are considering has a lower cost of living than their own. They would like everything (such as bread, beer, clothing, a meal out, a bus ride and a visit to the cinema or a theatre) that goes to make up a typical shopping basket to be cheaper than it would be at home. That will ensure that their money will go further, as will that of anyone holidaying in the country, thus making it a better rental proposition. But, at the same time, they would hope that the country would be as developed as their home country and the provision of services and the general well-being of those living in the country they are considering buying into is high. Needless to say, these two elements often pull in opposite directions, but they are not always diametrically opposed.

In many of the countries you will research, the cost of living is a fraction of that in the UK or the USA. You can live in a Romanian village for a year for what the average Brit would spend on groceries in a month. But you won't find a museum, a cinema with English films, a reasonable choice of restaurants, pleasing buildings, good roads, street lighting or perhaps even regular refuse collection. The nearest airport may be 4 hours away and the only hospital worthy of the name in the capital city or further away still. If you and your partner are self-contained and healthy, that may not matter. But for the socially minded, you may find it worth trading up to a higher cost and higher quality of living.

Checking out the following resources will help identify which countries are good value as a living experience rather than just cheap.

Realtor.com (`www.realtor.com`)

This is the website of the US National Association of Realtors. Select 'Moving' from the menu bar at the top of the screen, and then from the 'Moving Tools' menu in the middle of the left hand menu, select 'Salary Calculator'. Once in the Salary Calculator tool, select the term 'International Salary Calculator' highlighted in blue at the bottom of the first paragraph. Now, the purpose of this tool is to help you negotiate an appropriate salary package when your organisation, or one you are considering joining, has a job overseas. But this is just as effective at working out how far your existing income will go in a foreign country.

In this screen you are asked to enter the country where you now live and the one to which you are planning to move to. Put in 'United Kingdom' and 'Russia' respectively and then select the menu bar entitled 'Show Cities'. Now you will be given a choice of 7 UK cities (from Belfast to Manchester) and 2 Russian cities (Moscow and

St Petersburg). By selecting London and Moscow, you will see that for every $100,000 you make in London, you will need to earn $96,599 in Moscow. So the cost of living in Moscow is cheaper, but only just. Making the same calculation but comparing London with Cape Town in South Africa, you would need to earn only $68,707 to be as well off as you were in London on $100,000. In other words, the cost of living is around a third cheaper in Cape Town.

Realtor.com includes information for over 700 international cities, with costs using 162 different currencies. Its cost of living numbers are adjusted for the exchange rate that prevailed at that time it collected the data, so if that exchange rate has moved substantially since the data was updated, the cost of living comparison might be different. The components of the cost of living index are: housing cost (33%); utility cost (8%); consumables, food, drink, meals out etc. (16%); transportation (10%); and other services such as cinema, theatre attendance etc, (33%). It makes no allowance for local taxes and inflation, so you need to allow for those yourself.

(This a far from perfect model, but if you want the 'real thing', you will have to buy it from *The Economist* Intelligence Unit-EIU (www// eiu.enumerate.com) at a cost of around $520 per city-to-city comparison. You will also have access to the EIU's Quality of Living Index, which gives an indication of how pleasant or otherwise it is to live in a particular city.)

EURES The European Job Mobility Portal
(www.ec.europa.eu/eures)

This site is intended to help job seekers and employers but it has some general information about the cost of living and wages in each EU country. Select 'en' from the menu bar in the middle of the screen, then, from the 'Living and Working' pull-down menu bar, select the country you are interested in. Once in the country section, choose 'Living and Working Conditions' and from the 'Living Conditions' pull-down menu bar, select 'Incomes and Cost of Living'.

There is some other useful information on the site, on taxes and accommodation rental and selling prices. All information is updated twice a year.

United Nations Development Programme (www.undp.org)

The Human Development Index (HDI), published annually by the UN, ranks nations according to their citizens' quality of life rather than strictly by their traditional economic figures. The criteria for calculating rankings is a summary composite index measuring 33 aspects of a country's average achievements in three basic aspects of human development: longevity, knowledge and a decent standard of living.

From the main menu, choose 'Human Development Data' from the menu on the left of the page. Then select 'Get Data', from which you can choose the country you are interested in or you can 'Build your own table' and choose the countries and indicators you are interested in and download formatted tables, either on-screen or to an Excel file.

Mercer Human Resources Consultancy (www.mercerhr.com)

Its twice-yearly 'Cost of Living Report' covers 300 cities around the world and is calculated using 186 separate items considered to be a typical basket of goods and services. The items are selected from a range of supermarkets, convenience stores and department stores designed to reflect the typical spending pattern of an expatriate executive living in a foreign city. You can find the report by typing its title into the search pane on the company website. Unfortunately, the report itself is expensive (several hundred dollars for partial information), so you will almost certainly have to content yourself with the press release of the data which you can find by typing 'press release' into the search pane. The press release includes about three A4 pages of basic data which gives a ranking of cities from the most expensive to the cheapest.

Mercer also produces a 'World-wide quality of living survey' which checks out the 39 criteria which, in its opinion, make life bearable or otherwise. Once again, the report is costly, but the press release is free and helpful. It can be found by using the same search method as for the Cost of Living Report.

World Wealth Report (`www.ml.com`)

Enter the words 'Annual World Wealth Report', into the search pane in the top-right corner of Merrill Lynch's (ML) website and the product of a collaborative relationship between ML and Capgemini, initiated in 1985, will show up. The study was established to develop an understanding of the investment needs of the world's high net-worth individuals (HNWIs). Aside from the understandably selfish needs of the investment industry, the report provides a fascinating insight into where serious money is being made; and where the number of people becoming seriously rich is growing the fastest: property price rises can't be too far behind.

The World Wealth Report covers 68 countries which between them account for over 98% of global Gross National Income and 99% of world stock market capitalisation. Among the countries producing new millionaires at the fastest rate are: India, Spain, Korea, the Czech Republic and China. In 2006, the study was extended to include recent European Union entrants Cyprus, Slovakia and Slovenia, as well as Kazakhstan, Tunisia, Ukraine, Uruguay and Vietnam.

Inward investment and business climate

Key drivers for property prices and yields include the quantity of inward investment and the ease with which businesses can start up and grow. The reasons are simple to understand. International companies are most likely to locate subsidiaries, branches and joint ventures in countries which have signs of having a benign business environment. Sure, those countries need low labour costs, but they also need a workforce with skills and the ability to produce goods and services to compete in international markets. It doesn't matter too much what those goods and services are: for example, Romania has carved out a new niche as a centre for film production and the Czech Republic has seen new life injected into its motor industry when Volkswagen took Skoda under its wing.

The effect of a favourable business climate on the property market should not be underestimated. With inward investment come executives, usually on short-term contracts, who need suitable property to rent and who have the wherewithal to pay high rents, at least high by local standards. Also, this inward investment stimulates employment and creates new higher paid jobs for workers in the host country as businesses become established and expand. That in turn means that the pool of locals who can afford housing or move to better properties expands, which in turn stimulates demand and prices and rents start to rise.

A good forward indicator of property prices and rental yields is when inward investment picks up and businesses bureaucracies are simplified. There are few, if any, property markets which have seen strong profit performance that was not heralded by such conditions.

Organisation for Economic Co-operation and Development (OECD)
(www.oecd.org)

The OECD tracks economic and social data on some 100 countries, monitoring their progress towards becoming market economies. It is best known for its publications and its statistics, covering issues ranging from macroeconomics to trade, education, development and science and innovation.

Select 'Publications' from the 'Find' menu on the left of the home page. Then enter the title of one of its most useful reports ('Trends and recent developments in foreign and direct investment') into the search box. The latest report should appear at the top of the list of publications. In this report, as well as finding out where most foreign direct investment (FDI) is going, you can see countries whose FDI has stalled. For example, in June 2006 the OECD report shows that cumulative inflows of FDI for the period 1996–2005 put Poland, Turkey, the Czech Republic and the Slovak Republic in the top 30 countries for FDI. China, India, Brazil and Romania also showed up strongly in the statistics, while investment in Argentina and Chile was static.

The OECD produces over 200 reports on inward investment and related topics and most of the 'long abstracts', providing sufficient information for most property investor's purposes, are free. The 'Advanced Search' facility, at the bottom of the page once you are in the 'Find' section, allows you to search by country and topic for any report from 1997 onwards. Entering, for example, 'Albania' here throws up 5 relevant reports.

US Department of State Investment Climate Reports
(http://www.state.gov/e/eb/ifd/2005)

Investment Climate Statements are prepared each year as an aid to US businesses operating in overseas markets. The statements are updated each year as Chapter 7 in the Country Commercial Guides, which can be found listed by country at the US Department of Commerce's website: www.export.gov.

The statements cover general characteristics, such as openness to foreign investment and treatment of foreign investors, which, though not specifically directed to property investors, has a strong bearing on matters that will be of interest to them. For example, looking at Peru, you will find that that under the country's constitution, foreign investors cannot 'acquire or possess under any title, land, forests, waters, mines or fuel or energy sources' within 50 km of Peru's international borders. However, foreigners can obtain concessions and rights within the restricted areas with the authorisation of a supreme resolution approved by the Cabinet. Such authorisation requires a favourable opinion from the Joint Command of the Armed Forces. You will also see that while, in principle, secured interests in property are recognised, the Peruvian judicial system is often very slow to hear cases and to issue decisions. In addition, outcomes have been difficult to predict and enforce, and corruption is frequently alleged. All in all, both local and foreign investors find that contracts are often difficult to enforce in Peru. Neither of these factors would inspire much confidence in Peru as a place in which to invest heavily in property.

In the final section of each country statement is given information on FDI, showing how much money has been invested and by which overseas country. For Peru, Spain is the largest foreign investor, followed by the UK and then the US.

Doing Business (www.doingbusiness.org)

Provided as a collaborative venture by the World Bank Group in cooperation with the Lex Mundi Association of law firms and the International Bar Association, the Doing Business database assesses and measures business regulations and their enforcement across 155 countries. Its indicators identify specific regulations which enhance or constrain business investment, productivity and growth and provide yardsticks to gauge the cost of doing business in each country covered.

Information for the databases is collected from studies of existing laws and regulations in each economy; targeted interviews with regulators or private-sector professionals in each topic; and co-operative arrangements with other departments of the World Bank, the European Bank for Reconstruction and Development's Transition Report, the World Economic Forum's Global Competitiveness Report, the Fraser Institute's Economic Freedom of the World and other donor agencies, private consulting firms, business and law associations. The topics, whose contents are updated annually, include:

- Starting a Business
- Closing a Business
- Paying Taxes
- Dealing with Licenses

- Employing Workers
- Registering Property
- Getting Credit
- Protecting Investors
- Trading Across Borders
- Enforcing Contracts.

You can use the database to get a snapshot of each economy's aggregate ranking on the ease of doing business and on each of the 10 topics which comprise the overall ranking, by selecting the 'Explore Economies' facility. Using that and selecting, say, Estonia as your target country, you can see that it is the 16th-best country out of 155 in which to do business. The best country for doing business in is New Zealand and the worst the Congo. Estonia's weakest area when it comes to doing business is in 'Employing Workers', where it comes 111th, as hiring and firing is an expensive process.

Data is also provided for each country, for all the 10 topics covered in the database. You can also produce tailored reports on selected countries, using specific measures for ease of comparison.

The Economist Intelligence Unit (`www.eiu.com`) (fee payable)

The Unit claims, with some justification, to be the world's foremost provider of country, industry and management analysis, with more than 40 offices worldwide. Its mission is to provide executives with authoritative analysis and forecasts so that they can make informed global decisions.

Among the Unit's many reports is an annual survey of business environments. Type 'The Best Place to Do Business In' into the search pane and you will see its annual survey listed. While these surveys have to be paid for, if you go to the bottom of the screen, you will find a free press release which, as well as providing a table showing the ranking of all 155 countries covered, gives a brief summary of which countries are doing best and worst and why.

IPA World (www.ipaworld.com) **(fee payable)**

IPA World is published by Oxford Intelligence and provides a community site for professionals involved in cross-border business expansion and location as well as providing news and information about some 7,000 international companies on the move. Its four main interlocking services are:

- **Reports Index:** This is an archive of publications about FDI, international trade, global locations, industry sectors and economic forecasts.
- **Events:** This is a calendar of key international trade fairs, exhibitions, conferences, trade missions and inward investment events.
- **Jobs**: Provides a site where professionals working in investment and trade promotion can post their own recruitment needs and view job adverts.
- **IPA World Directory**: A comprehensive directory of government agencies and organisations offering location assistance and advice.

You can get a free trial by registering on the website; annual subscription to the service starts from £300.

European Investment Monitor (EIM) (www.eyeim.com)

EIM, produced for Ernst & Young, the international accountancy firm, by Oxford Intelligence, is the most comprehensive source of cross-border investment projects and trends throughout Europe. Since 1997, it has been monitoring over 9,000 sources daily and cross-checking its data with companies and other sources.

From this web page, select 'Download Ernst & Young's EIM Report on European Investment Announcements'. The report is free and full of useful data that will give pointers on the potential for property rental prospects in the corporate market. For example, the 2006 report shows that the new European heartland of automotive investment is centred on the Czech Republic, with Poland and Slovakia in the vanguard; 150 new automotive component plants have been established by inward-investing companies in the past 3 years alone. Russia is identified as the new hot spot for financial services projects, as a sector whose staff are renowned for their appetite for luxury penthouse apartments.

Corruption, crime and safety

Buying a property inevitably involves being confident that the asset you are acquiring actually belongs to the seller and that they have the right to dispose of it as they wish. It also means that, once in that country, you can enjoy a reasonably safe and secure life. Certainty in these matters depends on the application of the rule of law, in that contracts can be enforced and criminals properly prosecuted.

What we accept as the norm in more developed countries can by no means be taken for granted around the world. In many countries the judiciary either doesn't function effectively or favourable judgments can be bought with relative ease. In such countries the police, government officials, customs and tax inspectors, lawyers and indeed almost anyone in the bureaucratic process chain often regularly, and more or less openly, expect and accept bribes. In many countries an informal tariff operates, with a predicable fee expected for a particular service.

In countries where those whose job it is to maintain it openly flout the rule of law, the average citizen is hardly likely to pay much regard. In such countries your chances of being kidnapped, robbed, attacked and even worse may be significantly higher than in your home country. For example, in the UK, where fewer than one property in a hundred is likely to have an intruder alarm system, in some countries in Eastern Europe you would be considered insane not to have a security guard on the premises in an apartment block. In many remote rural regions you can expect houses to be regularly stripped of anything of the slightest value if they are left unoccupied even for a weekend. Aside from the unpleasantness of living in such an environment, the cost of protection can turn out to be highest ongoing property expense.

The following websites may be useful:

Transparency International (TI) (`www.transparency.org`)

Corruption, as defined by TI, is 'the abuse of entrusted power for private gain'. It claims that corruption 'hurts everyone whose life, livelihood or happiness depends on the integrity of people in a position of authority'. This is particularly true when it comes to buying, selling or renting out property, where investors of all descriptions are reliant on a myriad of officials, professionals and intermediaries, usually operating in a foreign language, who have ample opportunity to take advantage of their privileged position.

TI, established in 1986,is independent and impartial and operates through a worldwide network of over 90 locally established organisations. It is probably best known for its Corruption Perceptions Index (CPI). This is a composite of independent surveys studying 159 countries. In the most recent survey, 113 of the countries studied scored less than 5 out of a clean score of 10 and, of those, 70 countries scored less than 3, indicating 'rampant corruption that poses a grave threat to institutions as well as to social and political stability'. To download the latest CPI, go to: www.transparency.org>policy_research>surveys_indices. There you will find links to the latest CPI as well as the Bribe Payers' Index (BPI), which ranks corruption by source country and industry sector, and the Global Corruption Barometer (GCB), a public opinion survey which assesses the general public's perception and experience of corruption in over 60 countries.

The TI studies are survey based and depend for their accuracy on the responses of some 50,000 people around the word. Worryingly, around 1 in 10 of these respondents claimed to have paid a bribe in the past 12 months. Bribes and corruption are often fairly petty affairs, such as payments to officials ranging from police to escape speeding tickets, to hospitals to secure treatment and town councils to obtain planning consents.

The countries that TI sees as being seriously corrupt at nearly every level, and in which property is currently being marketed to the international community, include: China, Romania, Ukraine, India, Argentina, Russia and Albania.

Internet Centre For Corruption Research (www.icgg.org)

This is a Joint Initiative of the University of Passau, in Germany, and Transparency International. In addition to providing the TI Corruption Perceptions Index (TI-CPI), which can be obtained on the TI website, the centre also provides data on the past 5 years, so you can see favourable or adverse changes in a country's performance. As well all data for the 159 countries in the TI-CPI (which can be retrieved in the form of an Excel spreadsheet) there is also data for a further 35 countries. Because there were less than three sources available, these 35 countries are measured less reliably and are not included in the official list. You can also find on this site a number of background research papers explaining the trends for perceived levels of corruption from 1995 onwards.

United Nations Survey on Crime Trends and the Operations of Criminal Justice Systems (www.unodc.org/unodc/crime_cicp_survey_seventh.html)

This is a very detailed report on the amount of crime by all major categories for 92 countries, prepared periodically by the UN. The data can be downloaded into an Excel spreadsheet, from which you can carry out any analysis you care to make in order to find out where you are most likely to be murdered, mugged, have your car stolen, house broken into or be the victim of fraud.

Worldworx (www.worldworx.tv/safety/)

This is a general travel and information site on an extensive range of travel issues. It provides a quick summary of crime statistics for every country in the world. The entries are brief and selective, but cover the most important issues.

For example, the site's entry on Latvia warns of a common scam involving identity theft through false job offers aimed at foreigners planning to settle in the country. Usually this takes the form of a company claiming to be located in Latvia, but which has a non-existent address, offering employment as a UK- or US-based agent or freight forwarder. When the victim responds to the job offer, commonly posted on one of several popular internet job sites, a social security number and other identifying information-needed for the identity theft are requested, under the guise of conducting a background check. For Russia, the entry includes the comment that extortion and corruption are common in the business environment. Organised criminal groups and sometimes local police target foreign businesses in many cities and have been known to demand protection money. The Ukraine entry includes a warning that burglaries of apartments and vehicles represent the most significant threat to long-term residents.

Human Development Report (www.hdr.undp.org/statistics/data)

Published annually by the UN, this report assembles from various national and international sources the latest published data on the proportion of people for each country and major city studied who have been victimised by one or more of the 12 crimes recorded in the survey: robbery; burglary; attempted burglary; car theft; car vandalism; bicycle theft; sexual assault; theft from car; theft of personal property; assault and threats; theft of motorcycle or moped; and bribery.

At the above link, select 'Data by Indicator', then, from the alphabetical list, choose the crime you are most concerned about. Among the countries where property crime, for example, is most prevalent, in these statistics at least, are England and Poland and the safest are Switzerland and Austria. The least safe city when it comes to property crime is Buenos Aires (Argentina) and the safest is Beijing (China).

The Home Office (www.homeoffice.gov.uk)

Type 'international crime statistics' into the search pane in the top left of the screen and you will find a list of the latest studies. At the time of writing, 'International comparisons of criminal justice statistics', by Gordon Barclay and Cynthia Tavares with Sally Kenny, Arsalaan Siddique and Emma Wilby, published in October 2003, contained the most recent data.

These statistics reveal that while, overall, crime in England and Wales, Cyprus, Canada and Italy is dropping by over 2% a year, in Poland, Slovenia, Turkey and Lithuania it is increasing by over 4% each year. Over the period 1997–2001, for which these figures were compiled, there was an average fall of 10% in the EU for domestic burglary. The highest falls for such crimes were in Greece (28%), Germany (27%), England and Wales (26%), Finland (24%), Scotland (18%) and Sweden (17%). Among the other countries, there were high falls in Bulgaria (58%), Turkey (50%), Norway (39%), Switzerland (31%), Canada (28%) and New Zealand (27%).

Wired Safety (www.wiredsafety.org)

Cyber crimes, in particular 'identity theft,' are one of the most prevalent and fast-growing international crime areas. Buying, selling and renting out property is an occasion when you are most likely to be exposed to this danger. Wired Safety, operates what it claims to be the largest online safety, education and help group in the world. It is a cyber-neighbourhood watch and operates through more than 9,000 volunteers worldwide.

From the left-hand horizontal menu, select 'Scams and Frauds' where you can find information on the latest scams and how to protect yourself against them.

Privacy International (PI) (www.privacyinternational.org)

If you are looking for a country to move to where you will be better able to protect your privacy, then this organisation could help guide your research. Britain is the worst-performing democracy in Privacy

International's surveillance league table ranking 36 countries, including the 25 EU member states. PI, based in London, is a human rights group formed in 1990 as a watchdog on surveillance and privacy invasions by governments and corporations. Points are awarded, covering 13 areas such as the use of ID cards, the number of CCTV cameras, statutory and constitutional safeguards and data retention by government agencies. Britain was ranked in 2006 as being in a category of country demonstrating 'endemic surveillance', alongside China, Russia and Malaysia. Countries such as Thailand, Argentina and the Philippines rated better in terms of respect for personal privacy than Britain.

Also worth of attention are the site's 'Stupid Security Awards', an open competition run by PI to discover the world's most pointless, intrusive, annoying and self-serving security measures. The awards aim to highlight the absurdities of the security industry. They were first staged in 2003 and attracted over 5,000 nominations from members of the public from around the world. Recently, the 'Most Inexplicably Stupid' award went to Philadelphia International Airport for over-reaction to a bottle of cologne, with the runner-up being Heathrow Airport for quarantining a quantity of green tea.

From the horizontal menu bar on the right of the home page, select 'Global Studies'.

CHAPTER 7

Checking the Local Environment

In this chapter:

- Understanding what is on offer in terms of local healthcare.
- Checking out what medicine money can buy.
- Appreciating getting older.
- Educating children.
- Instructing older pupils.

While the economic climate and political stability are necessary elements for a healthy property market, they are not in themselves sufficient to guarantee either pleasure or profit from an investment. One unnerving statistic to keep in mind when considering buying a property overseas is that over 200,000 Brits sell up abroad and return home. In fact, the av erage period of ownership of an overseas home is little over a decade.

So, what goes wrong? While overseas property buyers may be successful in assessing their current needs, they often neglect to take into account the fact that personal circumstances, unsurprisingly, change over time. Childless couples may start a family, and young families may need to move nearer to secondary schools or university as children become teenagers. Healthy pensioners will find themselves becoming less full of life, or a surviving elderly relative might need to come and live under the family roof. See Table 7.1 for some of the

Table 7.1 What changing personal factors need to be taken into account when considering the local environment of an overseas property location?

Children attending or changing school
Children become teenagers and need jobs or attend university
Chronic illness
Death of spouse, perhaps the car driver!
Elderly relative needs looking after
Job or career change
Marriage
Need to return to home country more often than expected
Nursing home or hospice required
Redundancy
Retirement
Separation or divorce
Starting a family
Healthcare

factors that commonly change over time. These need to be built into your assessment of the local environment.

The majority of overseas property buyers are still between 40 and 50 years old and in good health. But circumstances may change and in any event one factor that does matter, even for the holiday rental market, is the availability of adequate healthcare services.

State healthcare

One important factor to bear in mind when it comes to state healthcare is that if you have taken 'residence' in your new country, that is elected to have your tax and legal affairs based in that country, you will be considered a foreigner in the United Kingdom, or wherever else you once lived. If your new country is in the European Union, you need a European Health Insurance card, or EHIC (the replacement for the E111) in order to receive emergency healthcare in the United Kingdom. If your new home is not an EU country, you can check out what you are entitled to as a visitor on the Department of Health website (www.dh.gov.uk).

Check out the following websites for information on state provisions for healthcare:

European Observatory on Health Systems and Policies (www.euro.who.int/observatory)

The European Observatory on Health Systems and Policies is a partnership between the WHO Regional Office for Europe; the Governments of Belgium, Finland, Greece, Norway, Spain and Sweden; the Veneto region of Italy; the European Investment Bank; the Open Society Institute; the World Bank; CRP-Santé Luxembourg; the London School of Economics and Political Science (LSE); and the London School of Hygiene and Tropical Medicine (LSHTM). It supports and provides comprehensive and rigorous analysis of healthcare systems in Europe and beyond.

Select 'Country Information' from the left-hand menu bar and, from there, choose the country or countries you are interested in researching, from the list of 80 presented. There you will find links to the country's Ministry of Health and to pdf files with information on the current state of healthcare in that country. For the Ukraine, for example, the valuable information includes the fact that there is a serious shortage of doctors in primary care, particularly in rural areas. That fact might influence a decision on whether to purchase cheap retirement property several hundred kilometres from Kiev.

World Health Organization (WHO) (www.who.int/en)

Usually known simply by its initials, 'WHO', the World Health Organization was established in 1948 with the aim of attainment by all peoples of the highest possible level of health. 'Health' is defined as a state of 'complete physical, mental and social well-being and not merely the absence of disease or infirmity'.

Select 'Countries' from the left-hand menu bar, then look through the countries in which you are considering living or buying a property. There you will find a range of information concerning health matters on WHO's 192 member countries. The data covers the most serious health risks; life expectancy of locals; and numbers of doctors, nurses and other health professionals.

By selecting 'Research tools' from the left-hand menu bar, then 'WHO Global InfoBase Online' from the middle menu bar headed 'A guide to statistical information at WHO', select the 'Compare Countries' icon. There you can compare several countries, using WHO estimates for certain available risk factors and other indicators.

By selecting 'Statistics by disease or condition' in the Research Tools menu bar, you can find the risks for almost every type of illness known to man, as well as a mass of data perhaps only of interest to those of a morbid disposition. For example, it is possible, by selecting 'Global Suicides' from the Mental Health menu bar, to discover that Ukraine, the Russian Federation, Sri Lanka, Slovenia, Moldova, Poland, Hungary, Lithuania and Estonia have suicide rates between 3 and 7 times those of the UK and the USA. In contrast, the Bahamas, Brazil, Mexico, Peru and the Philippines are among countries whose suicide rate is a fraction of that in the UK and China is the only country in the world where women are more likely than men to commit suicide. A very high suicide rate doesn't exactly inspire confidence in a local environment.

Department of Health (www.dh.gov.uk)

The Department of Health's overall purpose is to help improve the health and well-being of everyone in England and Wales, including those who travel abroad. From the 'Shortcuts' menu bar on the right-hand side of the screen, select 'A–Z Site Index'. Once there, select 'Overseas Travel' from the alphabetical menu bar. This section tells you how to get medical treatment abroad, including information on the European Health Insurance card, or EHIC (the replacement for the E111). You will also find frequently updated alerts on outbreaks all over the world, together with advice for travellers about staying safe.

Table 7.2 Countries with which the UK has reciprocal healthcare agreements

Anguilla	Montenegro
Australia	Montserrat
Barbados	New Zealand
Bosnia and Herzegovina	Romania
British Virgin Islands	Russia
Bulgaria	St Helena
Channel Islands	Serbia
Croatia	Turks and Caicos Islands
Falkland Islands	The Russian Federation
Gibraltar	Montenegro
Isle of Man	Montserrat
Macedonia	New Zealand

The UK has reciprocal healthcare agreements with some countries (including all EU countries and Switzerland), which enables travellers to receive free or low-cost emergency care. The countries with which the UK has reciprocal healthcare arrangements are shown in Table 7.2:

In most other countries around the world, you will have to pay for treatment so you will need to take out private health insurance and even in these countries you are likely to be entitled to emergency treatment only.

United Nations International Children's Emergency Fund (UNICEF) (www.unicef.org)

Although set up exclusively to help children in the 192 countries in which it operates, UNICEF publishes some useful general health-related statistics on its website. Select 'Info by Country' from the left of the top horizontal menu and you will find the latest information on basic indicators for each country, such as mortality rates, as well as information on diseases, hygiene, availability of drinking water, sanitation and so forth. The bottom table, entitled 'Rate of Progress', shows the rate of improvement being made in a country in particular areas. For example, you can see that in the Czech Republic, the average rate of mortality of the under-5s, a reasonable general indicator of health provision, improved by 3.1% a year over the 20 years to 1990. Since then, it has improved at the much faster rate of 8.9%. By contrast, in Brazil, the improvement rate has been static at 4.1% over the whole period since 1970, indicating that in this important area of health the situation in Brazil is not getting better.

World Health Organization (`www.who.int/en`)

Select 'Research Tools' from left-hand vertical menu bar, then 'Global Atlas of World Health Resources', followed by 'Data Query' on the top-right horizontal menu bar. From here you can find how many doctors, dentists, nurses, community care-workers and so forth there are in any country or group of countries. The more of the particular group of healthcare professionals that concern you that there are in a country, the more attractive it is – to you, at any rate. You can also find out about the prevalence of any and every disease in every country.

123world (`www.123world.com/hospitals`)

123world is an online database claiming to offer the best deals on everything including vacations, hotels, resorts, inns, vacation packages, travel packages, vacation rentals, attractions, show tickets and lots more. One unique feature is its source of authentic and reliable information about the hospitals of the world. The links in this directory will guide you to the official sites of the hospitals, ranging from Al-Shifa Trust Eye Hospital in Rawalpindi, Punjab, Pakistan, through to the Children's Hospital of Lima, Peru to the Women and Children's Hospital in Adelaide, Australia.

By clicking on the corresponding letter of the alphabet, you will be taken directly to the official home page of the particular hospital. Where there is no official site, 123 has screened a number of available sites and selected the most informative one on the subject.

Private healthcare: short term

If you intend to use your new property as a holiday home, you are likely to make several trips a year to the country concerned. As long as none of these trips is longer than 90 days, annual multi-trip holiday insurance should meet all but the most extreme medical and health situations.

Multi-trip holiday insurance policies exclude prevailing medical conditions, terrorist attacks, kidnapping, and bills over £2 million. More than 450 different holiday insurance policies are on offer in the United Kingdom.

The following organisations offer information on local paid healthcare:

Money Supermarket
(www.moneysupermarket.com/travelinsurance)

Using this site, you can get most of the research legwork done for you in choosing the best-value product. Launched in December 1999, Money Supermarket's website makes it easy for you to compare over 500 different healthcare insurance products. The company is an appointed representative of Moneysupermarket.com Financial Group Ltd, which is authorised and regulated by the Financial Services Authority in the UK.

Age Concern (www.ageconcern.co.uk)

If you or your partner are over 65 then Age Concern, established to 'promote the well-being of all older people and to help make later life a fulfilling and enjoyable experience', is a useful source of information. Select 'Shop' from the left-hand menu bar, then select the 'Insurance' icon, followed by the 'Travel Insurance' icon. There you will find information on all aspects of travel insurance.

You will also find some useful information by selecting 'How We Can Help' from the left-hand menu bar, followed by the 'Retiring Abroad' icon where you will find an information sheet containinga checklist of questions to think about.

Saga (www.saga.co.uk)

Saga is more of a commercially oriented organisation than Age Concern, whose stated aim is to provide high-quality, value-for-money services for people over 50. Aside from marketing cruises on its own fleet of ships, the company offers a range of travel insurance products which can be found by selecting 'Travel' under the main menu on the left-hand side of the screen, headed 'Insurance'. It also has a small directory to 'Care Homes Abroad' which you can find by selecting 'Resource Centre' from the left-hand menu bar, then in the 'Accommodation' area scroll down to 'Care Homes Abroad'.

MediCover (www.medi-cover.co.uk)

MediCover is a travel insurance policy supplied by Inter Group Insurance Services Ltd to provide travel insurance for travellers with an existing medical condition.

The insurance cover it can offer is only available for single trips, up to a maximum of 185 days per trip, and you must declare all medical conditions that you have and from which you suffer. Uniquely, MediCover don't seem overly concerned about the prospects of its clients dying, provided, that is, 'where a terminal prognosis has been given, the prognosis is expected to be more than four months after the end of the trip'.

Insure and Go (www.insureandgo.com)

Insure and Go is a good source for insurance if you are of a more intrepid nature. It includes over 40 adventure sports automatically in all its policies, covering everything from abseiling to 'zorbing' (hurtling downhill in a 3.2-metre plastic sphere).

Private healthcare: long term

If you want full private medical cover all year in your chosen country and anywhere else you may go, including the United Kingdom, expect to pay between 2,500 and 5,000 (£1,730 and £3,460) a year for a family of four, depending on age, sex and medical condition, for full medical and dental insurance cover. These figures will be influenced heavily by location, so, for example, expect to pay considerably more if you plan to live in Ukraine, where local medical provision is minimal and repatriation may be the only option in cases of serious injury or illness, than if you were going to, say, Malaysia or Singapore which have world-class local hospitals. Premiums for the elderly are punitive and it is virtually impossible to apply for private health insurance (PHI) for the first time if you are over 75.

Preferred Medical (www.preferredmedical.co.uk)

Established in 1995, Preferred Medical Ltd is an independent intermediary offering specialist advice for all matters relating to private health care protection. From the home screen, select 'Expat health cover' in the International Health Care section. There you will find six sections explaining the reasons for taking out international health care insurance and the range of services typically on offer. Start by reading the section headed 'Your International Checklist'. This will alert you to possible limitations on insurance cover in the case of war or terrorism, as well as how useful or otherwise such policies are should you fall ill on a visit to your home country, or to some other country that you may be travelling to or through.

Private Medical & Health Insurance UK (PHA)
(www.phahealth.co.uk)

PHA is an independent insurer broker advising on over 200 different health cover plans. From the left-hand menu bar, select 'Expat Healthcare'. There you will find all the information on the myriad of different healthcare insurance policies on offer. In the left-hand menu bar, once in the 'Expat Healthcare' section, there is some useful information in 'Expat Articles'. This include facts on living and travelling in various overseas countries; checklists on healthcare issues to plan for before leaving home; and a free question section where you can e-mail a request for information on any country and any subject. PHA staff aim to answer such questions promptly.

Nursing homes and care of the elderly

In many countries the proportion of elderly people is 20% and rising. However, in many countries the services available for the elderly and those needing long-term care are stretched or non-existent. Even where such care is well provided for, the costs are high. The absence of satisfactory provision is a principal reason for those buying properties overseas either returning to their home country or deciding against buying in a particular location.

In principle, citizens of countries such as the UK are often entitled to long-term care in the overseas country where they have chosen to live. But they will only be entitled to the care provision that is normally provided in that country, rather than the level to which they would have been entitled in their home country. In many countries, and not just the more remote and less civilised ones, there can be a wide disparity in provision between the two standards. For example, in Spain and many Mediterranean countries it is the norm for families and extended families to look after sick or elderly relatives. Those who have left their roots behind and retired abroad are unlikely to have any such family to hand and so will be reliant on an unfamiliar and often less generous state-funded provision.

There is no easy way to find comparative data on country-by-country provision, but the following organisations offer a route to productive research:

Direct Gov
(www.direct.gov.uk/BritonsLivingAbroad/BeforeYouGo)

Directgov, produced by the UK Government's Central Office of Information, brings together a wide range of public service information and services online from across departments, on topics ranging from travel safety and parental leave to special educational needs and local health services.

This link takes you straight to a menu for 'Britons Living Abroad', with a range of options covering such topics as voting rights, keeping safe and taking pets abroad – all interesting and important topics in their own right. Selecting the menu topic 'Preparing to Move or Retire Abroad' will bring you information including that on health where you will find further links taking you to information on: welfare rights abroad; facts concerning UK benefits not payable outside the UK; and healthcare costs in the country to which you want to move.

Selecting the link 'More about benefits if you live abroad' takes you to information on such topics as: continuing your Winter Fuel Allowance (which you can claim in certain circumstances when you are moving or have moved to certain other countries); pensions; sickness benefits; and further related links.

Should you need more information, the site gives you access to government directories, as well as links to relevant third parties who can offer additional trusted advice and support, including such organisations as are concerned with helping those caring for someone overseas.

The Foreign and Commonwealth Office (FCO) (www.fco.uk.gov)

There is a mass of valuable information on this website, but it is far from easy to find. From the opening screen, select 'Travel Advice' from the menu bar on the left-hand side. Then select 'Travel Checklists' in the new left-hand menu bar. Finally, select 'Retiring Abroad' from yet a further left-hand menu bar. Here you will find tips, sources of information and a list of organisations who can provide help, under the generic headings such as 'Before you go' and 'When you arrive'. The sting is in the tail of the list of what the FCO can and cannot do. It confirms that it cannot: give travellers any money; repatriate them (except as a last resort); pay for healthcare, accommodation or travel costs, except in special circumstances; or get travellers better treatment in hospital than is given to the local population.

You will also find links to information on retiring abroad by typing those words into the search bar at the Quick Search bar which appears in varying positions on the left-hand menu bar, depending on where you are on the site.

Heyday (www.heyday.org.uk)

Heyday has taken over the area covered by the Association of Retired and Persons Over 50. The only evident way to access information is to put the appropriate word or words into the search bar in the top left of the screen. Entering 'ill health abroad' yields 81 links to articles and information topics such as retirement homes; caring for someone at a distance; and some specific information on France and Spain. Generally, the information is free, but to join discussion forums and get questions answered you will need to take out an annual subscription at a cost of £20.

Age Concern (www.ageconcern.org.uk)

Age Concern is the UK's largest organisation working with and for older people. It has developed an increasing interest in the problems of a fast-growing population of people retiring abroad. Select 'How we can help' at the top of the left-hand menu bar on the home page, then, at the bottom of the screen, click on the text box 'Information sheets by number' followed by 'Retiring abroad IS1'. This will take you to a three-page summary of issues and some links to further sources of information and advice.

The International Longevity Centre (www.ilcusa.org)

This research centre, in partnership with a number of institutions around the world, is leading the World Cities Project, examining and comparing the social services, health and quality of life for persons aged 65. The study itself is currently relatively limited, but expanding. There are links on the site to other institutions concerned with the subject.

Elder Web (www.elderweb.com)

This is site in the early stages of development, but has ambitions to be a one-stop global information sourcebook for elderly people and those concerned about the subject. There is some basic information and a number of blogs covering an assortment of countries around the world. There are snippets of unnerving statistics, such as that the average stay in an 'old people's home' is 388 days. In fact 78% of residents won't last the first year.

International Association for Hospice and Palliative Care (IAHPC) (www.hospicecare.com)

The IAHPC's mission is to increase the availability and access to high-quality hospice and palliative care for patients and families throughout the world. It does this by promoting communication, facilitating and providing education, and by being an information resource for patients, professionals, healthcare providers and policy-makers around the world. From the horizontal menu bar at the top of the home page, select 'International Directory' where you will find a country-by-country listing of long-term care homes and institutions. Confusingly, the Bukit Mertajam Hospital Penang Palliative Care Unit, Malaysia is listed alongside the British Columbia Hospice Palliative Care Association (BCHPCA), but, overall, this is one of the most comprehensive world guides on offer.

Online healthcare

Over a fifth of American adults, or 55% of those with Internet access, have used the web to obtain health or medical information, according to recent research. Around half of those are in excellent healththemselves, but are seeking material to help someone else. The biggest benefit that Internet health site users have is that they appreciate the convenience of being able to seek information at any hour and the fact that they can do research anonymously. For those living in a foreign land, where doctors are thin on the ground and hospitals are themselves inhospitable, the Internet may be the first line of defence either to deal with minor ailments, or to decide whether the symptoms warrant a visit to a country with a more sophisticated healthcare system.

The following websites may be useful:

BestTreatments (`www.besttreatments.co.uk`)

BestTreatments is owned and produced by BMJ Publishing Group Ltd, the medical publishing division and wholly owned subsidiary company of the British Medical Association (BMA). It is best known for its weekly journal *BMJ* (formerly known as the *British Medical Journal*), established in 1840, and *Clinical Evidence*, the international source of the best available evidence for the treatment of important medical conditions. The aim of this website is to provide patients, doctors and other healthcare professionals with the highest-quality information, based on the latest research evidence.

On the left of the home page are a selection of topical healthissues and in the centre are two pull-down menus with A–Zs of ailments, conditions and illnesses. One menu is for doctors and one for patients.

Patient UK (www.patient.co.uk)

First launched in 1997 by (Patient Information Publications) (PiP), a partnership between Dr Tim Kenny and Dr Beverley Kenny, GPs in Tyne and Wear, England, this started as a directory of UK websites, which provided information on health, disease and related issues. Then, in December 2002, Patient UK, was re-launched as a joint venture between PiP and Egton Medical Information Systems (EMIS). The aim is to be a reliable and comprehensive source of health and disease information, mainly aimed at non-medical people. It also reviews health and illness related websites and links to many of these from the web directory are included on the site. The directory of websites can be accessed either in A–Z format; or by disease; or by topics such as 'travel health', 'health equipment' or 'help lines'.

MedlinePlus (http://medlineplus.gov)

This is a giant American website that will direct you to information to help answer almost every possible health question. It brings together authoritative information from the National Library of Medicine (NLM); the National Institutes of Health (NIH); and other government agencies and health-related organisations. Set searches are included in MedlinePlus to give speedy access to medical journal articles, extensive information about drugs, an illustrated medical encyclopaedia, interactive patient tutorials, and latest health news. Just be aware that the drug names are all American and can vary from those used in Europe and elsewhere.

Education provision

If you have children, or are planning to have any, then you have a number of additional factors to consider if you decide to live overseas more or less full time for a number of years. Taking children overseas and educating them there could add not just a foreign language to their skills, but give them a first-hand experience of another culture and way of life. Children are a popular feature of family life in most overseas countries and could well provide your ticket of entry into contacts and friendships that might otherwise prove difficult, if not impossible, to develop. Children make friends easily, even when they don't have a common language. Until they reach the teenage years, children have fewer inhibitions than adults and are prepared to try out words in a new language, even though the words and their pronunciation may be wrong or even ridiculous. According to research, children need only about 200 words to be able communicate effectively. So, in a few weeks, they will be trying out a few sentences, in a few months they will be able to hold a conversation of sorts with their peers and in 9 months they will be fluent, with most of the vocabulary of a foreign-language child of their age. The bit they will be missing is picking up some adult phrases and expressions in the foreign language from you, unless, of course, you already speak the language in question. With young children, you should speak your mother tongue at home, to ensure that they keep up their own language. Learning a foreign language should be seen as a bonus, but it still leaves you with the problem of what to do about your children's general education.

Pre-university education

Your main choices are the local state schools, which will conduct education in the local language. This will be 'challenging' for children over 10, who don't already have some grasp of the local language. However, children of up to 15 or so have adapted well. Otherwise, your safest option will be either an international school in the country or a boarding school in a country where the education is conducted in English.

Sources of information on pre-university education worldwide include:

Education World (`www.education-world.com`)

Founded in 1996, Education World is a free resource, funded by corporate sponsors and advertisers and designed primarily for educators as a place on the Internet where teachers can gather and share ideas. It is a complete online resource where educators can find the lesson plans, research materials and each other. It is a by-product of this last feature that is particularly valuable for those living or planning to live overseas. In the bottom right-hand menu box, entitled 'More Resources', double-click on the bottom link, 'See our complete site guide'. Once there, select 'School Directory' from the 'More Resources' menu box, also near the bottom-left of the page. Once in the directory, you can search all the different types of school – primary; secondary; charter schools (those freed up from the worst excesses of bureaucratic control); Montessori schools; private schools; and public schools – by continent and by country.

Independent Schools of the British Isles (ISBI) (www.isbi.com)

ISBI lists 1,700 schools worldwide on its online database. You can probably find an English-language school in the capital city of your chosen country Such schools often go by the title 'American school', with 'French' and 'British' as further options. These international schools are usually private, fee-paying institutions and members of professional associations, such as ISBI. Fortunately, school fees are modest by British private school standards, ranging from €400 to €10,000 (£277 and £6,900) a year. International schools take pupils from age 2 to 18. Many schools follow the British GCSE and A-Level system, while others use the increasingly popular International Baccalaureate (IB).

International School Review website
(www.internationalschoolsreview.com)

You can find a rating for over 600 international schools in countries from Angola to Zimbabwe, with Azerbaijan, China, Russia, Lebanon and Vietnam thrown in for good measure. You can access every school review on the site for just $29 a year and all other information is free.

United Nations Educational, Scientific and Cultural Organization (UNESCO) (www.unesco.org)

Founded in 1945, UNESCO is a specialised United Nations agency with the aim of promulgating knowledge about every country in the UN's success or otherwise when it comes to education. From the home screen, select 'Statistics' from the centre of the right-hand menu bar entitled 'Services'. Then, from the left-hand menu, select 'Statistical Tables' from the section headed 'Statistics'. From the centre of the screen, select 'Education'. Here you will find some fascinating tables, such as 'How does expected duration of schooling relate to national wealth?'. Surprise, surprise: the longer people spend at school, the wealthier the country's citizens are. There is a mass of other comparative data on each country's education level, literacy and numeracy attainments and so forth.

Higher education

Higher education in many overseas countries is competent, and in some cases more than competent. You will also find – in the capital cities, at least that – university tuition is conducted in English and is, by UK standards, relatively inexpensive, as are the living costs. You may even find that the programme is validated and the degree qualification itself offered by a UK- or US-based university, or from a country of similar educational status.

Find out about higher education overseas on the following sites:

British Accreditation Council (BAC) (www.the-bac.org)

The BAC is a registered charity (non-profit-making organisation) established in 1984 to act as the national accrediting body for independent further and higher education. It is independent both of government and of the colleges with which it deals. BAC's 230 accredited colleges undergo a thorough inspection every 5 years, with an interim visit after 2–3 years.

From the top-right icon, 'College Directory', and from the drop-down menu, select 'Overseas Colleges'. There you will find accredited colleges in the Czech Republic, France, Spain, Pakistan, the United Arab Emirates, Bulgaria, Greece, India, Germany and Switzerland.

Global Education and Training Service (GETIS)
(www.britishcouncil.org/getis.htm)

GETIS is offered by the British Council to provide information on international education in almost every country in the world. The British Council's purpose is to build 'mutually beneficial relationships between people in the UK and other countries and to increase appreciation of the UK's creative ideas and achievements'. GETIS is a subscription service, fees for which start at around £150, but these can be waived for individual users who are not using the information as part of their business activity. On the website you'll find information about overseas education systems which may help you decide whether a country has what you require in terms of resources and teaching institutions.

The Accreditation Council for International Universities & Institutes (ACIUI) (www.aciui.org)

ACIUI grew out of a National Task Force on continuing education commissioned by the Bureau of Education (now the US Department of Education) in 1985. It is dedicated to quality continuing education and training programmes, achieving that goal by certifying education providers on thousands of educational programmes worldwide. Countries covered include Argentina, Australia, Canada, India, Bangladesh,Brazil, Haiti, Italy, Nepal, Panama, Thailand and the Virgin Islands.

To find accredited overseas colleges and universities, select 'Member Institutions' from the left-hand vertical menu bar.

Braintrack (`www.braintrack.com`)

Over 8,300 links to higher educational institutions in 194 countries created by a partnership comprising Harvard University, the Directory of US State Universities and other colleges. It contains the contact details for universities, polytechnics, colleges and other higher educational institutions from all over the world, with direct links to their websites. Using Braintrack is free of charge for everyone but it takes a dim view of anyone copying the information or part of it and making profits from it in any form, and it threatens to prosecute offenders. You can search for an institution by name; use a continent-by-continent search menu; or search within each country on an alphabetical list of countries. Aside from contact details, there is no information, but at least by using this site you can quickly find whether a country or town has a higher education provision, or better still a choice of several institutions, then quickly find out what sort of courses are on offer.

University of Illinois at Urbana-Champaign, Education and Social Science Library (`http://www.library.uiuc.edu/edx/rankint.htm`)

In response to a steady stream of enquiries regarding the merits or otherwise of the degrees and teaching programmes of higher education institutions around the world, the Education and Social Science Library at the University of Illinois has, since 1997, published this online source of ranking information. The purpose of the rankings site is to draw together and provide links to websites ranking colleges, with criteria ranging from the academic to more frivolous factors intended mostly for entertainment. *The Times Good University Guides* and *Asia Week*'s survey of the best universities in Asia rub shoulders with the *College Prowlers Guide*, ranking categories ranging from academics, athletics, transportation, and computers to guys, girls, nightlife and campus dining. Since not all ranking services have the same goal, more information and current research on rankings are listed in the articles on the College Rankings Bibliography and the 'Caution and Controversy' page, both of which can be selected from the left-hand vertical menu bar.

CHAPTER 8

Getting To and Fro

In this chapter:

- Finding out about air routes to overseas destinations.
- Tracking train travel options across countries and continents.
- Voyaging overland.
- Sailing to foreign parts across seas and oceans.

One of the most important factors that influence both the attractiveness of a particular country or city is its accessibility. If the cost, journey time, timetabling or frequency of flights (or other methods of travel) to a destination are, or are likely to be, a limiting factor, then the market to which the property could appeal will be similarly restricted. There is almost a reverse 'pricing and rental' equation at work here. The less accessible a destination, the lower the purchase price of a property is likely to be and the lower the rental yield. The old property adage of the most important factor in buying property being 'Location, location, location' applies with a vengeance when that location is nearly impossible to get to.

Table 8.1 gives an idea of the cost and rental differences between properties in the highly accessible area around Bulgaria's Black Sea Coast. Both Varna and Bourgas, the cities which serve the region, are inundated with regular flights from dozens of major cities both in the UK and around the rest of Europe. Aside from the usual budget operators, new kids on the block such as Hungary's Wizz Air, Norway's Norwegian Air Shuttle and Slovakia's SkyEurope serve these routes,

Table 8.1 Indicative purchase prices and monthly rents for three-bedroom property in Bulgaria

	Purchase Price	Weekly Rent (Low to High seasons)
Black Sea Coast	€100,000	€500–€700
Veliko Târnovo	€40,000	€200–€400

along with national carriers such as British Airways. A total of 45 carriers have so far asked to be permitted to perform regular and charter flights to Varna and Bourgas. Contrast this with getting to and from Veliko Târnovo, Bulgaria's capital in medieval times before the Turks overran the country. This beautiful city is surrounded by bucolic areas, with the Danube and Romania nearby as an added bonus. But the only direct route from the UK, for example, is a 26- hour coach ride. The alternatives are a 3-hour flight to Sofia, Varna or Bourgas, followed by a 3-hour trip on a bus without air-conditioning.

Airport access

There is little debate about the fact that the arrival of budget airlines can make an area more popular, driving up property prices, but their arrival is not a guarantee of continuing access. EasyJet, for example, makes no secret of the influence it expects to have on property prices and regularly publishes property stories in its in-flight magazine. As a property investor, however, you must consider what can happen if the budget airlines pull the plug on your route, or if they go bust. Budget airlines dump routes at will and alter timetables and flight frequencies all the time. Make sure that at least two airlines service your destination and that a wide variety of major cities around the world also serve the area. While you may be happy to trek there by boat, bus or rail – indeed, it may even add to the sense of adventure for you – those looking for a holiday home to rent or a place to locate their business empire will almost certainly not share that view.

Keeping tabs on flying options

Fly Cheapo (www.flycheapo.com)

On this website you can find details of all the 2,497 European low-cost airline routes provided by 47 active low-cost airlines, to 298 airports in 39 countries. The simplest way to find information is to select 'Route Search' from the horizontal menu bar at the top of the screen. There you will find two parallel pull-down menus, the left-hand one asking where you are travelling from and the right allowing you to choose your destination. Entering a request for information on available low-costairlineflightsbetweenLondonandKrakow(Poland)revealsfour airlines (easyJet, Ryanair, CentralWings and Sky Europe) as operating the route. On the right-hand side of the screen you also have information on any relevant news on the airport and proposed new services. For example, on the day this entry was researched it was announced that Jet 2 was planning to fly to Krakow; CentralWings was expanding its service both in and beyond Poland; and Sterling was opening up new routes across the country.

If you can't find a suitable flight to and from your chosen destination, you can use the 'low-cost route search' tab, which will try to make alternative suggestions. This will help find useful information, such as that Trieste in Italy (which is well served by low-cost airlines) is less than an hour's drive from Croatia's desirable Istria Peninsula. In fact, Trieste is closer to Istria than Zagreb, the country's capital.

At the bottom of the screen showing 'Search results' (obtained by entering a search request) there is a 'Help' facility showing all the low-cost routes from around Europe to that destination. Tables 8.2 and 8.3 show all the low-cost airline routes to Krakow (Poland) and Sofia (Bulgaria), from which it is evident that while the former is readily accessible from 14 European countries and 40 cities, the later is served by only 3 routes from 3 countries.

From accessibility perspective, Krakow is significantly more attractive than Sofia, as more tourists and business travellers can reach the city from a wider range of countries and cities within those countries.

Table 8.2 Low-cost airline routes to Krakow, Poland

Belgium	Brussels (International)
Croatia	Dubrovnik; Split
Denmark	Copenhagen
France	Paris (Orly)
Germany	Berlin (Schönefeld); Cologne-Bonn; Dortmund; Frankfurt (Hahn); Hamburg (Fuhlsbüttel); Stuttgart
Greece	Athens; Heraklion; Rhodos; Thessaloniki
Ireland	Cork; Dublin; Shannon
Italy	Bologna (Guglielmo Marconi); Milan (Orio al Serio); Naples; Rome (all airports); Rome (Ciampino); Rome (Fiumicino); Turin
Netherlands	Amsterdam
Norway	Oslo (International)
Spain	Barcelona; Malaga
Sweden	Stockholm (Arlanda)
United Kingdom	Birmingham; Bristol; Edinburgh; Glasgow (Prestwick); Leeds Bradford; Liverpool; London (all airports); London (Gatwick); London (Luton); London (Stansted); Manchester; Newcastle

Table 8.3 Low-cost airline routes to Sofia, Bulgaria

Hungary	Budapest
Slovakia	Bratislava
United Kingdom	London (Luton)

Of course, accessibility is not the only factor affecting the relative desirability of one location over another. But for someone living in Edinburgh and wishing to spend occasional weekends in their overseas property, Sofia would involve a more expensive and lengthy journey, such as might rule that option out. Factor in the evidence that German and Irish people are major buyers of overseas properties and

Krakow becomes an even more attractive option when it comes time to sell up.

WhichBudget.com (`www.whichbudget.com`)

WhichBudget (no connection with the consumer magazine) was founded by Martino Matijevic and Isabelle de Cato who met while studying at Oxford. After Isabelle finished her year in Oxford, she returned home to Nice and, in order to see each other as often as possible on a student budget, they used the cheap flights offered by 'no-frills' airlines. Being keen travellers, they continued using budget airlines in order to escape for a long weekend several times a year and became known among their friends for their knowledge of the destinations one can fly to with budget airlines. After numerous requests, Martino decided to create a little utility to answer such questions and in the mid-1990s put it online so that their friends could use it –and so, WhichBudget was born. Today, the site attracts around 300,000 unique visitors a month, from as far away as Japan, Brazil, Australia and the USA.

The site covers 116 airlines, covering 19,409 routes to 760 airports in 113 countries. The opening screen invites you to answer two questions: I want to fly from' and 'I want to fly to'. By selecting the country – say, Albania – you will find that only Tirana, the capital, has a low-cost route. Selecting 'Australia' would open up the prospects of flying to 30 airports, from Adelaide to Whitsunday Coast.

SkyScanner (`www.skyscanner.net`)

SkyScanner is a search engine for cheap flights, started by three founders in 2003 and based in Edinburgh. Its goal is to become the number one online resource for travel information. Of particular value to prospective property buyers on this site is the additional information provided when you make a request. For example, when asking for routes and fares between London and Morocco, you will see that the site shows prices for only the low-cost airlines Atlas Blue, easyJet, Ryanair and thomsonfly. But on the right-hand side of the screen, in a box labelled 'Other airlines on this route', you will see that British Airways, First Choice, flythomascook.com, GB Airways and Thomsonfly also cover the same destinations. This will let you see how many airlines fly to the city and so reassure you that you are not likely to be dependent on the whims or financial stability of one airline. Currently, the site shows only flight prices for the low-cost airlines within Europe and Australasia. However, it does have a tool allowing you to search its supplier partners for non-European destinations. The link is within the search box and reads 'Can't find your route, or want worldwide and scheduled flights?' As SkyScanner becomes fully comprehensive, you will be able to search for worldwide destinations directly within its website.

Oh – and, of course, you can find the cheapest flights as well!

Seat Guru (`www.seatguru.com`)

Travellers today are not content with just being able to fly to a destination; they want to know something about how enjoyable or otherwise the flight experience will be. Airline comfort and amenities are important factors influencing incoming business executives following in the wake of inward investment, and a vital potential rental market for property investors. Matthew Daimler, a frequent flier who realised from first-hand experiences the vast differences between airline seats and amenities, started up Seat Guru in October 2001. It's a repository of his knowledge, currently providing comprehensive seat and aircraft information for 29 airlines. There are tips on check-in; baggage; unaccompanied minors; and travelling with infants and pets, as well as 'Amenity Icons' to show the in-flight services available on each flight.

World Airport Guide (`www.worldairportguide.com`)

This is a service provided on the World Travel Guide website. It includes almost everything you need to know, including the all-important information on how to get to and from the airport, which on some occasions is located up to 100 km away from the city or town it purports to service. The information includes public transport (bus, train and metro) routes, costs and timetables; taxi services and costs; and motorway links. There is also information on transfers between terminals; car parking; shop and restaurant facilities; and left-luggage. An airport that is costly and time-consuming to get to and has few facilities to appeal to travellers is hardly likely to act as a spur to property prices.

US Department of State Open Skies Tracker
(`www.state.gov/e/eb/tra/c661.htm`)

Open Skies agreements reduce government interference in the commercial decisions of air carriers, freeing them to provide affordable, convenient and efficient air service for consumers. As such, they are a precursor to budget airlines being allowed to operate on certain routes. There is a link on this web page to a free subscription to an e-mail list (DOSCIVAIR) to receive civil aviation agreements and announcements on Open Skies agreements around the world. By monitoring this news, you can know in advance if a country currently not party to international Open Skies agreements is likely to change that status. If and when it does, that could contribute to an improvement in the local property market.

Air & Business Travel News (`www.abtn.co.uk`)

Air & Business Travel News is a review published every Monday by -mail and on the web in partnership with OAG, one of the world's major scheduled airline information suppliers. Registration is free and the format is simple: comment, 20 news stories and a feature item on some aspect of travel. Readers are travel suppliers, travel organisers and regular travellers. A third of the way down the left-hand menu bar is an 'Archives' search facility where you can find, by topic, travel articles going back 4 years. News at the time of writing included announcements of a new low-cost airline – Macau Asia Express – established in the former Portuguese colony, flying to new destinations in China mainland and Asia; and that Ryanair had concluded a deal that will see the airline's entire fleet of Boeing 737 aircraft fitted with OnAir's onboard mobile communications solution, meaning that passengers will be able to call, text and e-mail using their mobile phones, BlackBerrys and Treos from mid-2007, at rates which will mirror international roaming charges.

Train travel

While train may not appear to be either feasible or desirable as a way to reach more exotic property destinations, it is surprising just how far around the globe can be reached in this way. For example, the Trans-Siberian Express – the name that applies not to a train but to the tracks spanning Russia from Moscow in the European East to Vladivostok on the Pacific Coast in the Asian Far East – covers 5,777 miles, taking 7 days to cross 7 time zones. Using trains with exotic names such as the *Rossiya* (Russia), it is possible to link a couple of thousand miles back to London from Moscow and a couple of thousand miles on from Vladivostok to Hanoi or even Saigon. While few would want, or could afford, to make this a regular travel method, it would add spice to the journey once in a lifetime.

Central and Eastern Europe as far out as Istanbul, though likely to take a couple of days to reach by train, may not be that much more expensive than flying.

Information sources for train travel

The Man in Seat Sixty One (www.seat61.com)

This website was established by Mark Smith, a career railwayman who was Station Manager for Charing Cross, London Bridge and Cannon Street stations in London, then Customer Relations Manager for two UK train companies. He now works, as he describes it, in 'the murky world of government regulation of fares and ticketing on Britain's railways'. In his work he has been able to travel around the world on trains and ships, taking in such exotic journeys as Marrakech (via Paris, Madrid and Algeciras); Tunisia (via Lille and Marseille); Italy; Albania; Malta; Istanbul; Aleppo, Damascus and Petra; Ukraine and the Crimea; and even as far as Tokyo and Nagasaki via Moscow, Vladivostok and the Trans-Siberian Railway. Seat 61, from which the site takes its name, is one of a pair of individual seats with table which actually line up with the window in a Eurostar 1st-class compartment. Seat61.com is a personal site, run as a hobby. It's not a business, and the information on the site is provided free of charge to users, though the site now generates some income through Google ads and affiliate schemes.

On this site you can find out details of every train and connecting boat route on every continent, with links through to booking agencies. The site provides a history of the countries' railways and a description of the level of service you can expect, together with an idea of cost, as well as pictures of the trains themselves. The entry on Malaysia, for example, includes sufficient information to convince users that the author has travelled the route himself.

Thomas Cook (`www.thomascookpublishing.com`)

The first edition of Thomas Cook timetables appeared in March 1873 and its publications remain the ultimate guides for global travellers planning a rail trip and for en-route reference. The two editions – the monthly *European Rail Timetable* and the bi-monthly *Overseas Timetable* – between them cover all the world railway routes. These are available singly for around £13; an annual subscription to the *Overseas Timetable* (6 issues) costs from £69.00 and to the *European Timetable* from £138.00, including postage and packing in the UK. You get more than just a timetable, as information on transport operators, rail and bus passes and useful telephone numbers are included for each country, as are features on health and safety and passport and visa requirements.

Heritage Railway Association (www.heritagerailways.com)

Although the principal aim of the association is to disseminate information about heritage and tourist railways and railway preservation groups, there is a useful directory that can be accessed by selecting the 'Railways around the World' icon at the bottom of the left-hand horizontal menu bar. There you will find links to railway websites around the world, including those such as 'USA by Rail' which has everything you need for train travel in North America and links to other rail and travel websites throughout the USA, Canada and the rest of the world.

Coach and bus routes

Coach and bus are hardly realistic ways to travel between continents, though within them, and particularly in the less developed parts of the world, they are cost-effective travel options. This is also one way in which secondary cities and towns within countries have been opened up to tourism and property buyers, where no viable airport yet operates. For example, Croatia, which has only a handful of regular flights between London and its three major cities (Dubrovnik, Split and Zagreb) has a regular coach service to those three plus Rijeka, Zadar and a dozen other towns, taking between 33 and 50 hours and costing around £175, comparable to the air fare.

One further advantage that coach operators claim, with justification, is that unlike, air travel, most of their services bring you directly to the city centre, with no need to pay for expensive transfers or wait for connections.

Overland voyage information sources

Eurolines (www.nationalexpress.com/eurolines)

Part of the National Express Group, Eurolines is the brand name that groups together 32 independent coach companies, who between them operate Europe's largest regular coach network. This network connects over 500 destinations, covering the whole of the continent from Athens and Moscow, taking in destinations such as Casablanca in Morocco. Eurolines' services are all non-smoking and use modern coaches with reclining seats, large picture windows, washroom facilities and a comfortable amount of legroom. Fares are competitive with those of the low cost airlines and the ones quoted on the website come with no hidden extras. Sea crossings, travel taxes and road tolls are all included in the price.

The Bus Station (www.busstation.net)

This is an eclectic collection of bus, coach, tram, trolley and transit-related links all over the world. It was started by Steve Annells, from Oxfordshire, an IT contractor, because he found it frustrating trying to find bus and transit sites through search engines. The Bus Station is one of the biggest resources for bus-related links on the web. There you can find links to bus-related topics as diverse as model shops, refurbishers, dealers and people who live in or race buses. Organised geographically, you'll find links to bus service providers around the world, country by country. The links are a bit 'hit and miss'. For example, 'Routes International' turns out to be something of a gem, providing onward links to bus service providers across all 5 continents, while 'Metro Planet', billed as a 'world guide' simply appears to invite e-mail questions, with no information whatsoever on the site itself.

Boats and ferries

Travelling by boat will almost certainly be slower and more expensive than other ways to reach an overseas destination. But for the determined traveller, or those in the growing number who dislike air travel for whatever reason, it is a realistic possibility. There are no countries with a coastline that can't be reached by either ferry or freighter; and there is the bonus of having time to forge relationships or at least have discussions with others who may know the country you are heading for, and have valuable knowledge to impart.

Sources of advice and information on sea travel

A Ferry To (`www.aferry.to`)

A Ferry To is the world's largest ferry-crossing gateway. You can find routes, timetables and fares for all major European ferry operators and then book travel simply and securely online. The opening screen includes a large map of the countries covered which stretch from Iceland in the north, Morocco to the south, the Canary Isles to the west and Turkey to the east. In all, 25 countries or major islands can be reached routinely by ferry.

The site offers two search options. You can select a destination from the map and see which countries offer direct ferry services to it; or you can select outward and return routes from the left-hand menu box and check out services and prices. All prices and availability are obtained directly from one of 65 ferry companies with whom the site collaborates, so you will know straightaway if there is space and will be able to make your ferry booking instantly at the price shown.

A Ferry.ca (`www.aferry.ca`)

Offers a service nearly identical to that of A Ferry To, covering North America, Canada and Alaska.

Dan Youra Studios (`www.youra.com`)

These publishers of travel guides and maps – in print, on the web and on cell phones – have an extensive coverage of world ferry schedules. From the menu bar on the left-hand side of the screen, select one of the four ferry guides offered. Selecting 'World Ferries' takes you to a menu bar in the centre of the page where you are offered 30 or so major country destinations, including China, Japan, Australia and

New Zealand. Each country has a variable selection of web links leading to local ferry services, timetables and fares.

Freighter World Cruises (www.freighterworld.com)

Freighter World Cruises was founded in 1975 and is a travel agency specialising in placing passengers on freighter ships. It spotted a market opportunity when – thanks to the increases in technology – ships needed fewer professional crew to operate them. Shipping companies took little convincing that they should sell their unoccupied officers' cabins to fare-paying passengers. Destinations cover the Orient; the South Pacific; Australia and New Zealand; South America; Europe; and the Mediterranean and journeys are sold either one-way, as round trips or in small segments. Freighter travel is more expensive than flying, with fares typically ranging from €90 to €130 per day, but well below conventional cruise ship rates. It is not an option for people in a hurry: Long Beach, California to Tokyo, for example, takes about 13 days. But it is one way of striking up relationships with people, including the crew, who may have an in-depth knowledge of the country in question and have a few invaluable tips to pass on to prospective property investors.

CHAPTER 9

Money Matters

In this chapter:

- Dealing in foreign exchange.
- Raising a loan at home and abroad.
- Using banks.
- Finding an offshore haven.
- Sorting out a tax base.
- Taking timely financial advice.

Money matters more than almost any other aspect of the property-buying process. It is vitally important for the whole process that you have access to sufficient funds in the appropriate currency, at a competitive rate of interest. In countries in which financial systems are inefficient, outdated or just plain corrupt, the transaction fees (that is, the expenses associated just with acquiring and moving money, even if it is your own funds, from one place to another) can add between 5 and 10% more to overall costs.

Financing is equally important when it comes to both handling the day-to-day expenses for items such as utilities and repairs and to moving income into the country in which you want access to it.

These matters may appear peculiar only to overseas buyers handling international cross-border financing, but that is not the case. If the locals, who are one of the most likely buyer groups when you come to sell up, have difficulty in raising a mortgage, changing currency from their local money into euros, dollars, pounds or what ever currency you, the seller, require, then the whole property buying and selling process can become torturously slow. In some countries, when selling properties costing over €150,000, it routinely takes over 18 months for the financial arrangements to be concluded.

Any profit made will be subject to local tax, probably tax in your home country and perhaps the value of your property will make you subject to a wealth tax (an inheritance tax should you or any co-owner die). There is also the possibility that you will need to make special arrangements to circumvent any local laws on inheritance rights of heirs, successors and any other family members who, due to a quirk of the rules, might be deemed entitled to a share of any estate.

All these finance and taxation matters need to be thoroughly investigated as part of your sizing up the world property market and identifying those countries acceptable to your needs.

Currency and exchanging money

Buying, selling or renting out a property abroad means handling money in at least two currencies: pounds sterling and the currency of the country in which you are buying property. You may even need to deal in euros, as many major transactions, including buying and selling property, are now conducted exclusively in that currency.

The amount you set aside in pounds can vary in its purchasing power in another currency by several percentage points over a few weeks or months – and perhaps by as much as 30–40% over 10 years or more. Any property purchase takes time and the longer it takes, the longer you are exposed to currency market forces which can make your payments unpredictable. The same potential for loss occurs when you sell a property or when you receive rent. Aside from the change in value of one currency against another, your bank or currency exchange service levies a transaction cost.

Many countries have their own currency, but not all currencies are equally stable. The less stable the currency, the more cost and risk are involved in any transaction.

The key factors to find out about a currency are:

- Is it '**not fully convertible**'? This would mean that the government of the country concerned exercises political and economic control over the exchange rate and the amount of its currency that can be moved in or out. China and India are among many countries falling into this category. Such constraints can mean that a currency drops sharply in value periodically, as the Government of the day tries to hold back international pressures. It can also make it more difficult and complicated to take money out of a country under certain circumstances. In almost any event, in such countries you will need 'permission' to repatriate funds to the UK.
- Is the currency '**pegged**'? For the majority of countries who have been anxiously seeking ways to promote economic stability and their own prosperity, the most favourable way to obtain currency stability has been to 'peg' the local currency to a major convertible currency, such as the euro or the dollar. This means that while the local currency may move up and down against all other world currencies, it will remain (or at least attempt to remain) stable against the one to which it is pegged. In total, 22 states and territories have national currencies directly pegged to the euro (including 14 West African countries, three French Pacific territories, two African island countries and three Balkan countries).
- Is the currency '**dollarised**'? This is a slight misnomer, as the term is used to describe a country which abandons its own currency and adopts the exclusive use of the US dollar or another major international currency, such as the euro.The euro, for example, is the official currency in 15 states and territories outside the European Union. In such cases the country in question takes on the risks and costs associated with the 'host' currency. Many of the economies opting for this approach already use the foreign currency informally, in private and public transactions, contracts, bank accounts, property transactions and even for more mundane events such as

hotel accommodation, restaurant meals and shopping for electrical goods and other relatively expensive items.

- Is the currency '**fully convertible**'? If so, it stands on its own two feet and fluctuates as the country in questions succeeds or fails. Russia, for example, lifted currency controls in July 2006 as a sign of economic confidence, making the rouble fully convertible. Now it is more attractive to invest in Russia while Russian businesses can freely, without worry and without any special permit or burden, participate in investments overseas. Barely 8 years earlier, the country defaulted on its massive domestic debt, devalued its currency and wiped out Russians' savings. Russia's macroeconomic situation had to become stable in order to allow this to happen, which has been achieved on the back of large gold reserves, a balanced budget and foreign investment that exceeded capital outflows, largely on the basis of oil and gas exploration activity.

Help with currency matters

HiFX plc (`www.hifx.co.uk`)

The Reuters Forex Poll ranks HiFX plc within the top three most accurate foreign exchange forecasters globally, beating many of the world's leading banks. Founded in 1998, it is a successful and fast-growing business featured in *The Times* Virgin Atlantic Fast Track 100 and in *The Sunday Times* Top 100 Best Companies to Work For. It has offices in the UK, Europe, North America and Australasia. As well as carrying out all the functions of dealing in foreign exchange and having the near-ubiquitous currency converter on its website, there is some further information useful to the property investor.

From the left-hand menu bar, select 'Press Section' and from that drop-down menu choose:

- **Article Library**: covering various aspects of buying property and living abroad, as well as the more popular locations such as Spain.

- **Global Property Hotspots**: where you will be invited to sign up for a free monthly report to find out where's hot and where's not. As, every year, over 25,000 private individuals use HiFX to buy and sell currency for overseas property purchases, it should have a pretty good idea of where most of the deals are being done.

From the left-hand menu bar select 'Market Information' and from that drop-down menu choose:

- **Charts**: where you can track currency movements over various time periods.
- **Interest Rates**: where you can get a snapshot of world interest rates. At the time of writing, these ranged between a low in Japan of 0.25% and a high in New Zealand of 7.5%. Vital information if you are considering parking some cash somewhere pending concluding a property purchase.

The site's glossary gives a description of the vocabulary used in the industry. Alongside 'Bulls' and 'Bears', acknowledged (if not fully understood) by many are terms such as 'OCO (One Cancels the Other) Order' (a combination of a linked limit order and a stop loss order at predetermined market levels where, if one is executed, the other order is automatically cancelled. It is used to hold foreign exchange risk within known parameters), 'PIPs' and 'Points' (currencies are usually quoted to five decimal points and a 'PIP' is the term used to describe 0.00001 of a currency, which is smallest part of an exchange rate. A 'Point' is 100 pips, or 0.001).

OANDA (`www.oanda.com`)

OANDA was spun out of Olsen and Associates, an econometric research and development firm founded by Richard Olsen and Michael Stumm in 1995. It was first to market in making comprehensive currency exchange information available over the Internet, and now has strategic distribution, licensing and other relationships with companies such as AOL, Travelocity, American Express, Air Canada, British Airways, Sheraton and FedEx to provide exchange rate information on their websites. From the left-hand menu bar you will find an extensive range of valuable tools:

- Select **FXConverter** (Foreign Exchange Currency Converter) to access the multi-lingual currency converter with up-to-date exchange rates covering any of the 164 currencies used around the world. Select the desired currencies from the drop-down lists, as well as the date, language and amount which you would like to convert. The date function is a neat addition, as you can see what rate you would have got in the past. For example, a British pound would have bought only $1.41 in 1985, while it bought $1.89 in September 2006 – a sizeable 34% appreciation.
- Select **FX History** to chart foreign exchange rate movements over time.
- Select **Cheat Sheet** to produce your own print-out of converted currencies for various countries and amounts of money. It can be useful on property-buying trips to have a ready reckoner to hand, rather than having to get the calculator out for every discussion.

British Bankers Association (BBA) (www.bba.org.uk)

This is the principal trade association for banks operating in the UK. It has 218 members and 75% of the membership is of non-UK origin, representing 60 different countries. BBA members hold 90% of the UK banking sector's assets and represent 95% of all banking employment in the UK.

From the horizontal menu bar at the top of the home page, select 'Members' and from there select 'BBA Member Banks', where you will find a directory to the websites of all its members. Most of these banks offer foreign exchange services, albeit that in some cases they may not be as competitive as the specialist 'boutique' firms. But they do at least offer the comfort of absolute certainty of the security of your funds. While you may be comfortable transferring a small sum through a small firm, you may feel less sanguine when it comes to hundreds of thousands of pounds and might want tolook for an established bank.

The Financial Markets Association (ACI) (www.aciforex.com)

This association was founded in France in 1955 following an agreement between foreign exchange dealers in Paris and London. In the years that followed, other national associations were formed and there are now affiliated financial markets associations in 65 countries and individual members in another 17 countries and it has the largest membership of any of the international associations in the wholesale financial markets. The Head Office is based in Paris, which explains the mismatch between the English-sounding name and the abbreviation.

From the left-hand menu bar, select 'National Associations' from which you will find links to the websites of country-affiliated associations, listed by continent. The country associations usually contain directories of members.

Getting a mortgage for an overseas property

Borrowing money to buy an asset, such as property, rather than to simply be spent on more consumption, is one exception to the rule 'Neither a borrower nor a lender be'. Generally, property prices rise on average at a faster rate of interest than the cost of money, so, usually, the more you borrow, the more you make, in the property game. But even though borrowing in the case of buying property is in principle a good idea, in practice you still have to be able to afford the repayments. So you have to balance two factors.

- How much do you need to raise to fund the purchase of the property and carry out any repairs and modifications?

Table 9.1 Interest and repayments per €100,000 in€

Interest rate	Period of mortgage		
	10 years	15 years	20 years
4%	12,329	8,994	7,358
5%	12,950	9,634	8,024
6%	13,587	10,296	8,718
7%	14,237	10,979	9,439
8%	14,903	11,683	10,185

- Can you afford the repayments, bearing in mind that interest rates may change over time? To work this out, you need to calculate how much free income you have (that is, money not earmarked for living expenses and other fixed commitments). To this you could add any income you expect to get from renting out your home in the UK or your new property.

Table 9.1 shows how much you should allow in mortgage costs to cover each €100,000 borrowed, for a range of time periods and different interest rates.

There are a number of mortgage options, which are explored below. However, as far as your budget is concerned, depending on time and interest rates, you will need to budget for between €7,358 and €14,903 in mortgage costs per €100,000 borrowed.

The options for overseas mortgages are:

Re-mortgage at home

This is by far and away the easiest (and may even be the cheapest) option, as well as allowing you to keep your house in the UK. Lender permitting, you could even let out your house in the UK and cover some or all of the mortgage repayments for your property overseas.

All you really need is a fairly substantial slice of unencumbered equity in the property (that is, the difference between what the property is worth and what you still owe the mortgagor). You don't even need to demonstrate an income in the UK, as you could go through a 'buy-to-let'-type scheme. You will also avoid any exchange risk exposure. (See 'Understanding exchange risks' in this chapter, for clues as to how to deal with exchange rate issues).

You should be able to borrow up to 70% of the value of the property, with an interest rate of between 1–2% or so more than a conventional mortgage (currently about 6% in total), depending on the 'lock-in' term you elect for. The arrangement fees will vary depending on your circumstances, but are unlikely to be more than a few hundred pounds and the arrangements can be made in a few weeks at the most, often much less. You may even be able to get an agreement in principle in a day or so, which at least would give you the comfort to get on with making an offer on any foreign property.

Talk to your current mortgage provider and also the organisations listed below:

UK Mortgage Brokers Directory (`www.mortgages.co.uk/brokers`)

This service is provided by Financial Services Net Ltd, a small non-regulated business which does not offer advice but does list and describe the services of 50-plus mortgage providers. On the left of its home page you will find a menu bar with a number of useful tools, including one to calculate the maximum amount you can borrow under varying circumstances.

Money Supermarket (`www.moneysupermarket.com`)

This business is part of Moneysupermarket.com Financial Group Ltd, which is 100% privately owned by the group directors of which the majority of shares are controlled by Simon Nixon (chief executive) and Duncan Cameron. They decipher the key requirements (based on the information you give to them in an on-screen questionnaire covering such factors as whether this is a buy-to-let, a re-mortgage etc.) and then present the information in such a way that it can be sensibly compared with the thousands of mortgage products on the market. This makes it easy to find the best product to meet your needs and save you money.

From the home page, select 'Money' from the horizontal menu bar at the top of the page, then 'Mortgages'. From here you will find options, which mostly lead you to a short questionnaire, intended to establish your needs and circumstances.

Using a UK or an international bank

If putting your UK home on the line with a re-mortgage appears too risky then you could look to either UK or international banks to finance a property overseas. All the UK banks impose conditions, such as lending only on amounts above £60,000; advancing up to 75%; lending for no more than 20 years; or restricting use to owner occupation only. There are not many banks in this market and not every lender will arrange a loan on every type of property, lend the same proportion of the purchase price or lend in both sterling and euros. The situation is, however, changing fast, though new entrants appear to be focused on specialist opportunities. For example, in October 2006, Prudential, Britain's second-largest insurance company, became the first foreign company to receive permission to sell financial products, including mortgages and loans, in Vietnam. The Pru, after 7 years of doing business in the country, holds a substantial amount of savings for Vietnamese customers and has been looking for ways to recycle that money without exposing it to the exchange rate risks that would arise from using it elsewhere.

The banks to try for a mortgage include:

Newcastle Building Society (`www.newcastle.gi/mortgage/`)

Newcastle is one of the strongest mutual building societies in the UK and, since August 1990, it has served the expatriate community out of its Gibraltar office.

The vertical menu bar on the left of the home page offers all the options required, including eligibility, repayment methods and an application form.

Norwich & Peterborough Building Society (`www.npbs.co.uk`)

This is a strong mutual building society with an active interest in the overseas mortgage market. Follow this thread, for example, to find out about its Spanish mortgage facilities: `www.npbs.co.uk>mortgages>spanish-mortgages.asp`. You will also find menu options for other useful topics, including: 'Additional Borrowing'; 'Financial Advice'; 'Insurance'; and 'Credit Card'.

Lloyds TSB(`www.lloydstsb.com/mortgages.asp`)

From this screen, select 'Other mortgages and home finance' at the bottom of the vertical menu bar in the centre of the page.

Also, international banks (such as those listed in this chapter in the section on banking offshore), also offer mortgage finance for overseas properties:

Trying the locals

Many banks overseas are happy to provide mortgages for foreigners buying properties in their countries, though some are very new to the game. In at least one case, the country's banks have only been offering mortgage finance since 2003 and by 2006 demand was so great that the brakes had to be slammed on, severely restricting supply. Few developing countries offers a larger proportion of the purchase price, an interest rate closer to the prevailing bank rate or the hassle-free, speedy service that you can obtain in the UK, the USA, Australia and throughout the major European countries. But the big plus of having a mortgage in a local currency is that you will have no exchange rate worries. It pays to shop around for a mortgage abroad, as interest rates and terms vary considerably, depending on the bank, the amount and the period of time. Mortgages are generally available in even the most unlikely countries for up to 70 or 80% of the property valuation, repayable over up to 20 years, with interest rates 2 or 3% above the local base rate. But banking services are evolving quickly in these countries, especially as the banking sectors are privatised and new owners from Austria, Germany and such countries breathe fresh life into the sector.

Guide to country-specific sources of finance

The Move Channel (www.themovechannel.com/websites/services/financial/mortgages/world)

Founded in November 1999 by Dan Johnson, The Move Channel started life as a simple guide to the buying procedures for residential property purchase in the UK, coupled with a small directory of website reviews covering property sales and rentals, again primarily in the UK. Now it straddles the world and this slightly torturous web address will take you straight to 249 overseas mortgage providers in 49 countries from Andorra to Thailand, by way of China and Turkey.

European Federation of Building Societies (www.efbs.org)

The Federation is an association of credit and other institutions promoting and supporting housing finance. It stretches the concept of 'Europe' beyond the normally accepted boundaries, covering some countries in the EU (though not all) and a few which are further away. From the left-hand vertical menu, select 'Members' and from there the country in which you want to raise funds, from directories of members in Austria, Belgium, Croatia, Cyprus, the Czech Republic, Egypt, Germany, Hungary, Israel, Italy, Luxembourg, Morocco, Romania, Russia, Slovakia, Spain and Tunisia.

Managed currency mortgages.

Financial professionals have been using managed currency mortgages for years, as an effective way of managing a significant mortgage debt over an extended period. Such a mortgage works by transferring debt around the world, taking advantage of reduced interest rates and fluctuations in the currency markets. These fluctuations can reduce your debt painlessly. For example, if a £100,000 debt were transferred into US dollars at an exchange of 1.90 USD to the GB pound, you would owe $190,000. If the dollar weakened to €1.95 to the pound (a decline of 2.63%) then, after transferring the money back to GB pounds, your debt would be reduced to £97,370: a saving of £2,630. Now, envision what would happen if these transactions were being made several times a year, as currency dealers take advantage of changing conditions. But tracking one currency can be very risky, so a safer route is to link your borrowing to overseas interest rates in a sterling-denominated loan which tracks borrowing costs in other countries. The following organisations can help with this type of financing:

Managed currency specialists

ECU Group (www.ecugroup.com)

This firm is a specialist currency manager, catering to companies, institutions and high net-worth individuals. Its flagship product is the Managed Currency Mortgage Programme, which has a successful 17-year track record with over $1 billion under management. From the home page, select 'ECU in the Media' where you will find a refreshingly eclectic range of press articles from heavy weights such as the *Financial Times*, the *Daily Telegraph* and *Money Management*, giving the pros and cons of this type of mortgage finance.

Kaupthing Singer & Friedlander Group plc
(www.singer-friedlander.com/privatebanking/residentialcurrencymortgage.htm)

This is a financial services group providing banking, investment management and asset finance services. It was listed on the London Stock Exchange from 1987 until August 2005, when it was acquired by Kaupthing Holdings UK Ltd, a subsidiary of Kaupthing Bank hf (the largest bank in Iceland) and listed on the Icelandic Stock Exchange. Its minimum loan is £500,000, with no maximum (subject to its discretion). The typical initial loan-to-property value is 70%, with a maximum overall limit of 80%. It will lend to 100%, subject to additional collateral being provided.

Banking for overseas transactions

Banking in even the most unlikely parts of the world has come a long way in the past two decades. The factors which have had the greatest influence are the collapse of the Iron Curtain; entry (or prospect of entry) to the EU; and the effects of globalisation. The EU rules, for example, require that a country must have a 'functioning market economy', which, among other things, means there must be banks providing a comprehensive range of services to a wide cross-section of the populace.

That's a healthy development from the property buyer's perspective, because having a banking facility in local currency in the country in which you plan to buy is essential to get the buying process underway. You will not only have to be able to put down a deposit quickly in order to secure a property but, once you have bought, utility bills and other local expenses will need to paid and that can be done most conveniently by standing orders using a bank based in the relevant country.

Anti-money laundering regulations

'Money laundering' is the name given to the process of moving money through various transactions so as to distance the funds from their original (criminal) source. The money may have started its life as a backhander to an official for awarding a contract. That money could then be put into a property development project, which is then sold to foreigners by showing just half the value on the title, with the balance being passed under the table. After a few more transactions, perhaps also asking customers to pay their deposits into offshore banks, the exact source of the cash becomes more and more difficult to trace. Also, the more legitimate transactions that take place using 'dirty' money, the 'cleaner' it becomes, as those transactions are seen as the source of the cash.

If you last opened a bank account in the UK a decade ago, you may be in for a shock if you try to do so again now. In the past, banks were most concerned to see you thump some money on the table and, until you needed an overdraft, few questions were asked about you or where your money came from. Now, in an effort to prevent criminals moving money around, the banks have been required to be much more circumspect in those to whom they 'grant permission' to open one of their accounts. Now you will need to prove who you are and where you live. The bank will also be required to alert the authorities if they notice suspiciously large transactions going through your account.That, in theory, gives the government information as to who the criminals might be.

Currently, opening a bank account in many other countries is still a fairly relaxed process but the processes on monitoring for suspicious transactions are being tightened up. Also, you need to be on your guard to see that you are not drawn unwittingly into a laudering activity.

Using a local bank

Most countries covered have at least two or three locally owned banks with an established network. Generally, such banks are soundly based and unlikely to go to the wall in the foreseeable future. For the most part, the requirements for opening an account are currently little more than a formality: usually, presenting a passport will suffice.

Local banks will usually be quite secure for transferring money through to pay for a property and for handling small sums on an ongoing basis. It may not be prudent, however, to leave large sums either on deposit or even in the bank's vaults. In the first instance, unlike in the UK, where even large deposits are protected by the Government in the case of default, that is rarely the case in less-developed markets. In the second place, bank robberies are more frequent in certain parts of the world and unless you can prove the amount of cash held in a bank safe you will have little chance of recovering your money after a break-in. One developer who left €250,000 in cash in a major Bulgarian bank, which was being held in that form to protect it from currency fluctuations, lost all their money in this way. The bank was robbed, the money taken and it took the developer 18 months of hard legal threats to recover just a portion of their funds.

Things to look out for in choosing a local bank

- Check out all charges, especially those for using ATM machines which can be up to $7 a time.
- Make sure that someone in the branch can speak and read English.
- See that the bank has the facilities to send and receive money from overseas and that the costs are competitive.
- Choose a bank with a convenient branch, as you will be spending a lot of time there while arranging to buy a property.
- Establish the opening hours. These often vary from bank to bank.
- Make sure that the bank can pay standing orders and, ideally, has an Internet banking facility.

Help with finding a safe overseas bank

Business Link (`www.businesslink.gov.uk`)

This mammoth website, run for the UK Government, is primarily for those running or considering setting up a business. From the home screen, select 'International trade' from near the bottom of the left-hand vertical menu bar; then, from the central vertical menu bar, select

'International trade finance'; then, from that central menu bar, select 'Foreign currency and exchange rate risks'. You will then find an extensive range of information of value to overseas property buyers, including such topics as: 'Identify foreign exchange risks'; 'Forward foreign exchange contracts'; 'Opening foreign currency accounts'; and 'Opening an account with a bank overseas'. Select the last of these menu options and you will find a brief description of the pros and cons of this process. In the middle of the screen there is a link to a directory of foreign banks which are licensed to take deposits in the UK. The attraction for property buyers is that they can have the best of both worlds, in some countries at least: a bank with a local presence in the country of their choice, yet being around in the UK too, in case of problems.

HKSB (`www.us.hsbc.com/1/2/3/international-services/relocation/overseas`)

HSBC offers a wide range of international banking products and services for individuals relocating abroad and these could also be of benefit to property buyers. Through a chain of HSBC International Banking Centres, it helps clients to establish their finances in a new country by using its streamlined account-opening process. You can see a directory of the 50 countries in which they can help you open a bank account at this web page.

Worldwide-Tax (`www.worldwide-tax.com`)

This site is a very comprehensive one, dealing with a host of taxation and financial subjects for some 70 countries. The information for each country includes a general and economic survey. The site includes tips for investors, including those buying properties, who are not residents of that country and lists any investment benefits available. It has around 3,000 links to providers of supporting services such as accountants, lawyers, government sites, as well as a complete and comprehensive section on the embassies in that country.

Thislink (`http://www.worldwide-tax.com/banks/bankssites.asp`) will take you to its directory of world banks, sorted by country, and includes the major banks in each country, including local banks and international banks having branches there. Most of the banks on this site have an English website which includes an explanation of how to open a bank account in the bank's country, as well as online application procedures.

Offshore banking and tax havens

Banking in one of the world's 50 or so tax havens, such as the Channel Islands, Gibraltar or the Isle of Man, may sound like quite a smart thing to do. There is a lot of mystique, or perhaps it would be more accurate to say 'misinformation', surrounding such banks. There are some attractions to offshore banking, and quite legitimate ones such as relative secrecy, the facility to deposit funds in a variety of currencies and the fact that interest can be paid without any withholding tax being deducted. However, the advantages are not usually all they are cracked up to be. In Europe, at least, the secrecy is being eroded by anti-money laundering legislation and the tax advantages are often only a 'smoke and mirrors' illusion. Just because the bank doesn't deduct tax doesn't mean that you are not liable for tax. In whichever country you are domiciled, you are liable for tax on your worldwide income, wherever and however it is earned. It is just that with an offshore account you get to declare the income yourself, rather than the bank doing it for you as with most of the onshore variety of banks.

If you do decide that you need an offshore bank, then look for these attributes:

- **High credit rating**. Some offshore banks, indeed some tax havens, themselves look decidedly shaky. You need a safe home for your money: one with a credit rating as close to AAA, the highest standard given by the agencies such as Standard & Poor's, who rate this sector. You might be wise to stick to the offshore operations of the

UK and American banks whose names you will recognise and can trust.

- **Minimum deposit levels.** Many offshore banks are really only looking for high net-worth clients. They set their minimum deposit levels high with that in mind (some as high as €15,000 and many above €150,000). You may feel that for your first exposure to this type of bank you would prefer to put a toe in the water rather than jump straight in at the deep end.
- **Credit card facilities.** Does the bank offer international credit card facilities?
- **Access to funds.** For how long do you have to tie your money up and what are the penalties for early withdrawal? You may have to commit your capital for upwards of 3 months to get the best interest rates, but that could be too long if your property search is successful more quickly than that.
- **Costs.** For what and how much does the bank charge?
- **Internet and telephone banking.** Is either of these facilities on offer?

The UK HM Revenue and Customs (HMRC) in 2005 proved to the Special Commissioners (independent arbitrators on tax matters) that one un-named bank had 1,847 customers with overseas bank accounts, of whom only 327 had owned up to the fact on their income tax returns. HMRC estimates that several billion pounds in undeclared interest and income is involved and it is determined to get a good slice of it back. As a result, HMRC has been given the go-ahead to probe further into personal banking details of all those domiciled in the UK. (See the PriceWaterhouseCoopers tax investigation website (`http://www.tax-investigations.com`).) HMRC can probe into your financial affairs for the previous 6 years if it doesn't suspect fraud or negligence, or up to 20 years back if it does. As well as recovering any taxable income undeclared, it can impose an interest charge on the amount of the under-declaration as well as up to a fine equivalent to 100% of the amount involved. There will also be a hefty bill for professional assistance, not to say the worry and time spent in dealing with the tax enquiry.

Finding an offshore bank

The Sovereign Society (www.sovereignsociety.com)

The Sovereign Society, headquartered in Waterford, Ireland, is a membership organisation founded in 1998 to provide proven legal strategies for individuals to protect and enhance their wealth and privacy, lower their taxes and to help improve their personal freedom and liberty, with a focus on offshore banking and asset protection. It advises by publishing efforts and seminars on: 'Asset Protection Strategies'; 'Tax Management Solutions'; 'Global Investment Opportunities'; 'Second Citizenship and Residency'; and 'Offshore Structures.'

Select 'Visitors' from the horizontal menu bar across the top of the screen. From there, you can select from a range of free services including: 'The Sovereign Society Offshore A-Letter', containing new information monthly and including an index to past editions; 'Offshore Economic Analysis By Country'; and 'Events' (covering seminars and lectures).

Escape Artist (www.escapeartist.com/taxhavens/taxhavens.htm)

This link will take you straight to the directory of the 50 countries recognised as being potential tax havens. Once on the relevant country page, you will find a further directory of web links taking you to sources of help and advice on tax haven issues in that country. Alongside this information are thousands of articles, contacts, resources, links and tools for finding overseas real estate, international employment, hidden enclaves, artists' havens, unique destinations, offshore investments and the requirements for living an international lifestyle. Since 1995, this organisation has been helping 'escape artists' to restart their lives abroad. Over 350,000 subscribe (free) and read *Escape From America* Magazine and the *Offshore Real Estate Quarterly.*

Banking online

Many online retail banking services operate from the UK, most of which are full-service operations offering inter-account transfers, bill payments and automated transactions for direct debits and standing orders. You still need a physical location to pay in or withdraw cash, but otherwise virtually anything goes. In the UK, online bankers require you to be over 18 (some ask that you be over 21) and resident in the UK.

Banking online will work for you if you think these benefits are important:

- **Convenience**. You can set up your own standing orders, direct debits and one-off bill payments and apply for overdrafts and personal loans online, as well as off-set credit balances against mortgages and other loans. More importantly, you can operate the account anywhere, at any time.
- **Planning**. Many services let you download your financial data to Microsoft Money, Quicken and Sage software packages, to help you with financial planning and money management.
- **Value**. Online banks said they would be cheaper to run than conventional banks and they would pass some of those cost benefits to customers. Its certainly true that many online banks offer better interest on deposits and lower costs for services, though that is not a universal truth.

Ever wondered just how safe online banking is? Online bankers use the 128-Secure Socket Layer (SSL) protocol to protect data communication across the computer network. SSL relies on a system of encryption 'keys' comprising a unique combination of 128 zeros and ones (hence the '128' in the title). This protocol results in 2,128 possible permutations of ones and zeros, so it is just not economic for profession fraudsters to hack in. They rely on the careless disclosure of passwords and PINs and on 'spyware' which can burrow into your computer and find your banking details. Look out for a yellow padlock symbol indicating an SSL certificate.

But however secure the system may be, you are advised to take the following precautions:

- Ignore all e-mails appearing to come from your bank and asking for account details.
- Always enter the bank's web address directly in your web browser, rather than following a hyperlink in some text.
- Do not disclose your personal access data to anyone.
- Always log out using the bank's log-off icon.
- Check your accounts regularly and report any suspicious transactions immediately.
- Use current anti-virus and firewall software.
- Use a pos-2001 operating system and browser, as these will incorporate higher levels of security.
- Use public access points (such as Internet cafés) sparingly, as these are rarely completely secure.
- Avoid wi-fi, as hackers can site themselves within 'earshot'.

Finding an online banker

Find (www.find.co.uk)

Find is owned and operated by Omnium Communications Ltd and is authorised and regulated by the Financial Services Authority (FSA Reference No. 435537).

Its financing comes from FF&P Private Equity Ltd, the private equity division of Fleming Family & Partners, and Electra Quoted Management.

To get to itsdirectory of recommended online banking services, follow this thread: www.find.co.uk>banking>current_accounts_centre>online_banking

Business.com (www.business.com)

This site's mission is to help the business professional find exactly what they are looking for through the use of its business-focused search engine and directory. Developed by a team of industry experts and library scientists, the Business.com directory contains more than

400,000 listings within 65,000 industry, product and service subcategories. From the home page, typing in the words 'Directory of Online Banking' will yield a list of 60 banks around the world, with direct web links to their online banking service.

Understanding the tax regime

Buying a property abroad in many ways is the relatively easy part of living overseas. More complex problems to tussle with are: who will own the house (you, your partner, your children, any combination of those parties, or a more anonymous offshore company); what will happen to your tax or pension position if you start to spend more and more time in your overseas property; and, of course, how will any profit you make on your property be treated if and when you finally sell up?

The answers to all of those questions depend entirely on your personal circumstances and the country in which you choose to buy property. For example (see Figure 9.1), in some countries while you can die rich, as there is no inheritance tax, taxes on business activities or capital gains on the sale of properties may be higher than in your home country. There are few, if any, universal guiding rules. Added to this, dealing with matters such as tax and its minimisation, for example, depend greatly on your appetite for risk and complexity.

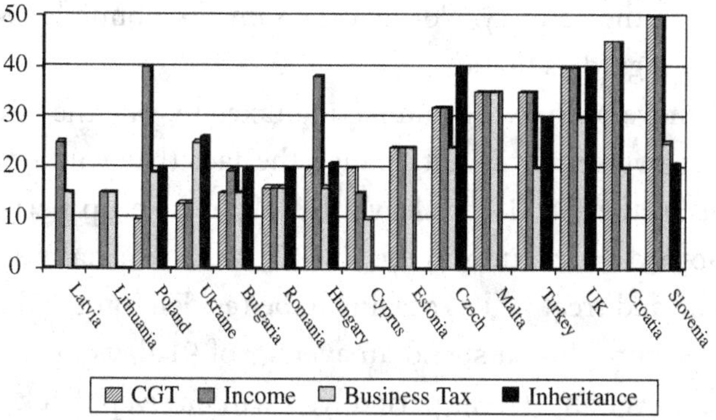

Figure 9.1 Tax regime differences in Eastern Europe

Those who prefer little paperwork and fewer dealings with lawyers and accountants might elect for a path that could end up giving a greater share of income and gain to the tax authorities or some other third party. But that might matter less to them than a peaceful life. Others would cross hot coals in order to keep money out of the hands of the tax authorities – within the bounds of the law, of course. The subject has serious implications for property owners and if handled properly can eliminate the tax on any gain in value and reduce the burden on rental income by as much as half.

What follows is a brief guide as to how tax and legal issues might impinge on the main decisions which could affect your overseas property affairs – be they a temporary or more permanent arrangement – and where you can find information on the tax regime in your chosen country. You should always seek professional advice on these matters, to be sure that your own personal position has been properly taken into account.

Rules on residency

There is usually no way of avoiding paying tax somewhere, but you do have some choice as to where you end up paying it. The governing rule on to whom you pay your taxes is not so much about where you live, nor necessarily where your income comes from, as where you are resident. The word 'resident' has a particular meaning when it comes to taxation and is not necessarily the same as having a residence card or living in the country. Nor is it the same as 'domicile', which is the place you regard as home.

If you have been living and paying taxes in, say, the UK, then simply going overseas will not change the fact that you are 'ordinarily resident' in the UK. If you leave the UK to take up permanent residence abroad and so inform the HMRC, it will normally accept this at face value and treat you as ceasing to be resident on the day following your departure. If you spend an average of 91 days or more per year in the UK over any 4-year period, you will be swept back into the UK tax net. The days of arrival and departure are not normally counted, so in theory you could spend an awful lot of long weekends in the UK before you used up your allowed days. You are, since a rule-change in 1993, even allowed to have accommodation available for your use in the UK.

For most of us, the arcane rules of tax residence will be largely irrelevant. However, if a large sum of tax (say from selling up your business or the capital gain on your house) is at stake, the Revenue might become a bit more rigid as to how the rules are applied. You may have to take steps to prove your movements, using travel and hotel receipts; you may be wise to have no accommodation available to you in the UK.

If you spend more than 183 days in Spain during one calendar year, you usually become liable for taxes in a foreign country whether or not you take out a formal residence permit. These days do not have to be consecutive and you become resident for tax purposes on the morning of the 184th day. Temporary absences from the overseas country in which your property is based are ignored for the purpose of the 183-day rule, unless you can prove you were resident in another country for more than 183 days in a calendar year.

Doubling tax troubles

At first sight, a tax regime abroad can look more attractive than the one operating in the UK (or wherever your home country is) but, sadly, it is not always a matter of 'either or', as many buying property or moving abroad find out. It is possible to be tax resident in both countries if you meet both sets of rules. For example, if you spend 200 days abroad, 100 days in the UK and the remaining days elsewhere, both the foreign and British tax authorities or your home tax authority could reasonably lay claim to you.

Many countries have 'double taxation' agreements designed to settle the argument. 'Tie-breakers', as the relevant clauses in the double taxation agreement are known, deal with such cases as where people have homes, assets and income in roughly equal proportions in both countries. In those circumstances, you are normally deemed to be a resident of the country of which you are a national. The worn 'normally' should be a sign to the wary that this is not an area in which to tread without taking timely advice.

The aim of double taxation agreements is to help make sure that you don't pay tax on the same taxable event twice: once in a foreign country and again at home. But you could well end up paying different taxes in each country.

For example, you will almost definitely pay capital gains tax in the country in which your overseas property is situated when you sell up – wherever you base your tax affairs. On the other hand, income from UK property rents is normally taxed at source in the UK.

UK non-government pensions are taxed abroad, if that is where you receive the money, but government pensions are taxed in the UK. And capital gains on UK property sold once you move overseas will still be taxed in the UK.

General taxes (and inducements to invest)

Most, though not all, countries have some form of taxation. Often, the taxation rules are different for foreigners who want to either live or invest in the country. In some cases the taxes can be an inducement while in others they can act as a brake on what might otherwise seem a worthwhile property purchase. For example, capital gains tax rules often favour the local population over foreign non-residents, either by extracting a higher rate of tax by requiring that the asset is owned for a longer period before it is free of tax liability. The same may be true of income from rents. These are the key taxes to consider.

- **General income tax**. This is a tax on income earned in a particular country, from employment or any profitable activity. This almost invariably applies whether or not you live in the country where the money is generated or have elected for it to be your tax base. Some countries operate a flat-rate structure (such as Estonia, where 23%

is applied on all income). This tax favours those on high incomes. Other countries (such as New Zealand and Morocco) have a sliding rate with a 0% band, favouring those on low incomes; others (such as Thailand and Mexico) tax even the lowest earners by between 3 and 5%; and others still (notably the Netherlands, Denmark, Spain, Austria, Slovenia and China) have rates of tax on fairly modest levels of income of between 45 and 59%.

- **Income from rents and investments**. In many countries the income from renting out a property falls into the same bands as for personal taxation. But that is not always the case. For example, in Hungary individuals pay tax at 20% on all rental income, while the general income tax level starts at 18%. Other quirks of the tax system include variations in what is and is not a tax-allowable expense against any rental income. Taking Hungary as an example again, it is not until a property has been owned for 6 years that the full range of expenses which it is usual to incur in renting out a property can be offset against income before calculating the tax base.
- **Business tax**. If you plan to start or operate a business in the country in which you are buying property, you will be subject to tax on any profit made. The rates of business tax worldwide vary widely. The Maldives (9%) and the United Arab Emirates (15%) are towards the low end of the scale, while Italy (76%) and India (81%) are among countries with the highest business taxes. All business taxes are complicated, but in some countries they are more complicated than others. For example, it takes over 1,000 hours to prepare and file all business taxes in countries such as Ukraine, Brazil and the Czech Republic, while in Singapore, Switzerland and the Seychelles the whole task can be completed in less than 70 hours. (Also see below 'Legal structures'.)
- **Capital gains tax**. This is the tax charged against the profit made on the gain from investment in an asset, such as property. As with other taxes, there is a wide variety of rates and conditions to look out for. For example, owning a property for 1 year exempts investors from capital gains tax liability in some countries (Latvia, for example),

while you have to wait 5 years in others (for example, Bulgaria) for the same concession. Other conditions sometimes apply. For example, in Lithuania property owners are exempt from capital gains tax on the sale of one property in any one year, after a year of ownership. In Serbia and Montenegro, any proceeds of the sale of a property reinvested into personal housing are exempt from tax if the purchase is made within 60 days. You can reclaim any capital gains tax paid if such a reinvestment is made within 10 months.

- **Value added and sales taxes.** These are taxes levied on transactions rather than on income earned. So if renovations, repairs or any extensions are made to a property, or it is furnished or enhanced by the addition of a swimming pool, sauna or hot tub, such expenditure will attract a tax. The different ways in which this tax is levied can add as much as 18% to the cost of improving or furnishing a property. Also, such a tax will be due whether or not the property is let out or to be used solely by the owner for his or her own purposes. Even within Europe these taxes are levied at widely different rates – anything between 15% and 22% being the norm. Canada's VAT rate of 7% is one of the lowest and Brazil's and Denmark's 25% the highest. In addition, some items are exempt from this tax in some countries.
- **Import duties.** Within the European Union, import duties are largely a thing of the past. Also, many countries exempt personal effects brought into a country, including furniture, computers and even motor vehicles. But not all countries are equally forgiving. For example, you can import virtually anything into Iraq free of import duties, while taking anything into the Dominican Republic will be liable to a local tax of up to 40%.
- **Tax holidays and inducements to invest.** Many countries offer individuals and businesses tax or grant inducements to buy property or business assets in certain areas. These are often short-lived opportunities and, like all such offers, are intended to encourage some risk-taking. The degree of risk and reward varies enormously. For example, at the time of writing, Russia was offering new tax

incentives for investors in Kaliningrad which would all but eliminate tax charges for up to 12 years. For a rather smaller investment than the 150 million roubles the Russians wanted for the doubtful privilege of buying a slice of Kaliningrad, the US Government offers Green Cards (work and residence permits) to entrepreneurs willing to invest $500,000 in starting a business there.

- **Annual property tax**. Simply owning a property usually lands either the owner or the occupants with a tax bill. In the UK, the community charge puts the onus for paying the tax on those living in the property, while in Croatia a tax of between 5 and 15 kuna per square metre per year is levied on holiday homes and undeveloped land and buildings.

Information sources on local taxation matters

The Trade Information Centre (www.ita.doc.gov/td/tic/tariff)

This is a comprehensive resource for information on all US Federal Government export assistance programmes operated by the International Trade Administration of the US Department of Commerce. As part of its service you can find on the website information on the import and export tariffs applicable to most goods and services throughout the world. From this link, select 'Country Specific Tariff and Tax Information' from the vertical menu bar in the centre of the screen. That will take you to pages containing country-specific tax information, as well as Internet links to online sources

Doing Business (www.doingbusiness.org)

This is the World Bank's database providing objective measures of business regulations across 175 countries. It indicates the regulatory costs of business and can be used to analyse specific regulations on a country-by-country basis. Follow the thread: www.doingbusiness.org>ExploreTopics>PayingTaxes. There you will find the taxes that a small- to medium-size business must pay or withhold in a given year, as well as measures of administrative burden in paying taxes. The opening table in this section shows the total number of taxes paid; the time it takes to prepare, file and pay (or withhold) the relevant tax; the value added tax and social security contributions (in hours per year); and total amount of taxes payable by the business, except for labour taxes. To see the full details of the tax regime for a specific country, use the drop-down box on the top-right of the screen or click on the relevant country link on that page. By clicking on the column headers, you can sort the relevant data to show, for example, which country has the highest or lowest taxes, requires the most or least time to deal with or involve the most or fewest separate tax payments.

Also, by selecting 'Trading Across Borders' from the left-hand vertical menu bar on the home page, you can find out about the procedural requirements for exporting and importing goods. Every official procedure is counted – from the contractual agreement between the parties to the delivery of goods – along with the time necessary for completion. You can see that to import goods into Hong Kong requires only two documents, while getting the same goods into Rwanda calls for 20 separate documents to be completed. Clicking the 'Time for import' column heading shows that while it takes only 3 days to import goods into Singapore, you need to allow 139 to get good into Uzbekistan.

While all the information on this site is aimed primarily at businesses, it also gives a reasonable approximation to the complexity or otherwise that an individual might experience in carrying out similar tasks in the countries covered.

Worldwide Tax (`www.worldwide-tax.com`)

This site is a very comprehensive site that deals with a host of taxation and financial subjects for some 70 countries. From the central menu on the home page, select 'Tax Rates Around the World – Comparison' to find a quick summary of income and corporate tax levels as well as value added tax for all the countries covered. From the vertical menu bar on the left of the home page screen, select from the 'Shortcut to countries' section the countries you are interested in researching. Once on the country page, scroll down to the country taxes menu in the centre of the page and, from there, select the appropriate tax from the menu offered. At the bottom of that menu you can select 'Tax News 20' where you will find the latest changes in tax rules for the country in question. For example, at the time of writing, the Maltese tax authorities announced that individuals having an employment income, derived mainly outside Malta, will pay tax in Malta, subject to certain conditions, at a flat income tax rate of 15% from 1 January 2006.

PWC [Price Waterhouse Coopers]
(`www.pwc.com/uk/eng/main/home/index.html`)

This is the site of PricewaterhouseCoopers which employs more than 130,000 people in 148 countries and covers every aspect of tax and business affairs in each of them. From this page, select 'Tax' from the left-hand vertical menu bar in the centre of the page. You will be asked to register on the site before you can uncover much useful information from this section, but that takes no more than 5 minutes and is free. The tax site contains up-to-the minute breaking tax news and a range of publications including *Worldwide Tax Summaries*. Select 'Worldwide Tax Summaries Online' from the menu box centre right and you will be taken to an up-to-date overview of the corporate and individual tax rates and rules in operation in over 109 countries worldwide as well as important aspects of the relevant laws that shape taxation in the countries covered.

Tax News (`www.tax-news.com`)

The Lowtax Network of sites was launched in 1999 by Michael Bell, an established international business publisher. Except for the Lowtax Shop and a subscription newsletter, content is free to the user, with revenue being derived from advertisers and 'syndication' clients. The fives sites, directly accessed from the home page are:

- `www.lowtax.net`: 1,500 pages of detailed, factual information covering the tax and legal regimes in 35 offshore and 15 onshore countries.
- `www.tax-news.com`: a daily worldwide tax news service with a 12,000-story searchable archive.
- `www.investorsoffshore.com`: news and reference data for alternative investors and expatriates.
- `www.offshore-e-com.com`: news and background on offshore e-commerce.
- `www.lawandtax-news.com`: news and reference material on law and tax for international businesses, covering 20 key worldwide countries, to be expanded to 50.

Wealth tax

Property is difficult to conceal and can make owners ready targets for a particularly pernicious form of taxation not known in the UK. However, some countries (such as Finland, France, Greece, Iceland, Luxembourg, Norway, Spain, Sweden and Switzerland) levy a tax each year on the value of their citizens' assets. In some cases, (in France for example), the reach of the tax goes further still where anyone resident in the country on 1 January is taxable on his or her worldwide assets, and non-residents with assets in France are taxed on the value of their French assets as at that date. The tax is often based on the wealth of the household, including any spouse or partner and any infant children (with a reduction for each dependant child under the age of 18). Taxable assets usually include: property; cars; other vehicles; furniture; horses and other livestock; jewellery; shares; bonds; the redemption value of any life assurance; endowments; and debts due to the taxpayer. The amount of the tax varies, as does the level of wealth required before it becomes due. For example, the 'Impot de Solidarité sur la Fortune', as this tax is known in France, is assessed annually, with progressive rates ranging from 0.55 to 1.8% for people whose worldwide assets are greater than €732,000. In Iceland, you only need to have net assets in excess of €53,000 to become caught up in the wealth tax net. Other names by which wealth tax is known include: 'capital tax', 'equity tax', 'net worth tax', and 'net wealth tax'. Countries which have shed this tax include Austria, Denmark, Finland, Ireland, Germany, the Netherlands and (from January 2006) Russia.

Organisations helping with managing wealth tax issues

Word Tax Payers Associations
(`www.worldtaxpayers.org/statnet.htm`)

This organisation has as its mission to form 'a united front for lower taxes, less waste, accountable government and taxpayers rights all over the world'. It is a non-profit organisation officially established at the Foreign Press Club in Washington DC, USA in 1988, to join the fight for lower taxes. Until 2000, the name of the organisation was 'Taxpayers Associations International'. This link leads directly to the statistics of wealth tax rates around the world, showing which countries do and do not levy such a tax.

Worldwide Tax (`www.worldwide-tax.com`)

This website is a very comprehensive one dealing with a host of taxation and financial subjects for some 70 countries. From the vertical menu bar on the left of the home page screen, select from the 'Shortcut to countries' section the countries you are interested in researching. Once on the country page, scroll down to the country taxes menu in the centre of the page and, from there, select the appropriate tax from the menu offered. For example, at the time of writing, Russia had announced a new law, effective from 1 January 2006, abolishing the inheritance and gift tax; and stating that close relatives would pay no personal income tax on gifts (e.g. real estate, cars, shares etc.) and only non-close recipients would pay personal income tax on gifts.

Inheritance tax, death duties and related issues.

Whichever of the ownership structures you choose, you will have to concern yourself as to who inherits when you die or any joint owner of the property dies. You will also need to express your decisions in a will. If you don't, the death in question will be dealt with under the intestacy laws, which are a nightmare to deal with, especially if there is scope for ambiguity as to whether the matter should be handled under UK law or the law of the country in question.

Unlike in the UK, under the law of many overseas countries certain family members have automatic inheritance rights. For example, it may be that spouses and children (even illegitimate ones) may not be cut out of a will. However, if you are still a British citizen, irrespective of your tax residency arrangements, your will, as long as you make one, will usually be dealt with under English law.

While an English will is usually valid under the law in most foreign countries, it is advisable to draw up a will in the country in question in order to save time in being able to distribute the estate and the ensuing additional administrative costs. No matter in which country your domicile is, the local authorities will be interested in the disposal of any assets (for example, the house you are buying now), so a will in that country will smooth the process and ensure that the deceased's wishes are faithfully carried out. Your foreign will needs to drawn up in the local language and signed before a notary, with witnesses present. Your foreign and English wills must not conflict in any way, otherwise that will leave scope for interminable disputes, delays and additional costs.

You will need an executor for your foreign will. While in the UK it is not uncommon for lay people to act as executors, proving a will abroad, especially for a foreigner, can be complex, so it may make good sense to appoint a local lawyer to steer the inheritors in the best direction.

Organisations helping to minimise post-death taxes

The American Council for Capital Formation (ACCF) (www.accf.org/publications/reports/sr-intcomp-deathtax.html)

This is an organisation dedicated to the advocacy of tax and environmental policies to encourage saving and investment. The ACCF was founded in 1973 and is supported by the voluntary contributions of corporations, associations, foundations and individuals. This link leads directly to a table showing an international comparison of inheritance taxes. Japan has the highest rate (70%), followed by the USA (55%), with the UK and France coming in at 40%. Argentina, Australia, Canada, India and Mexico are among the countries not levying an inheritance tax. The starting point for levying the tax ranges from the relatively low figure of €30,000 in Denmark up to $3 million in the USA.

The tax rate can also vary according to the type of asset left in the estate of the deceased. For example, in Brazil property value is taxed at 4% while all other assets attract a rate of 6%. Some countries try to dodge the emotive title of death duties. For example, Argentina imposes a court filing fee ranging from 2 to 3%, based on the market value of the estate, with the fee being paid by the beneficiaries.

Inheritance Tax Planning World
(http://inheritance-tax.openchallenge.org)

This service is delivered by TaxWorld and provides free tax information from around the world, including such esoteric topics as the history of taxation; tax statistics; tax terms in different languages; and a tax directory. This link is to its guide to inheritance tax planning, with an interesting closing gambit. If your wealth is over £1 million, you are invited to e-mail to arrange to meet an inheritance tax expert!

Deciding how to structure the ownership of your overseas property – tax and other considerations

You may be forgiven for thinking that the only way to own a property is for you to buy it. That would be just too simple. In general, there are five main different types of ownership structure, each with a number of variations. Choosing the right structure for you will call for professional advice from a lawyer or accountant conversant with tax and inheritance law in the UK and in the country in which plan to buy a property.

At stake is the potential to liberate thousands of pounds while you are alive and to save your dependants a small fortune in tax when you die. But in order to secure these savings you may have to relinquish a degree of control over your property – not something about which many of us would be too enthusiastic. If you are considering putting the property in your children's or partner's name, make sure you give yourself a life interest in the property. This will protect your right to live there for as long as you live, while saving your dependants a hefty inheritance tax bill when you die. Your lawyer can arrange this for you.

As well as owning an overseas property in your own name, it is possible to use a company, formed expressly for that purpose, to hold all or part of the property asset on your behalf. In many cases the company is little more than a 'front' for personal ownership, as a sole individual can also own the whole of the company. In some countries (such as Bulgaria, for example), foreigners cannot own the land on which a property stands in their own name, and so have to form a company. There are also some tax advantages to owning a property through a company. For example, in Hungary a company pays capital gains tax at 16% while individuals pay 20%. The same rates apply to rental income from property.

There are three possible corporate options for owning property overseas: each is has potential attractions and in some cases an equal or greater number of associated problems. This is definitely not a way

Table 9.2: Pros and cons of ownership structures

Structure	Pros	Cons
Sole ownership	Simple	Could leave a big inheritance tax (IT) bill for dependants. Miss out on potential for tax savings if you plan to rent out property, as there are more tax-efficient ways to own the property.
Joint ownership with spouse	Reduces IT liability	Co-owner can force sale at will. Also, could miss out on tax savings if you plan to rent out property.
Adding children to title	Reduce IT liability further	Children can also force sale at will. Still miss out on tax savings if you plan to rent out property.
Put property in children's name only	Virtually eliminate IT liability	You will all but lose control of property in your lifetime. You need permission to sell. Still miss out on tax savings if you plan to rent out property.
Buy using a UK or offshore limited company or a company formed in the country in which you plan to buy a property	Could reduce taxes if you plan to rent out property. Can help with IT. Leaves you in control	Complicated and you will have to be sure that any tax savings you could achieve are worthwhile (company taxes are mostly lower than the rate individuals pay).
Form a buying syndicate	Can be very tax-efficient if you are allowed to put the property into a SIPP (self-invested pension plan)	Even more complicated than using a company but if you are investing over £300,000, could be worth exploring.

to property ownership for any but the very well advised. The common feature of all three types of company ownership is that it is possible for the ownership of the asset to be concealed from the casual observer. Any determined party could find out who owned the shares in the company and hence break the superficial code.

- **UK limited company (or one in your home country)**. This will offer the same advantages as would generally be achieved by using a corporate structure to own assets. But if you own only one or two properties and the sums involved are relatively small, this may not result in a lower overall tax bill
- **A company in the country concerned**. There is a potential tax advantage here, in that companies in overseas countries pay tax a lower rate of tax than the top marginal rate for individuals. But it is doubtful whether this alone is sufficient reason for buying a property through a company.
- Use an **offshore company**. Over the past few years, governments around the world have introduced legislation intended to eliminate the benefit of buying property through an 'offshore' company. For example, in Portugal they have introduced an IMT (*Imposto Municipal sobre Transmissões*) payable on offshore owned property at a flat 5% of value and also imposed a tax on a presumed rental income calculated as 1/15th of the '*Valor Patrimonial*' (rateable value). However, there may still be three advantages to holding an overseas property in an offshore company, but as all of them will only pay out when and if you sell up and all the costs of forming and running the company are up front, you may think this particular light is not worth the candle. The benefits lie around possible saving on capital gains tax by shifting the gain offshore, saving on notarial and registration fees and the fact that transferring shares in an offshore company may avoid the lengthy procedures necessary to register a fresh title. The sale and purchase can thus be achieved more quickly, easily and cheaply.

Organisations helping with deciding ownership vehicles

Business Link (www.businesslink.gov.uk)

This is the main contact point for support, information and advice for small businesses and owner-managed businesses in the UK. From the left-hand vertical menu bar, select 'Taxes, returns and payroll'. From there, select 'Choosing and setting up a legal structure' from the central menu bar headed 'Legal structures, records and returns'. Here you will find an overview of the pros and cons of using a limited company as a vehicle for your business activities, the rules of which are generally applicable to property activities.

Doing Business (www.doingbusiness.org)

Provided as a collaborative venture by the World Bank Group in co-operation with the Lex Mundi Association of law firms and the International Bar Association, the Doing Business database assesses and measures business regulations and their enforcement across 155 countries. From the left-hand menu bar, select 'Starting a business'. There you can see the bureaucratic and legal hurdles you are likely to encounter in forming a company. The columns in the centre of this page give a summary of the position in each country and, by selecting a particular country, you can get more detailed information. Using the database you can see, for example, that starting a business in Haiti takes 203 days and involves a dozen different procedures, whereas in Australia it takes only two days and two procedures are involved.

Offshore Companies House (www.offshore-companies.co.uk)

Despite its official-sounding name, this is a freelance operation founded by a group of professional bankers, accountants and lawyers, with a wealth of offshore experience from different onshore and offshore jurisdictions. The best place to start is in the FAQ (Frequently asked questions) section, which can be selected from the left-hand vertical menu bar. There you will find answers to such questions as what types of offshore companies there are; how much they cost to form and run; and what the real advantages of using them are. The organisation is selling its services from this site, so expect to have to pay for anything beyond general information. It aims to keep up to date on the international legislation and, for example, have, due to changes in tax policy in the countries in question, crossed the Cayman Islands, Switzerland and the Bahamas off its recommended places to form an offshore company while suggesting BVI, Belize, Dominica, Seychelles, Panama and Gibraltar as places where you can save on taxes when buying and selling property.

(See also the advisory organisations listed below.)

Getting financial and tax advice

Back in 2004, SIPPs (self-invested pension schemes) were originally supposed to include overseas residential property in the allowable asset class. This allowance would have made buying overseas property very attractive indeed: effectively knocking off up to 40% from the purchase price, depending on your tax rate. At the last gasp, the Chancellor of the Exchequer backed away from allowing residential property to be held in individual SIPPs, though a more complex group investment is still on the cards.

The UK investment advice community was miffed, to say the least, as it was gearing up for a possible bonanza. Its loss is your gain. As part of getting prepared, a lot of financial advisers acquired the necessary knowledge on the investment aspects of overseas property deals. They became versed in such topics as potential profits; tax implications of letting and selling; disposing of British assets; and managing pensions and wills.

Financial adviser associations and bodies

The Association of Investment and Financial Advisers (AIFA) (www.aifa.net)

AIFA is the trade association for independent financial advisers (IFAs), representing around 70% of the market. From the left-hand vertical menu bar, select 'Find an IFA'; from there you will be invited to enter a UK postcode which will lead to a localised directory of IFAs. Expatriates will need a UK postcode in order to get into the directory. You will be invited to fill out a request form for the area in which you seek advice. Select 'Expatriates' from section 3 and continue as meets your needs.

The Institute of Financial Planning (www.financialplanning.org.uk)

The Institute is the UK professional body which can help you understand more about how comprehensive financial planning differs from the more product-oriented broking service. It can also help members of the public search for a qualified financial planner to assist them in organising their personal or corporate financial affairs in order more readily to achieve their goals, which includes advice on buying property overseas or relocating to another country. Select the term 'search for a qualified Financial Planner' from the 'How we can help you' option in the centre of the home screen. From there you will be asked to look in more detail at other areas, including 'Expatriate Financial Planning' and 'Offshore Investments'.

International Tax Planning Association (www.itpa.org)

Founded in 1975, this is a multi-disciplined association of over 1,000 bankers, trust officers, finance directors, accountants, lawyers and others with a practical interest in the tax aspects of cross-frontier transactions. It examines tax mostly from the point of view of the taxpayer; membership is limited to practitioners who act for or in the interests of taxpayers. You can find a directory of member firms in the *Green Book* which you can find in the horizontal menu bar across the bottom of the screen (or use this link: `www.itpa.org/services/gb.php`). From there, select a tax jurisdiction (by country) and a service (such as estate planning; immigration; or tax planning), then click 'Search'.

Worldwide Tax
(`www.worldwide-tax.com/consultants/financialconsult.asp`)

This website is a very comprehensive one dealing with a host of financial subjects for some 70 countries. From this page, select the county in which you require a financial consultant.

CHAPTER 10

Researching the Legal Environment

In this chapter:

- Checking out rights to reside.
- Looking into earning a living, and more.
- Sorting out ownership rights.
- Looking into property-buying measures.
- Entering enterprise.

For the most part, those living in the USA or the 30 or so countries comprising the European Union (EU)and the European Economic Area (EEA) (Norway, Iceland, Liechtenstein and Switzerland are members of the EEA, allowing them to participate in most aspects of the EU Single Market without actually joining the EU), have within their own vast continents almost complete freedom of movement. An American citizen can buy a property in California or Massachusetts, as the mood takes them, and live and work there, enjoying the same rights and privileges as those born and bred in that state. Similarly, a Frenchman or Spaniard could move to England with much the same freedom.

However, not all of the world operates under such a benign freedom of movement. Even within some areas which are apparently open to all comers, some constraints apply. For example, Malta is a fully paid-up member of the EU and, in theory, a citizen of any other member state can buy a property there on the same terms as the locals. Citizens of countries other than the EU need to apply for an AIP (Acquisition of Immovable Property) permit in order to purchase property: a process that usually takes about 3 months. Even with that permit, restrictions are still placed on what a foreigner can and cannot do with any property for which an AIP is granted. Whereas, since 2004, when Malta joined the EU, fellow EU citizens do not need an AIP permit to buy one property, provided it is intended to be their primary and principal residence (regardless of whether they actually choose to live in Malta), they still need a permit for any additional properties.

Many subtle and not so subtle restrictions apply to constrain or discourage foreigners from buying property, owning land, working or setting up in business overseas. Such issues contribute greatly to the relative desirability of a country as a place to buy property and to the prospects of fully enjoying that property once bought.

Visa and residence rules

A visa (shorthand for the Latin *carta visa*, which literally means 'the document having been seen') is a paper issued by a country, giving a named individual permission to enter that country for a given period of time and for certain reasons. With the exception of member countries of the EU and the EEA, who accept each other's passports as sufficient permission to enter, most countries require a valid visa as a condition of entry for foreigners, though there exist exemption schemes which allow foreigners to stay for periods (typically ranging between 30 and 90 days) without one.

For some countries getting a visa is little more than a formality. For example, just turn up at any airport in Turkey, pay the equivalent of £20 and you can stay in the country for up to 90 days, with just a small stamp in your passport to verify your status. However, without applying in advance with supporting documentation, it is impossible to get a visa to enter the USA.

Visas come in a variety of forms directly affecting what you do in a country. The most common is the tourist visa, which allows entry for a holiday or to visit relatives and friends. A business visa allows you to engage in commercial activities, but not to take up an employed position in the country. Work, temporary-work, working holiday and student visas are other forms which explain the constraints and time in which you are allowed to live in a country without applying for residence.

If you want complete freedom to come and go in a country as you will, then you will need to apply for a residence permit. Often, this can be done from the country in question prior to your visa expiring, but sometimes you will have to return to your home country and apply from there for the necessary permision. In any event, this is an area to be explored prior to deciding in which country to buy a property, as any serious restrictions in ths area will limit the people to whom you can rent and ultimately sell on and consequently influence future property values.

Sources of help and advice with visas and residency

BBC (www.bbc.co.uk/radio1/onelife/travel/travelbasics/rpermit.shtml)

The BBC website has some basic information on residence, work and job permits in a range of countries. From this page, headed 'Residence permit', select countries you are interested in exploring from the 'Country A-Z' web link in the centre of the screen.

All Visa Info (www.allvisainfo.com) (fee payable)

This site makes the grandiose claim that it provides 'Visa and Country Information for 250 Countries'. However, the United Nations recognises only 192 countries and even if you add the couple not recognised by the UN you still arrive at only 194, so it is hard to see where the rest come from. Nevertheless, the site provides valuable information. The main strength and competency is that it provides specific visa information and/or links to find the information for all types of visas 'for all citizens of the world', so it claims, for example, to be able to provide the correct visa information if an Albanian wished to work in Andorra on a business visa. If the information is not on its website it aims to reply to queries within 24 hours. It does not provide or issue visas but simply informs the client of exactly what the requirements are and then suggests where they should go to get the visa if needed. The information is updated on a weekly basis each Saturday, to ensure that it is accurate. In the event of unusual circumstances, the visa information would be updated the same day.

From the home page, select 'Visa Information' from the left-hand vertical menu bar. From there, you are invited to complete a questionnaire asking about your nationality, the country you want to visit, what type of visa you require (e.g. business, tourist, single or multiple entry, 1 month to 5 years etc.). To get the information, you have to pay a €5 fee by credit card or PayPal.

Also on the above menu bar is a section headed 'Visa Definitions', where you will find explanations of the different types of visa that can be obtained.

Henley and Partners (www.henleyglobal.com)

Henley and Partners are specialised private client and business advisers with particular expertise in providing 'residence solutions'. The firm also has a reputation in multi-jurisdictional real-estate advisory, tax-planning and fiduciary services. Select 'Residence' from the vertical menu bar on the right of the screen. From there, you will find a series of options including 'Overview', then options to examine countries within continents. The final option in this section – 'Visa Restrictions' – takes you to the Henley Visa Restrictions Index, a global ranking of countries according to travel freedoms their citizens enjoy, as well as the international relations and status of individual countries relative to others.

The top ranking in 2006 was held by Finland, Denmark and the United States, with a score of 130 each (such a score means that a citizen of, say, Finland, may enter 130 countries and territories without a visa). They are followed by other European nations and Japan.

Canada and New Zealand are joint 6th together with Luxembourg and Austria. Singapore (8th) ranks before Malaysia, which is ranked 9th together with Iceland, Greece and Australia. Further down the scale, one will find Turkey (46th), Russia (62nd, together with the United Arab Emirates), India (71st) and China (78th). Not surprisingly, Iran, Iraq and Afghanistan score lowest, i.e. their citizens have the least travel freedom.

Federation of European Employers (FEDEE) (`www.fedee.com`)

FedEE membership is a resource for employers to ensure that they achieve legal compliance in European employment issues. There is also some useful free information on the website. Follow this link (`www.fedee.com/entryrights.html`) where you will find details of the most relevant trans national measures regulating the freedom of movement of EU citizens.

Foreign and Commonwealth Office (FCO) (`www.fco.gov.uk`)

The purpose of the FCO is to work for UK interests in 'a safe, just and prosperous world'. It does this with some 16,000 staff based in the UK and an overseas network of over 200 diplomatic offices. Its website is a mine of invaluable and up-to-date information that is near-impossible to find easily. Using the 'Quick search' box will result in an almost impossibly long list of options. By far the easiest way to get at information is to go to the websites of the countries you are interested in and search from there. From the FCO home page, select 'UK Embassies Overseas' from the left-hand vertical pull-down menu. From there, click on the links below to view the contact details of the UK's embassies, high commissions and consulates in the overseas countries you are interested in. At the bottom of each country's home page you will find a web link to the embassy or high commission website. Once on the country website, look under 'Services' in the left-hand vertical menu bar, or select 'Site Map' and look for a term such as 'Settle, work or buying property in … '. Here you will find guidance on current legislation concerning foreigners setting up residence in the country.

European Immigration Lawyers Group
(www.eilg.nl/network.html)

This is a group of lawyers specialising in immigration law. This link is direct to its country membership directory. Its work includes advice on visas, residence, work permits and citizenship.

Working and setting up in business

Salaries and wages are usually relatively low in most of the countries in which it is desirable to buy properties. Even if working for a multinational business, unless you have been lured to the country by an employer, you are almost certain to be paid less than you could expect at home. If you are an EU citizen then you have more or less the same opportunities in any of the 30 or so EU or EEA countries as you have in your home country. Citizens from outside the EU will find it harder to get into an EU country to work, as will EU citizens looking for work outside the EU. In such circumstances you will need to apply for a work permit, a subject also covered above in the 'Visa and Residence rules' section.

Most people buying properties abroad are simply looking for a modest additional income from employment of some sort that will be sufficient to make the venture of buying a property and living in their new country less of a financial strain. Working is certainly a good way to get to know a country and its inhabitants.

A further, and usually more practical, option is to start your own business. Most countries welcome entrepreneurs, especially if they create, or look like being able to create, jobs in the country concerned. If a country is desirable from a property investment perspective then by definition it will either have or have good prospects for tourism- and leisure-related business such as bars, restaurants, guest houses, riding stables and so forth.

For those without a business idea of their own, franchising – a marketing technique used to improve and expand the distribution of a product or service – is a good route to creating an income stream. The franchisor supplies the product or teaches the service to the franchisee, who in his turn sells it to the public. In return for this, the franchisee pays a fee and a continuing royalty, based usually on turnover. They may also be required to buy materials or ingredients from the franchisor, giving the franchisor an additional income stream. The advantage to the franchisee is a relatively safe and quick way of getting into business for themselves, but with the support and advice of an experienced organisation close at hand.

The franchisor can expand their distribution with the minimum strain on their own capital and have the services of a highly motivated team of owner-managers. Franchising is not a path to great riches, nor is it for the truly independent spirit, as policy and profits will still come from 'on high'.

Franchising can be a good first step into self-employment for those with business experience but no actual experience of running a business – often the case with those who are looking for something to do following a corporate career. However, while franchising eliminates some of the more costly (and at times disastrous) bumps in the learning curve of working for yourself, it is not without risks. Wild claims are made about how much safer a franchise is when compared with a conventional start-up. While it is true that the long-established big franchise chains are relatively safe, though a few big names have got into trouble, the smaller and newer ones are as vulnerable as any other venture in their formative years.

The cost of a franchise varies enormously. Anything from €3,000 up to €600,000 will be needed, depending on the type of franchise and its location. For example, taking out a McDonalds franchise in Spain will require an investment of €450,000–€550,000; running a Subway sandwich franchise will cost €10,000 in fees plus 12% royalties and advertising budget contribution plus, of course, the shop rent and fittings. A Coffee News franchise, which claims to be the most widely read publication in coffee shops and restaurants in Europe, is on offer for €3,500. This last franchise was only launched in 2002, but already it claims to have over 250 franchisee-run outlets and a further 5 run by the parent company. You will need to find a town with at least 20,000 inhabitants for a Coffee News franchise to have a reasonable chance of success. English4U, an English language school franchise launched in 2003, is one business where you might already have better skills than the locals can provide, but charges €17,500 for its franchise.

Help and advice with working and setting up in business abroad

Any Work Anywhere (`www.anyworkanywhere.com`)

This organisation was founded by Jo Drury and John Davie in January 2000, after 5 years of travelling and working around the world, as a means of sharing and capitalising on their knowledge as well as vicariously continuing their globe-trotting. 30,000 jobs have been advertised on the website on behalf of over 500 companies, ranging from large recruitment agencies and tour operators to independent farms and hotels, with hundreds of job vacancies being filled every week. Select 'Visa info' from the left-hand vertical menu bar. From there you will be presented with three pull-down menu bars in the centre of the screen: 'Work Visas, Permits And Restrictions'; 'Working Holiday Visas'; and 'Embassies And Consulates Worldwide With Web Sites'.

The pages in these sections contain a brief and general summary, visa requirements and the number of working holiday visas allocated in each country. There is a caution stating that each year the rules can vary and new agreements are being made regularly, so the site recommends that you obtain complete and up-to-date official information from the embassy or consulate before making any work and travel plans. There are also dozens of links to other useful websites, with information on work opportunities and conditions in countries around the world.

British Franchise Association (www.british-franchise.org)

This is the website of the UK trade association representing the interests of franchisors in the UK. There is information about the process of franchising, case studies and pros and cons. Select 'International' from the left-hand vertical menu bar and from there 'Franchise Associations – a list of franchise associations around the world'. There you will find links to the franchise associations in A–Z format, from Argentina to Turkey. Within each country association you will find links to a directory of franchisors operating in that country.

From the 'International' menu you will also find a tab entitled 'Intl Franchisees Sought – British Franchise Association members seeking overseas investors', where you will find a directory of UK franchisors looking for franchisees overseas.

European Business Innovation Network (EBN) (www.ebn.be)

If you are looking for a forward-thinking country to which to relocate and perhaps set up in a business in which technology or the Internet will be well received, then that will be a factor in your research for an overseas property. Using technology as the criterion would bring countries such as Estonia to the forefront of your planning. The Global Growth Competitive Index (www.weforum.org/) ranks Estonia 20th out of 117 countries in the world, higher than any other Eastern European country and higher than even Hong Kong which ranks in the 28th position. Estonia plans to cover the entire country with wireless Internet broadband and so become the first country in the world to be totally wi-fi. No matter where you are in Estonia, you will soon be able to connect to the Internet through any network.

EBN is the leading network for Business and Innovation Centres (BICs) and similar organisations in Europe. There are now more than 150 European Commission-recognised BICs in regions throughout Europe, from the Algarve in Portugal to the east of Finland; and from the west coast of Ireland to Košice in the east of the Slovak

Republic. (You can find any of the 150 BICs' contact details via the website in the heading above.)

These BICs are a regional focal point for innovators and entrepreneurs, co-operating with other organisations to ensure an A–Z range of assistance to new and existing small businesses: from detection and assessment of innovative business ideas, through business planning guidance, launch advice and business accommodation to post-start-up support.

The European Employment Service (EURES)
(www.europa.eu.int/jobs/eures)

EURES operates a database of jobs available throughout Europe. Vacancies on the EURES system can be found by first selecting 'en' from the horizontal menu bar at the bottom of the screen to enter the English language section of the website. From the drop-down menu in the centre of this screen, entitled 'Living and working-moving to another country', select the country or countries you are interested in exploring. In the country pages you will find: labour market information (such as the unemployment rate); living and working conditions (including information on social security and wage rates); and facilities to search for a job (where you can state your qualifications, experience and whether you are looking for permanent or temporary work). At the date of writing, 2,424 jobs were on offer in Cyprus, 1,536 in Slovenia and 4,254 in Lithuania.

Global Watch Service (www.globalwatchservice.com)

If you want to assess a country's potential as a benign host for a technology-based business, you can do so by subscribing (free) to the Global Watch Service). To help UK firms become and remain competitive at home and overseas, the Global Watch Service is a government initiative run by the Department of Trade and Industry (Dti) that keeps them aware of new technological developments and management practices from across the world. The main elements are:

- Information: in particular 'Online Technology Information', bringing together technical developments and policy information from overseas.
- *Global Watch*: a monthly magazine of important technology developments from around the world. It leads readers to Global Watch Online.
- British Embassy Science and Technology websites: British Embassies in Bonn, Germany; Paris, France; Tokyo, Japan; Washington, USA; and Seoul, Korea provide information on current scientific and technological developments and policies within their specific countries.
- Missions: for first-hand experience of overseas management technologies and practices.
- International Technology Promoters: for help with accessing specific technologies or information from overseas.
- Secondments: for financial and practical help to second key UK managers or specialists to a world-class overseas company for between 3 months and a year.

Select 'Information' from the horizontal menu bar across the top of the home page, where you will be taken to a vertical menu with the same heading. Select 'Countries' where you will see a continent-by-continent list of countries. On each country page you will find the following information:

- Science & Technology Overview.
- Science & Technology Organisation.
- Science & Technology Statistics.
- Embassy Reports.
- Technology News.
- Events.
- Key Contacts.
- Related Links.

Job Centre Plus (www.jobcentreplus.gov.uk)

This is the UK Government website covering all employment-related subjects. From the home screen, select 'Looking for a job' from the top of the centre vertical menu bar. From there, select 'Search for a job' from the menu bar entitled 'Customers' in the top-left of the screen. There you will find a six-stage questionnaire, the first three of which are intended to define and refine the description of the job you are looking for. The fourth stage invites you to select a location and at the bottom is a pull-down menu bar next to the heading 'Choose from the EEA or other international countries'. Select the countries in which you are interested and from there you will be directed to a fifth stage inviting you to state how many hours a week you would like to work, whether you prefer evening or weekend work and whether you want temporary or permanent work. Then you will be shown brief job descriptions of any vacancies, salaries, location and a web link for more information on available jobs.

You can also find details of how to claim the Job Seeker's Allowance (JSA) while looking for a job anywhere in the EU and EAA. Select 'Want to make a claim' from the vertical menu bar on the home page screen. Then select 'Check what benefits you may be able to get. Are you: Able to work and looking for work?', where you will be directed to information on the JSA that can provide an income of between £34 and £68 per week for a period of up to 3 months while looking for a job abroad. Women must be under 60 and men under 65 to be entitled to JSA.

National Business Incubator Association (NBIA)
(www.nbia.org/resource_center/links_to_member_incubators/index.php)

The *Oxford Dictionary* lists 'incubator' as a noun used to describe the apparatus providing warmth for hatching eggs. A business incubator is the commercial equivalent. It is a place where small, technology-based businesses can locate to obtain help, advice, resources and perhaps even finance in their formative weeks and months. The more incubators a country has, the more attractive it will appear to anyone looking to set up in a technology- or innovation-based business.

The NBIA claims, with some justification, to be the world's leading organisation advancing business incubation and entrepreneurship. It has over 2,000 members and has the most comprehensive directory of business incubators around the globe.

From the link 'International Incubators Online', select the country you are interested in viewing from the pull-down menu, then click on the 'View' button.

For Singapore, you will find two incubators listed, including the iAxil Venture Accelerator Centre. Itsr aim captures the essence of this type of service and its value to aspiring entrepreneurs: 'iAxil is a venture accelerator centre that helps entrepreneurs to translate a good business idea into a commercially-viable venture. It provides incubation and venture acceleration programs to nurture and grow new businesses. iAxil also supports and connects its portfolio companies to its wide network of local and foreign strategic partners.' The National Information Technology Park (NITP), founded in 2002, is the spur to encourage a technology renaissance in Mongolia, so don't necessarily rule out far-flung and remote countries from your property research. The Internet means that many business ventures can flourish almost anywhere.

PatentCafe.com (`www.patentcafe.com`)

Although largely US-based, this site provides intellectual property-related news. Andy Gibbs, author of books on the invention business and owner of an inventor's services company, originally established the site and is still its CEO. It has lots to offer, including downloadable 'inventor assessment forms' for helping you gauge whether your invention can really sustain a business; a comprehensive web directory to patent forms and offices all over the world; business and legal forms; and much more.

Riley Guide (www.rileyguide.com/internat.html)

The fastest-growing route to find employment is (surprise, surprise) via the Internet. Despite a sceptical view taken by the professionals when Internet-classified advertisements for jobs were launched in the mid 1990s, the number of websites offering employment opportunities has exploded. The advantages of Internet recruitment to both candidates and clients are obvious. Internet recruitment offers fast, immediate and cheap service compared with more traditional methods of recruitment.

The Riley Guide is a directory of employment and career information sources and services on the Internet. It is intended primarily to provide instruction for job seekers on how to use the Internet to their best advantage, but recruiters and other career service industry professionals will find information here to help them too. From this link you will be taken directly to the International Job Seekers screen, where countries are listed by continent and country. Selecting Poland, for example, will direct you to the Jobs Poland website (www.Jobs.pl), which claims to have over 3,750 employers registered, including over 620 foreign firms making active use of its services.

Grant Thornton International (www.gti.org)

International business report, formerly known as International Business Owners Survey (IBOS), is produced by Grant Thornton, a firm of accountants operating in 112 countries worldwide, with offices in 519 locations focusing on owner-managed businesses. This report provides insight into the expectations and plans of over 7,000 business owners across 30 economies. It builds on data collected in Europe as part of the former European Business Survey (1993–2002) so, in one form or another, the basic data has been around for over a decade.

Select 'Publications' from the horizontal menu bar at the top of the screen, then 'International Business Owners Survey' from the drop-down menu. From here you can obtain a copy of the IBOS summaries; or benchmark your opinions on business topics against those of other businesses in your own country and industry sector, or in other countries' and industries' sectors.

World Wide Chamber of Commerce Guide (www.chamberfind.com)

A chamber of commerce can be the best and most reliable source for finding a local business in any country. While chamber members are not necessarily professionally validated, they have usually signed up to a rule book governing their business behaviour. Chambers are also the repository of all information concerning doing business in the area. From the home page, select 'World Chambers' from the left-hand vertical menu, followed by the world region in which the country you are looking for is located. From there you will find an A–Z country directory of web links. A chamber's member directory may be listed in one of several ways within the chamber website, such as: 'Membership directory', 'Business listings', 'Community guide' or 'Business resource guide'. The chamber's membership directory can usually be accessed by keyword, by company name or by category.

Fair Guide (www.fairguide.com)

The Fair Guide is a global business-to-business and trade fair directory. Attending such fairs is an ideal way to find out about business opportunities in a new country. You can find out where and when which fair is scheduled by using its online database.

This global directory also contains fair exhibitors and a list of the fairs in which they have participated. Everything you need is on the home page. To find a fair, an exhibitor or a fair organiser, simply enter the name or title, select the country and click 'SEARCH'.

The Federation of International Trade Associations (FITA) (www.fita.org)

FITA, founded in 1984, fosters international trade by strengthening the role of local, regional, and national associations. Its affiliates are 450 independent international associations which fall into six categories:

- **World Trade Clubs** (world trade clubs, centres, councils; international trade associations etc.) Examples: Washington International Trade Association; World Trade Center Miami; World Trade Club of St Louis; Women in International Trade Chapters.
- **Associations/Chambers of Commerce** with regional/bi-lateral interests Examples: the German American Business Association; the British-American Chamber of Commerce; the US–Russia Business Council.
- **Associations focused on international logistics.** Examples: National Customs Brokers & Freight Forwarders Association; Women in Transportation; Containerization & Intermodal Institute.
- **Associations supporting international trade**, such as small business development centres/organizations, etc. Examples: Coalition for Employment through Exports; Florida Trade Data Center.
- **Associations supporting exporters.** Examples: Small Business Exporters Association; National Association of Export Companies; Export Managers Association of California; National Association of Export Companies.
- **Professional associations.** Examples: British Academy of Film and Television Arts Los Angeles; Foundation for International Meetings; International Licensing Industry Merchandisers' Association; American Translators Association.

The 400,000 organisations linked to FITA through their membership in a FITA member association represent a broad cross-section of the international trade community: manufacturers, trading companies, contractors, freight forwarders, custom house brokers, airlines, shipping companies, port authorities, banks, insurance brokers and underwriters, associations and a wide range of service providers including telecommunications companies, law firms, and consultants.

FITA does not offer membership to companies or individuals, but rather provides a direct link to one of its member organisations.

Euro Info Centres (EICs) (www.euro-info.org.uk)

EICs provide local access to a range of specialist information and advisory services to help companies develop their business in Europe.

EICs are multilingual teams accustomed to the demands of a transnational environment, familiar with local, regional and European circumstances and practices, and trained to use advanced telecommunication and information tools. They have direct links to the European Commission in Brussels and can plug into a business support network consisting of more than 250 centres across Europe. EICs are therefore a powerful local resource.

EICs offer a range of services, which are of practical assistance to anyone moving overseas and seeking to develop new markets and products. These include:

- **Specialist business enquiry services** dealing with the spectrum of questions which different companies have on the European business environment, ranging from EU and national legislation to technical standards; and from research and development programmes to EU funding.
- **Help with market information** through their network contacts and specialist information services. They utilise the various business contact and business co-operation initiatives also provided by the European Commission, thereby opening up further business opportunities for local companies.
- **Alerting companies to invitations to tender** issued by public agencies in Europe and beyond. By tapping into an up-to-the-minute database, EICs can supply those setting up overseas with a daily, weekly or monthly selection of opportunities relevant to their business.

With the breadth and diversity of their services, and their local knowledge, EICs can help you develop your business in Europe.

Trade Partners UK (`www.tradepartners.gov.uk`)

Trade Partners UK is the Government's central site for all its services and schemes to help exporters and, to a lesser extent, importers. The services include:

- Running 'Information Centre', a free self-service reference library for exporters. Its goal is to help you identify, select and research the export markets offering the most potential for your products or services.
- Provides access to all the data you are likely to need in order to find an export market or export partner.
- Help with both finance and arrangements for visiting overseas markets.
- Support in exhibiting at international exhibitions.
- Help to join other British companies on trade missions to our major markets.
- English-speaking commercial experts in every major international market to help you make the most of your visit.
- Help for all businesses and organisations involved in exporting from the UK to promote goods and services abroad at overseas seminars.

Property title and foreign ownership rights

There are a number of restrictions as to where foreigners can buy property in Turkey, which at first sight may seem onerous, but in practice are not that much of a problem. For example, properties in what are known as the 'Military Forbidden Zones' and 'Safety Regions' can't be sold or rented to foreigners and, as a matter of course, the Land Registry contacts Army Headquarters for clearance. These restrictions apply to a fairly minute area, for the most part on Turkey's borders where disputes are likely to flare up.

Foreign nationals were limited to purchasing property within the boundaries of major municipalities prior to July 2003, when the law was amended to permit them to purchase property outside these areas. However, foreign nationals are not allowed to purchase property within village boundaries with more than 2,000 registered inhabitants or to buy land or farms larger than 74 acres without special permission from the Turkish Government. As of July 2005, the legislation, revised in July 2003, applicable to foreigners who wish to purchase land or property in Turkey has been ruled to be unconstitutional by the Turkish Constitutional Court. The amended law, which was presented before the court, has unfortunately been rejected. Therefore, until the law is ratified and approved by the Parliament, any applications made by the foreigners to the Land Registry office will not be processed.No timescale has been given for when the matter may be resolved!

Organisations and publications who provide information on foreign ownership rights

Foreign and Commonwealth Office (FCO) (www.fco.gov.uk)

The purpose of the FCO is to work for UK interests in 'a safe, just and prosperous world'. From the FCO home page, select 'UK Embassies Overseas' from the left-hand vertical pull-down menu. From there, click on the links below to view the contact details of the UK's embassies, high commissions and consulates in the overseas countries you are interested in. At the bottom of each country's home page you will find a web link to the embassy or high commission website. Once on the country website, look under 'Services' in the left-hand vertical menu bar, or select 'Site Map' and look for a term such as 'Settle, work or buying property in … .'. Here you will find guidance on current legislation concerning foreigners buying property.

US Department of State (www.state.gov/e/eb/ifd/2005/)

The Department of State has as part of its mission statement the aim to 'Create a more secure, democratic, and prosperous world for the benefit of the American people and the international community'. While the jury may be out on its achievements in this respect, the Department's website is a mine of valuable information for overseas property owners. In particular, the Investment Climate Statements found at this link provide a thorough description of the overseas environments in which international. investors must operate. The statements cover general characteristics, such as openness to foreign investment and treatment of foreign investors, as well as details about procedures for licensing and similar administrative matters. The statements are updated each year as Chapter 7 in the Country Commercial Guides, a series to be found by country at the US Department of Commerce's website (http://www.export.gov/).

From this site you are offered a menu of counties which you can select to examine in detail. For Brazil, for example, you can see that 'an overburdened court system is available for enforcing property rights but decisions can take years. Judicial reform measures enacted in December 2004 streamline administrative procedures, and, by introducing the concept of binding precedent, should, over time, make judicial decisions more predictable'. For China, you can see 'Land: Chinese law provides that all land is owned by "the public," and individuals cannot own land. However, consistent with the policies of reform and opening to the outside, legal and natural persons, including foreigners, can hold long-term leases for land use. They can also own buildings, apartments, and other structures on land, as well as own personal property'.

Channel 4
(www.channel4.com/4homes/buyingabroad/countryguides)

This is the TV programmes website. Select 'Homes' from the horizontal menu bar at the top of the page. Then select 'Buying abroad' from the vertical menu bar on the left of the screen, followed by clicking on the 'Country guides' icon in the centre. For Russia, you will find information confirming that all property ownership is registered in a very comprehensive property register, which keeps details of every single change in ownership right down to a copy of every single purchase contract. There is no stamp duty on purchasing, although there is a fee to register the contract (approximately £200). There are no restrictions on foreigners buying residential property in Moscow and land can also be purchased in most of Russia.

International Real Estate Handbook: Acquisition, Ownership and Sale of Real Estate Residence, Tax and Inheritance Law,
by Christan Kalin (an international real estate, tax and estate-planning specialist and a partner at Henley & Partners, Zurich)
(John Wiley & Sons, 2006), price around £80

This 704-page colossus contains both a general chapter on ownership and title issues, as well as a complete and extensively researched address section listing selected contacts (lawyers, tax advisers, real-estate brokers, banks etc.) for each country. There are also tables of international overviews and comparisons covering ownership title issues, purchase costs, tax rates and inheritance laws relating to real estate.

Grant Thornton (`www.grant-thornton.co.uk`)

This is the UK arm of Grant Thornton International, one of the world's leading international organisations of independently owned and managed accounting and consultancies with around 520 offices in over 110 countries worldwide. Follow this thread: Home>Publications and events>Publications >UK foreign property ownership report to download their 40-page free booklet containing an analysis of foreign property ownership by UK individuals, published in association with Lombard Street Research, covering title and ownership topics among others.

Amberlamb (www.amberlamb.com)

These are publishers who specialise in international property investment. Their objective is to provide property investors and overseas homebuyers with the critical information that they require before making any investment or property purchase decisions. Their worldwide database of property investment guides give property investors a better understanding of the variations in different property markets and the potential pitfalls or advantages of investing in any particular property market. Like any publisher, their revenue model includes selling advertising space and links to other services such as Amazon's book website. But the basic data on over 100 countries, including tips and strategies on ownership, is free to registered subscribers, who can sign up for free too.

Buying procedures, costs and restrictions

The legal process by which property changes hands can be a disincentive to potential buyers, as well as a brake on property prices. By its very nature, property is an illiquid asset, unlike, say, shares and bonds that can be readily bought and sold. The more complicated, time-consuming and costly the process of buying and selling property is, the less attractive it is to outside investors. For example, in Turkey, many property transactions have first to be referred to the Army to check whether the land has any strategic importance, as the country has hostile relationships with both neighbouring states and ethnic groups within itself. In Slovenia, foreign buyers need only to get an EMŠO (Identity) number and a Tax Number, as do Slovenians. These cost about €15 each and take no more than a couple of days to organise. However, Slovenia has has kept its options open in respect of fellow EU members, who are the most likely foreign property buyers to flood the market, and could, should it wish make use of a general safeguard clause provided for in Article 37 of the Accession Treaty allowing it to reapply restrictions on purchases by non-nationals until 2011.

There is an argument that claims that however difficult the process, the first into that market will accrue certain benefits – known in business circles as 'first mover advantage'. Beguiling though the theory of first mover advantage is, it is probably wrong. A thorough review of the research studies that supported this theory was published in the *Sloan Management Review*, and the findings were found to be flawed. (The authors of this paper also drew on many other studies, which lent support to their views.) Among the many errors in the earlier research, the authors of the Sloan paper revealed that the questions used to gather much of the data were at best ambiguous, and perhaps dangerously so. For example, the term 'one of the pioneers in first developing such products or services' was used as a proxy for 'first to market'. In fact, the only compelling evidence from all the research was that nearly half of all firms pursuing a 'first to market' strategy were fated to fail, while those following fairly close behind were three times as likely to succeed. The moral here is that just because it is hard to buy property in a particular market and you are first on the scene, there is no guarantee that there is a fortune to be made.

Organisations offering information and advice on buying procedures and costs

International Consortium of Real Estate Professionals (ICREA)
(www.icrea.org)

ICREA is a membership association for leading national and international real estate organisations It claims to represents 2 million brokers and agents worldwide, each of whom adheres to a code of conduct. From the home page, select 'Country Information' from the horizontal menu bar at the top of the screen. From there, you will find a list of ICREA member countries/associations, with links to the member association's 'ICREA home page'. There you can access information about each country's real estate business practices, country and market data and links to the association's website and other key organisation and industry links.

Research Worldwide (www.researchworldwide.com)

This is a colossal site, providing a consolidation of real estate information with knowledge and advice sourced from local experts covering 1,400 cities and towns in 240 countries worldwide. The site has links to 16,450 research reports, 783 property-related trade associations and 113 benchmark indices covering property prices and other related information. Research Worldwide (Pty) Ltd is an independent research company registered in the Republic of South Africa and claims not to be involved in any conflicting activity such as real estate consulting, investing, financing, developing, broking, real estate/property managing or any other activity which could impair its total independence. Neville Berkowitz, a pioneer of research and forecasting in the South African property industry, who launched *The Property Economist*, formed the organisation in 1994. It has an advisory organisation with leading real estate research companies as associates in 17 countries: Australia, Brazil, Canada, China, Denmark, Germany, Hong Kong, Italy, Korea, Mexico, the Netherlands, Russia, South Africa, Sweden, Taiwan, United Kingdom and the United States.

Select 'Associations' from the top-right horizontal menu bar and from there choose a country, then the link to the country's main property association's website. For example, selecting Canada in the country pages reveals 21 associations, with the Canadian Real Estate Association (CREA) representing 65,000 realtors across Canada as the main association. Following the link to CREA's website contains a near-universal help for buyers and selection. There you will find information on the complexity or otherwise of the buying procedure.

The Overseas Property Professional (OPP) (www.opp.org.uk)

The OPP was launched in 2004 as both a magazine and a website. Aimed primarily at companies and individuals working in, or with an interest in, the overseas property industry, it is also a useful source of information to professional property investors. Every month, the magazine includes: the latest industry news; industry trends; analysis of issues;

profiles and interviews; research and statistics; product reviews; and new real estates development reviews. OPP magazine is only available by subscription, at a cost of £55 a year. While some information is available on the free subscription membership, you will require a paid-up subscription to access all the information. This service will keep you up to date with changes in the buying procedures around the world.

CHAPTER 11

Tourism Potential

In this chapter:

- Seeing why tourism matters.
- Understanding why not all tourists are equal.
- Tracking future trends.
- Spotting the factors that make for appeal.
- Contrasting between what attracts you and what will appeal to others.
- Appreciating the potential for health tourism.

Nine out of ten buyers of overseas property intend to generate at least some income from their investment; many of those expect the property to begin to pay its way right form the outset. One of the key factors that will determine both the prospects of renting out the property, of it being a pleasure to live in or visit; and ultimately of it being worth substantially more when you sell it than it was when you bought it, is the volume and nature of the country's tourist appeal. You will have to buy in a country (and, of course, a location within that country) which tourists as well as prospective residents, perhaps including yourself, want to visit. It follows that the more esoteric your own needs for a country are, the more restricted your holiday market potential is likely to be. To take an extreme example: if your ideal is to find a secluded old house, miles from anywhere, high in the mountains, where you have to hew your own wood for heating and cooking, draw water from a well and motor up and down a torturous mountain road for 2 hours in order to find the nearest shop (a description that fits much of Romania and Ukraine, for example), don't be surprised if few people coming for a week's relaxing holiday share your dream.

Old tourism versus affluent tourism

Dreary beeches and inaccessible mountains appealed to the mass tourist market of the former Soviet bloc countries, who were just delighted not to be in their own country for a while. It was a relief to know that the pain was being spread more or less evenly around the 'dark empire'. A country meeting this specification may have ridiculously cheap property but that property will be hard, if not impossible, to use as a holiday let. A busy, prosperous (and so expensive) part of the Croatian coastline may be a much better bet, from a holiday rental point of view. Despite being expensive, a property in a highly desirable location may make a better return on the money invested than a more remote, cheaper property that is harder to let and harder eventually to sell.

So you need to check out just how attractive to others a holiday destination in the countries appealing to you might be to others: not just the numbers of tourists going, but where they come from. The average British or American tourist spends between 5 and 10 times as much in the former Soviet countries as do fellow East Europeans.

Simply finding out, for example, that Romania was the world's fourth-fastest developing tourist market in 2006 is interesting but not sufficient on which to base an informed decision as to tourist prospects. Despite that country's fast growth, before you get carried away and put down a deposit on a new property there, it is salutary to note that barely 6 million people arrive in Romania each year. That is half the number going to Hungary, for example, and Romania ranks 65th most popular destination in the world. A quarter of those tourists come from Moldova and Bulgaria and other local countries whose populations couldn't afford to go on holiday anywhere else and who consequently spend very little money in the country. But, more encouragingly, your research could establish that in the last 3 or 4 years there has been a sea change in the country's fortunes and around half a million tourists a year come in from Germany, France, Austria and the UK.

Planning future tourist appeal

You can see what future plans a country has for its tourist industry by researching in the sources listed. Cyprus, after a few years of declining numbers plans, to hit back by opening 18 new golf courses, giving it a higher density of course to tourists than almost anywhere else, including Spain and the US. New Zealand, after promoting its dramatic landscape brought to prominence in the *Lord of the Rings* films, is re-branding itself as a 'foodies' destination. For decades, New Zealand's food relied on a dismal combination of boiled vegetables and under-seasoned meat. Now, cooking classes are all the rage, wines win international competitions and, according to George Hickton, Professor of Tourism at New Zealand's University of Canterbury, saffron, walnuts, truffles and olive oils will be marketed abroad in an effort to develop food tourism.

Sources of information on tourism potential

Tourism Offices Worldwide Directory (www.towd.com)

The *Tourism Offices Worldwide Directory* is a guide to official tourist information sources: government tourism offices; convention and visitors' bureaus; chambers of commerce; and similar organisations providing free, accurate and unbiased travel information to the public. Businesses such as travel agents, tour operators and hotels are not included. The *Directory* has been operating since 1994 and, as of 2008, contains 1,437 entries.

From the A–Z pull-down menu bar 'Tourism offices for countries other than the USA', select the countries in which you are interested. The USA, which has no centralised tourist information source, has a separate menu listing the various states. Selecting 'Moldova', for example, brings up the web address for the Departamentul Dezvoltarea Turismului (Department of Tourism Development) which, as with most entries in the guide, mercifully has an English site just one mouse click away from its home screen. Selecting 'Mexico', however, brings up a positive rash of agencies, as does New Zealand and other more developed tourist markets.

A useful feature is the 'Most frequently requested destinations this week' feature which lists the top 10 destinations people are researching that week, though, of course, that doesn't mean that they will necessarily go there.

SPRIG (www.sprig.org.uk)

SPRIG is an organisation which promotes information sources in leisure, tourism and sport. It claims to be 'The guide to Internet resources in hospitality, leisure, sport and tourism' and by taking a librarian's approach to information management it has produced a creditable volume of data sources. Financed by an annual membership fee, it represents all those who have an interest in information relating to leisure, tourism, sport, recreation and hospitality management. While it aims to be relevant not only to those who work in libraries and information services but also to publishers, academics and students, it is also, by default, an invaluable reference source for property buyers, who use information sources and materials.

Much of the information on the site is free. Start by selecting 'Guides' from the left-hand vertical menu bar. From there you will be offered 10 areas to explore, perhaps the most useful of which from an overseas property buyer's perspective are: 'Statistics' and 'Tourism'. In 'Statistics' you will find a selection of key sources for statistics and market research in hospitality, leisure, sport and tourism. The 'Tourism' section contains a very general introduction to the literature of tourism, highlighting some of the principal texts and resources.

Tourism Research Links by René Waksberg (www.waksberg.com)

This is a private initiative, established in 1996, intended to foster collaboration between those in tourism research. It contains links to around 200 organisations which manage, consult or research the tourism markets. There is also a small directory of universities and colleges which specialise in tourism studies worldwide. Going on to those university websites reveals a rich seam of valuable data. For example, following the thread through to the UK's Bournemouth University's Hospitality and Tourism Department's research programme (http://icthr.bournemouth.ac.uk/ICTHRhtml/research.htm) yields the following studies.

- *A Five-year Programme into Tourism in the peripheral areas of Europe*
- *Regional airport development for the Croatian Adriatic Islands*
- *Three Tourism Strategy Plans for the Hungarian Counties of Szolnok*
- *Romanian Tourism Master Plan, Spa Development Strategy*
- *The Economic Impact of Tourism on the Economy of Gibraltar*
- *Airport Development Strategy for Cyprus*
- *An analysis of the fiscal regimes of the East Caribbean States with special reference to tourism development*
- *An exploration of a tourism development strategy for north-east Brazil*
- *Survey, evaluation of resources and preparation of Master Plans for Tourism Development in Vanuatu*
- *Survey, evaluation of resources and preparation of Master Plans for Tourism Development for Egypt.*

World Tourism Organisation (www.world-tourism.org)

The United Nations WTO's membership comprises 150 countries with more than 300 Affiliate Members representing the private sector, educational institutions, tourism associations and local tourism authorities. Select the 'Facts and Figures' icon from the right-hand vertical menu bar. There you will find information on such gems as: 'Tourism Highlights', a concise overview of international tourism in the world, based on the results for the previous year. This report includes statistics and analysis on international tourist arrivals; international tourism receipts; a summary of tourism results by region; top tourism destinations by arrivals and receipts; outbound tourism by generating region; and the ranking of the top tourism spenders. The full document costs €75, however a press release with key data is available free and, once you know what to look for, tracking down this report in your nearest business reference library shouldn't be too difficult. You will also find the 'Tourism Barometer' in this section, which provides an overview of short-term tourism data from destination countries and air transport, a retrospective and prospective evaluation of tourism performance by the UNWTO Panel of Tourism Experts and selected economic data relevant for tourism. A 10-page summary of the 30-page report is available for free download.

Info Please (`www.infoplease.com/ipa/A0855290.html`)

Information Please has been providing authoritative answers to all kinds of factual questions since 1938 – first as a popular radio quiz show, then, starting in 1947, as an annual almanac and, since 1998, on the Internet, providing reliable information in a way which 'engages and entertains'. At this web page you will find links to a score of sites with statistics on travel, ranging from the mundane 'World's Top Ten Tourism Earners' to the more exotic 'Top Ten Best Honeymoon Destinations'.

Holiday Truths (`www.holiday-truth.com/resort _ report.php`)

This is a moderated blog, which is cleaned up to keep it respectable, but no effort is made to check the veracity of the information. It shows 'reports' on what tourists really think about resorts around the world, by listing the comments by country and by key destination within that country. You can certainly get a feel for how good or bad an area is from reading the comments, and hence the real income potential. But comments, for example, dated a couple of days previously, stating 'The place is like a building site' or 'The beach was dirty and the umbrellas were broken' might cause an anxious moment if you were planning to buy a property in Bulgaria's towns of Bansko or Nessebur. Each commenter scores using three ratings: cleanliness, resort entertainment and beach (slightly bizarre for the ski resorts listed, but people seem to understand and adapt their rating to meet the resort features). Unfortunately, there is no overall rating for a country or resort, so you will have to make a judgement based on the volume of comments and what each of them says.

Mintel (`www.reports.mintel.com`)

Mintel has been publishing market studies for over 30 years and produces some 600 reports into European, UK-specific and US consumer markets every year. Each report provides a unique overview of a market's dynamics and prospects, aiming to give the reader the knowledge to devise an informed and profitable strategy. From the top horizontal menu bar, select 'Reports' and from there 'Travel and Tourism International'. From the middle of this screen, select ' International Travel Series' where you will see a list of 40 reports including 'Home Ownership Abroad and Timeshare' and 'The World's Leading Outbound Markets'. This report provides an analysis of the 15 most important tourism-generating countries in the world, and examines a number of contributory factors in each of those countries, including population, the economy and exchange rates. It also takes an in-depth look at each outbound market; focusing on leading destinations, average length of stay, seasonality, purpose of visit, mode of transport and traveller demographics. The structure of the travel industry is also considered, as are booking practices and the role of the Internet. Throughout the analysis, the impact of the world events outlined in the opening paragraphs is considered, and a forecast for the future development of each market is also given. The outbound markets analysed in this report are: Germany; the US; the UK; Japan; France;

Italy; China; the Netherlands; Canada; Russia; Belgium; Austria; Hong Kong; the Republic of Korea; and Sweden. Mintel reports are fairly expensive, ranging from £500 to £1,500 each. But summaries are available free, as an appetite whetter, and business libraries usually carry a selection of its reports.

Medical tourism

Medical tourism, described as the act of travelling abroad to obtain healthcare, has emerged in recent years as a major new trend in the global healthcare and tourism industries. Residents of the United Kingdom, America, Canada and other countries where either medical treatment is either prohibitively expensive or waiting lists are excessive are seeking out affordable and high-quality medical care in India, Costa Rica, Thailand and 30 or so other countries where there are pockets of medical excellence, even if the general standard of healthcare in such countries is poor. New Delhi's Apollo Hospital, for example, treated 12,000 patients from across the world, including developed countries such as the United States, Canada and Britain.

There are signs that medical tourism is becoming accepted at the institutional level in some important markets. For example, Blue Cross Blue Shield Association has included Wockhardt Hospital in India among its worldwide network of participating hospitals; Insurer Health Net of California contracts with Mexican clinics near the US border; and United Group Programs in Florida, which caters to self-insured companies, offers options for obtaining medical care at Bumrungrad Hospital in Bangkok, Thailand.

A recent study of the sector by TRAM (Tourism Research and Marketing) indicates that the global medical tourism market comprised over 20 million trips in 2005, with a total value of €20 billion. The market is forecast to grow to 40 million trips (or 4% of global tourism volume) by 2010.

There is strong evidence that medical tourists arrive well before the operation or procedure they are undertaking and will then stay on afterwards. They also bring family members with them. While some undoubtedly stay either in hotels or in private hospitals, most are likely to rent comfortable apartments. As such a commodity is often in short supply in developing countries, where many of these emerging medical facilities are, there is likely to be higher demand and an upward pressure on rental prices.

The case for medical tourism

Europe has a long tradition of medical tourism, going back to the water cures of the spas in Georgian times, where the healing mineral waters offered miracle cures for all known diseases. Germany, Italy and Austria were popular destinations then. Today, private Swiss clinics, looking to lure the new capitalists of Eastern Europe, have placed ads in Swissair's in-flight magazine with the slogan 'Get well in Switzerland', reputedly netting some €340 million in additional revenue.

But miracle cures are not the primary drivers of this market today, where more prosaic needs dominate.

- This year alone, upwards of 500,000 Americans are expected to travel overseas to have their bodies fixed, at prices 30–80% less than at home. For Americans (and, indeed, the citizens of many other countries), medical tourism is usually prompted by the desire – or need – to cut costs. Around 43.3 million Americans lack health insurance, so having a hip replaced in India for $3,000 is much more affordable than having one replaced in the US for $39,000. And having a heart valve replaced in India for $10,000 (including air fare) is a bargain compared with the $200,000 it could amount to back home. And it is not just expensive treatments where costs diverge. An MRI scan, which costs about £1,000 privately in Britain, without a consultation, appointment or diagnosis, costs only £100 in India with consultation and diagnosis included.

- For Canadian and British citizens, the imperative is to cut waiting times. In Canada, the conservative think-tank The Fraser Institute claims that the total waiting time between referral from a general practitioner and treatment, averaged across all 12 specialties, averages 18 weeks. In the UK, waiting times range from 6-months to 2 years or more for non-emergency operations in NHS hospitals. Norwich Union Healthcare's 'Health of the Nation' index reported in December 2006 that 74% of GPs said they were seeing more of their patients travelling abroad for operations because of dissatisfaction with British waiting lists.
- Across the world, people are living longer. Life expectancy at birth in the United States in 1901 was 49 years and by the end of the century it was 77 years – an increase of 57%. Similar gains have occurred throughout the world. Life expectancy in China was around 35 years in the 1950s. Today, it has risen to around 71 years. Over the same period, life expectancy in India has doubled from 32 to 64 years. These gains were due largely to improved hygiene and water supply and the eradication and control of infectious diseases. The net effect is that billions of people are now living long enough to need surgery to replace hips or insert heart bypass valves, when previously they would have died prior to such problems becoming evident. Many older people also require cosmetic surgery to make longevity more acceptable.
- More people can now afford either to resort to medical tourism to cut hospital waiting time or to to indulge in medical treatments of choice such as cosmetic surgery or fertility treatment, as long as the price is competetive. According to the World Wealth Report compiled annually by Merrill Lynch and Capgemini, the number of millionaires is growing faster than the number of people in the world in 2005 (6.4 %). They estimate that there are 8.7 million high net-worth individuals (HNWI), defined as people with net financial assets of at least US $1 million, excluding their primary residence.

- Governments are being forced to accept the concept of a global health market in which they must play a willing (see below) or unwilling part. In May 2006, a court backed a British woman, Yvonne Watts, who went to France for a hip operation because she faced a year-long wait for an NHS procedure. Judges ruled that patients facing 'undue delays' in waits for operations should be entitled to treatment in other EU countries. Under 'health tourism' plans unveiled by the European Commissioner for health, Markos Kyprianou, there will be a big expansion of cross-border choice for patients allowing them to go anywhere in the EU for treatment if their home country doesn't meet their needs. The bill in such cases will be passed back to the patient's own country. A pilot project managed by Guy's and St. Thomas' Hospital has already explored this approach. The project offered (mostly elderly) patients who had been on the waiting list for more than 6 months the option of orthopaedic surgery in Belgium. In total, nearly 500 UK patients travelled to the five selected Belgian hospitals for orthopaedic surgery between June 2003 and April 2005.
- Governments are increasingly seeing health tourism as a serious market opportunity. A report by McKinsey & Co, consultants, commissioned in 2005 for the Indian Government, claimed that medical tourism in India would be a £2 billion business by 2012. In the Philippines the Government launched the Philippine Medical Tourism Programme in June 2006, with the goal of attracting 700,000 medical tourists annually, netting $300 million annually from 2007. In Singapore the Government is targeting to attract 1 million foreign patients annually and push the GDP contribution from this sector above US $1.6 billion, while Malaysia expects medical tourism receipts to be in the region of US $590 million by 2010.
- There is no longer the certainty that your home country provides the best medical care, whatever the cost. There is no doubt that the actual or perceived risks of MRSA and hospital-acquired infection in the UK have convinced some patients that they will

be 'safer' in a hospital overseas. Data published by the European Antimicrobial Resistance Surveillance System shows that the proportion of Staphylococcus aureus bacteria which is methicillin resistant is certainly higher in the UK (44.5%) than in countries such as Belgium (19.2%), Czech Republic (6.2%) and the Netherlands (1.0%).

The risks

Medical tourism is not without risks. While many overseas hospitals indicate that their doctors were trained in Western nations, there's less assurance that the nursing and other staff are equally qualified. In some other countries, standards are well below those in more developed nations. For example, an Associated Press article from 6 February 2005, reported that some Mexican plastic surgeons (who draw on trade from Texas) operate in an unregulated manner, with neither licensing standards nor adequate facilities. The results in some cases include disfigurement and even fatal infections, often linked to unaccredited hospitals and unlicensed surgeons.

In summary, the main risks are:

- Follow-up is difficult when the patient returns home, and expensive care may be required if complications occur.
- Medical qualifications vary greatly around the world and as a consequence quality assessment is problematic. The language barrier can complicate matters further still.
- Malpractice laws around the world vary greatly and are often problematic to enforce.

Medical market segments

Cosmetic surgery still comprises 80% of medical travel, according to providers. It's also teeming with suspect discount deals. It is also the sector that receives the most complaints. Australia's Government recently issued a special travel advisory warning against medical tourism in Thailand, as an increasing number of Australian women experienced complications after having cosmetic surgery in uncertified clinics. But with savings of close on 70% for such routine operations as a hip replacement, the market looks set for expansion.

The main market segments are:

- **Elective surgery** covers almost every non-emergency branch of medicine. Hospitals in countries as diverse as Estonia, France, Hungary, Malta, India, Switzerland, Latvia, Thailand, Bulgaria, the Philippines, Norway and Belgium have excellent medical and surgical facilities and offer cost saving private treatment covering such diverse fields as:
  - Heart surgery; hernia operations; and advanced prosthesis surgery involving total prosthetics for hips and knees as well as uni knee prosthetics.
  - Spinal surgery; brain tumours; and cervical or lumbar disc problems are dealt with in neurosurgical centres.
  - Weight and dietary conditions are treated in hospitals with world-class teams of specialist obesity surgeons, personal dieticians, psychologist and personal trainers working together to deliver proven and effective weight-loss treatments and obesity surgery.
  - Eye surgery such as cataract, glaucoma, squint, myopia, hyperopia, astigmatism or presbyopia.
- **Cosmetic surgery** is fast becoming acceptable, perhaps even essential, in the developed world. The plethora of personal makeover and cosmetic surgery programmes on television has helped to fuel a boom in cosmetic surgery. Whereas, 5 years ago, major healthcare providers including the UK's BUPA and BMI Healthcare only dabbled in the cosmetic surgery market, they are now taking the business very seriously and have seen year-on-year growth of around 25% to 30%. Sainsbury's Bank, in a recent estimate, concluded that, every day, around £1.8 million is spent on cosmetic surgery in the UK alone. It estimates that this year, in the UK, over £5 million

will have been taken out in personal loans for cosmetic surgery, and around a fifth of this will be in loans for men. The average size of loan for cosmetic surgery is around £6,500. Mintel estimates a 240% growth during the period 2001–2006, and predicts that by 2009 British adults will be making a trip to the cosmetic surgeon at least a million times a year.

- **Wellness and spa treatments** is a fast-growing market offering health, relaxation and rehabilitation in centres which can help conditions from allergies rheumatism, disc prolapse, to circulatory and nervous system problems. Spa physicians are on hand to recommend a regimen of tailor-made treatments. At the World Travel Market 2006 exhibition at ExCel, London, in November 2006, health and wellness was the major new tourism sector that travel agents were encouraged to see as a major opportunity. There was also a launch of a new generation of international spa accreditation by the British International Spa Association (BISA). International statistics indicate that the wellness market is growing by at least 17% a year. In Dubai alone there are at least 120 spas, health clubs and clinics offering wellness services and Estonia's Tourist Board announced last year that wellness and spa tourism was up by 34%, its fastest-growing market segment that now accounts for around one in nine of all foreign visitors.
- **Dental treatment** – considered increasingly costly in the UK and the USA – is increasingly being served by other countries such as Latvia, Hungary, Poland and Croatia. Package savings of up to 61% can be made on dental implants, 52% for wisdom tooth extraction and 44% for full acrylic dentures. High-end elective treatments such as titanium dental implants – prohibitively expensive in developed countries – are now an affordable proposition in many overseas centres.
- **Fertility tourism** – for many people experiencing fertility problems, the costs of investigation and infertility treatment in the USA or UK may be beyond their budget. Indeed, the treatment itself may be banned in the home country in question. In Italy, for example, people are voting with their feet after new laws were passed meaning no

screening or freezing of pre-implanted embryos; no sperm or egg donation; and no surrogacy or embryo research. Also, the availability of assisted reproduction techniques such as IVF varies from country to country. In 2005, for example, Denmark carried out 1,923 cycles per million of its population. In contrast, the UK carried out only 593 cycles per million. Costs for treatment also vary widely – treatment in countries such as Hungary and Slovenia cost around £1,608 compared with up to £4,000 in the UK. Specialist fertility facilities such as the Centre for Reproductive Medicine at Villa Del Sole offer standard and advanced fertility treatments from insemination to ICSI, PGD and AH with excellent clinical pregnancy rates. The Centre boasts over 3,000 babies born to date. Egg donor and surrogacy programmes are on offer for both married couples and single parents in IVF centres located in Moscow and Ekaterinburg, Russia, as well as the Jinamed Hospital in Istanbul, Turkey. But while IVF success rates are as good in Eastern Europe, as elsewhere, clinics are often unregulated.

- **Long-term care**: In many developed countries the proportion of elderly people is 20% and rising and the affordable services available for the elderly and those needing long-term care are stretched or non-existent. Some developing countries are starting to market what are, in effect, nursing homes for elderly foreigners, offering high standards of comfort and medical care at a fraction of the cost prevailing in their home countries. Organisations such as the International Association for Hospice and Palliative Care aim to increase the availability and access to high-quality hospice and palliative care for patients and families throughout the world. They do this by being an information resource for patients, professionals, healthcare providers and policy-makers around the world.

The Medical Tourist (`http://themedicaltouristcompany.com`)

This is a UK-based operation sending customers requiring medical treatment abroad. Founded by Dr Premhar Shah, who has been practising medicine for the last 30 years, the company has been sending patients abroad for treatment since 1998. It offers a complete service package, from arranging treatment, travel, concierge services, accommodation and visas to directly contacting the hospitals and doctors who will treat you in a hospital selected for the expertise of the medical team. The countries most used for common operations such as hip replacement, heart care, dental treatment and cosmetic surgery are in India, Cyprus, France, Poland and Malaysia. At the bottom of the left-hand vertical menu bar you can select 'Get a Quote', where you will be required to complete a short questionnaire covering subjects such as your current state of health, any medication taken and the treatment for which you would like a quote.

Medical Nomad (www.medicalnomad.com)

This site was founded in 2004 by a team of medical professionals, academic scholars and technology professionals who established it as a resource for people who want real choice when considering their healthcare options.

Growing medical costs, expensive insurance systems and delays in health provisioning (to name a few) have caused many of them to look for alternative healthcare solutions. At Medical Nomad, the aim is to provide comprehensive information as well as the resources needed to make informed choices about acquiring high-quality and affordable healthcare in the international medical market.

From the left-hand menu bar there are listed several ways to access the databases. By clicking on 'by country' in the 'Providers' section of this menu you are presented with an A–Z country list of medical facilities, starting with Plenitas in Buenos Aires, Argentina and finishing with the Florence Nightingale Hospital in Istanbul, Turkey. Alternatively, you can search by procedure, or browse an extensive library of articles and news cuttings on related topics.

Treatment Abroad (www.treatmentabroad.net)

This site is owned and managed by Intuition Communication, based in Berkhamsted, Hertfordshire. It also manages the Private Healthcare UK site, providing easy access for the public to information about private healthcare services and facilities across the UK, and the Harley Street Guide, for patients from the UK and abroad who are seeking information about doctors, dentists, hospitals and medical and clinical services available in London.

It also produces an annual report, Treatment Abroad PriceWatch (www.treatmentabroad.net/aboutus/pricewatch-survey-2006), an independent survey of medical tourism prices, carried out by European Research Specialists Ltd and compiled data from 108 clinics, hospitals and healthcare providers in 30 countries, roughly a third of the estimated number of overseas hospitals and clinics promoting their services to the UK market. The latest survey shows that savings of over 80% can be made by going abroad for some surgery and treatment. The report (64 pages)on medical tourism prices embraces elective surgery (e.g. hip replacement or knee surgery abroad), cosmetic surgery and dental treatment abroad. The pricing tables within the report provide direct comparisons of procedure costs (including doctor and hospital charges) and also package price comparisons taking into account likely costs of flights and accommodation for the expected length of stay.

A brief summary is free but a full copy of the report costs £100.

There are two ways to search the site. From the vertical menu bar on the left you can select a country (from 'Argentina' to 'Venezuela') and see what it has on offer. Alternatively, from the same menu you can slect from a list of surgeries various treatements and see which countries offer services in those areas.

CHAPTER 12

Property Performance and Appraisal: Narrowing Down your Choice of Country

In this chapter:

- Finding out about global property price trends.
- Getting a feel for properties and countries.
- Organising your data on different options.
- Preparing your shortlist of countries to examine.

All the factors identified so far in these chapters of Part 2 are intended to help you get a handle on what makes a particular country an attractive proposition in which to buy property and what does not. This chapter is by way of a bridge between carrying out a general overview of property prospects around the world and picking one country, or at most a handful of countries, to research thoroughly. The first part of the chapter examines ways to grasp how property prices have changed over time in various countries. Now, while, as they say on all investment advertising, 'the past is not a good guide to the future', the professionals know that it is usually the most reliable indicator there is. That can be considered as the hard-headed business side of the investment decision.

The second part of the chapter is intended to help you get a feel for the types of property on offer in different countries. The emphasis here is on the main property exhibitions that have as their goal to bring together a comprehensive range of countries into one arena, so that those attending can get a reasonable flavour of each country and so narrow down their choice further.

The final part of the chapter is tried and tested method, enabling you to bring all the factors that impinge on your choice into a weighting system so that you can rank the options. This method helps turn more nebulous factors (such as political stability or accessibility) into quantifiable outcomes.

Price appraisers

These are organisations which provide pointers on property price trends across different markets: They are not always scientific studies, nor are they all unbiased. To date, governments have been shy of getting too close to producing statistics on their housing markets, as properties have become an important and integral part of a country's economic life. That means that rises and falls in house prices directly impact on people's feeling of financial well-being, and governments don't want to be too closely involved in bringing bad news. It is also unlikely that taxpayers who are not themselves property owners (around 40% of householders across the developed economies) would welcome having their tax money spent in this way.

So read carefully the statistics and data provided by these organisations, using your judgement as to how much reliance to place on them.

Sources of data on global property prices and yields

The Move Channel (`www.themovechannel.com`)

Founded in November 1999 by Dan Johnson, The Move Channel started life as a simple guide to the buying procedures for residential property purchase in the UK, coupled with a small directory of website reviews covering property sales and rentals, again primarily in the UK.

Select 'Investment' from the right-hand side of the horizontal menu bar at the top of the home page.

On the left-hand side of this screen you will find a colossal ranking of different countries by almost every criteria that matter to a property buyer. So, for example, if you want to know in which countries property has appreciated the most in recent years, where the lowest-cost properties are, or where you can get the highest rental yield, just select the relevant link (See Table 12.1.)

Table 12.1 Ranking countries by property performance

Growth investments:
High capital appreciation
Low deposit required
Cheapest property on the market
100% finance available in the market
Proportion of off-plan available
Land investment proportion
Rental investments:
High rental yield
Guaranteed rental income on offer
Buy to let – Residential
Buy to let – Corporate
Buy to let – Student
Buy to let – Tourism
Serviced apartments
Fully managed rental services on offer
Self-managed
Specialist investments:
Land for development
Buy-to-renovate
Portfolios for sale
Project finance for own developments
Property funds wanting to invest in country
Syndicated deals
Whole developments for sale

The Economist (www.economist.com) (fee payable)

A 3-year subscription to *The Economist*, with the hard copy mailed to your address and access to the Internet database, will cost £50 a year. Some information on this site requires an additional payment, but the vast majority is covered in the annual subscription cost. You can access 10 years'worth of data on *The Economist*'s website, using the 'Research Tools' pull-down menu at the top left of the screen. Select 'Articles', where you can find coverage of 'property' from the topics menu. Here you will find *The Economist*'s Global House Indicator as well as individual studies on the Japanese and Indian property markets, for example.

Assetz Overseas (www.investors.assetz.co.uk)

Founded by Stuart Law, an active property investor himself, this organisation is active in selling overseas property through specialist divisions in France, Spain, Cyprus and Bulgaria. Assetz Finance Ltd, another company in this stable, has an overseas mortgage business of around £1.6 billion. From the home page, select 'Overseas Property' from the horizontal menu bar at the top of the screen. From there, select 'Which are the best countries to invest in'. There you will find Assetz Property Investment Tracker,™ a tool designed to provide investors with information to help show the return-on-investment for property in overseas markets, allowing for the size of deposit required, the house price growth for the last year and also factoring in buying costs in each country, which allows for the complexities in buying procedures. Assetz claims that this data is not available anywhere else in the world and is the result of very detailed research by the Assetz investment team. The data is updated monthly and can be accessed free.

Research Worldwide (www.researchworldwide.com)

See above for more information on this organisation. To find house price indices worldwide, select 'Benchmarks' from the top-right of the horizontal menu bar. That will take you to a page showing links to both commercial and residential property price indices. Select 'Worldwide House Price Indices' and you are taken to the latest quarter's house price movement, country by country. The data is consolidated from various sources including *The Economist*'s Global House Price Index.

European Council of Real Estate Professionals (`www.cepi.be`)

This is a trade association for property brokers whose aims, aside from improving professional standards across the sector, include collecting information among the European authorities on matters regarding real estate professionals' and consumers' interests and to inform the professionals, public and private organisations and the public on real estate legislation, regulations, local customs and practices in force in the various member states by publishing the results of questionnaires and surveys sent to the national member associations. It produces an annual report which can be downloaded by selecting 'Annual Reports' from the left-hand vertical menu bar. There you will find, for all European countries, the average property prices for apartments and houses; the increase (or decrease) in property prices over the past year; the cost of heat, light, power and water; the change in the number of properties bought and sold (giving a measure of the interest in a particular country); and the average rent for property in the capital and the second city. There is also information on commercial property. Though only 1 year's data is available in the report, the past 5 years' reports can be downloaded free from the website, so it is possible to use the particular data in which you are most interested in order to calculate your own trends.

Knight Frank (`www.knightfrank.com`)

Knight Frank has over 140 offices in over 30 countries across 5 continents. With over 4,500 brokers, it handles some $41 billion worth of commercial, agricultural and residential real estate annually, advising clients ranging from individual owners and buyers to major developers, investors and corporate tenants. Its strong local presence in established and emerging markets around the world, combined with powerful central research and intelligence-sharing, enables it to identify opportunities for clients to capture value in every aspect of their property dealings. Its research is freely available and downloadable from this website.

From this page, select 'Worldwide Research Reports' from the bottom horizontal menu bar. From there, you will see, across the top horizontal menu bar, a continent-by-continent option to narrow down the choice of reports to view. From the hundred or so reports on offer, the latest addition to the research portfolio can be found by selecting 'global/worldwide' from the horizontal menu bar. There are two strands here: one is 'International Residential', which is a bi-annual report giving a review of prime residential markets around the globe. Key areas of focus include recent supply and demand trends together with an outlook for short -term prospects. The market comments are supported by detailed statistics including price trends. A special topic is featured in each issue, focusing on an area of particular relevance to international homebuyers. Also within this strand is the Knight Frank Global House Price Index, claimed to be the first serious attempt to analyse pricing trends in residential property across the world on a standardised basis every quarter. Operating since 2005, the index show property prices in 34 countries, with more planned to be added. Prices are based on an assessment of price changes in the mainstream housing markets of the countries covered. Where possible, the Knight Frank index relies on an official national statistical source or a well-respected national financial institution, usually a large mortgage provider (as in the case of the UK where it adopts figures provided by the Nationwide Building Society). In some cases these sources of data are not available and Knight Frank has had to rely on valuation assessments of market movements – effectively assessing the value of a basket of properties from quarter to quarter. In certain cases the findings are related to capital cities (as in Lithuania, Latvia and Estonia) as a proxy for the wider national market.

The second strand of research is forward-looking, where the 'Global Real Estate Forecast' attempts to access the prospects for office, retail and industrial property worldwide.

Property exhibitions

Unless you have a clear idea of what type of house you want and where you want it, start with wide search criteria. You can now attend hundreds of exhibitions, all over the world, focusing on various aspects of overseas house and property buying. Some exhibitions focus on a particular country, such as Bulgaria, while others group together a clutch of neighbouring or similar (at least in the eye of the organiser) countries. So, Hungary, the Czech Republic, Slovenia and Croatia are often bundled together; as are Malta, Cyprus and Turkey. Though this might be administratively convenient, from a property buyer's perspective these countries have as much in common as chalk and cheese.

Other exhibitions, such as EMIGRATE, the emigration show run by Outbound Publishing, start from the supposition that attendees are planning a new life in a new country. These exhibitions typically have on hand immigration officials from a number of countries to explain the relocation procedures or actually to process applications. At many exhibitions, you see firms specialising in building and renovation, removals, insurance, overseas mortgages, medical and health services, pet passports and transportation. You may even be able to enjoy food and wine from the region, which adds to the overall experience of the event.

Exhibitions run by a single selling agent or by a particular developer showing its portfolio of properties, while a useful starting point for research, should never be seen as the conclusion.

Property exhibitions in the United Kingdom

There are dozens of major overseas property exhibitions throughout the United Kingdom, running throughout the year. In addition to these, look in the press for details of other exhibitions: more are being launched every year and many national exhibitions now run regional roadshows. As well as researching different countries, attending exhibitions is another way to meet local brokers (see below). Even if you don't attend in person, you can find details of all the brokers exhibiting on the show's website. Usually this will take the form of a searchable database, which can be filtered by country or type of property handled. For example, from the Property Investor Show website (see below), select ' Exhibitors' from the left-hand vertical menu bar. From there, you can either view all exhibitors; filter by category such as estate agent, lawyer, surveyor, tax advisers and so forth; and/or filter by country dealt with by the exhibitor.

Directory of major UK overseas property shows

The International Property Show
(www.internationalpropertyshow.com)

This runs six times a year: at least three times in London, twice in Cheshire/ Manchester and once in Dublin. The exhibitions are run in association with the *Daily Mail* and admission is free.

The Homebuyer Show (www.homebuyer.co.uk)
This runs once a year, at ExCel, London, usually in March. Sponsored by the *Evening Standard*, the show has been running since 1990 and claims to be the UK's largest and longest-running dedicated property event.

Homes Overseas Exhibition (www.homesoverseas.co.uk)
This exhibition is operated by the magazine of the same name and is run twice a year at both Olympia, London and the National Exhibition Centre, Manchester, usually in February and March.

World Class Homes (www.worldclasshomes.co.uk)
This is principally a web-based real estate brokerage running local exhibitions monthly around the United Kingdom and annually at the Galleria Shopping Centre near Brent Cross on the A1(M) at Hatfield.

The World of Property Show (`www.outboundpublishing.com`)
These shows are held three times a year: once in the north of England and twice in the south. The organiser is the publisher of *World of Property* magazine.

***Daily Mail* Ideal Home Show** (`www.idealhomeshow.co.uk`)
This show runs usually at Earls Court, London, in March. It is primarily intended for those who already have a property and want to furnish it. However, in recent years a growing number of overseas property firms have taken to participating. Tickets cost between £10 and £14, making it one of the few property shows charging for entrance. The numbers attending are massive and selling tickets at least does make sure that those attending are reasonably serious.

The Property Investor Show (`www.propertyinvestor.co.uk`)
This runs at the G-MEX Centre, Manchester, in June and in London's ExCel in October. The show, operated by Homes Overseas, attracts some 150 exhibitors – including major house builders, developers, estate agents, lenders, brokers, landlord associations and other leading property experts. There is a comprehensive programme of information seminars at the shows, covering all aspects of buying, selling, financing and managing your property.

EMIGRATE: Emigration Show (`www.outboundpublishing.com`)
This exhibition runs at Sandown Exhibition Centre, Esher, Belfast, York, Coventry and Edinburgh, at various dates between February and October. Despite the show's name and its avowed aim 'to help anyone to emigrate abroad, from those who are just thinking about emigration to those who have a visa and are ready to emigrate', three-quarters of the exhibitors are real estate brokers. There are, however, emigration experts on hand, to advise.

Aside from these major exhibitions, you can attend hundreds of smaller property shows, usually run in hotels, taking place throughout the year. Look for advertisements in local newspapers.

Finding a property exhibition abroad

If there are hundreds of property exhibitions run each year in the UK, as you can imagine, there are thousands around the world. Most countries now have at least one or two major shows each year, usually in the capital city. These will not always give you the breadth of property markets that you would find in the UK, Ireland, the USA, Germany or Holland, where the local market's appetite for overseas properties is well proven. They will often concentrate on their home market and feature a number of neighbouring countries too. But what they lack in breadth they more than make up for in depth.

Sources of information on overseas property exhibitions

Trade Show Week (www.tradeshowweek.com)
This is a Los Angeles-based magazine, serving the trade show and exhibitions market. From the home page, select 'Tradeshow directories' from the left-hand vertical menu bar headed 'Directories'. From there, you can search for an exhibition by name, country, topic, month or year. While there is a heavy US bias, shows the world over are listed.

TSNN (www.tsnn.com)

It calls itself 'The Ultimate Trade Show Resource', operating the most widely consulted event database on the Internet. It contains data on more than 15,000 trade shows, exhibitions, public events and conferences worldwide. You need to register (free) for full access to the database. From the home page you can chose an industry from the pull-down menu bar of that name on the top-right of the screen. You can also select a month or country or put in part of the exhibition name if you know it.

Trade Shows Alert (www.tradeshowalerts.com)

This service is provided by eindia Business, the business directory of India. Despite the parochial-sounding name, the exhibition search facility throw out links to real estate exhibitions around the world. Searching for a 1-month period showed up property exhibition in Sofia (Bulgaria), Madrid (Spain), Dortmund (Germany), Abu Dhabi and Palmeira (Portugal) as well as Jaipur (India).

Warning on property seminars

Before you even reach the airport, you may be tempted by one breed of rogues: property investment seminars and clubs. Organisations offering seminars and clubs have sprung up, claiming in their literature that they can show people how to get rich by investing in properties. These schemes often offer the near-certainty of building a £1 million property portfolio by signing up for a seminar costing between £2,500 and £6,000. (Don't confuse these seminars with the wholly worthwhile property exhibitions and seminars listed above, which can provide a valuable role in linking buyers and sellers.)

What you get for your money from the rogue seminars, according to one industry professional, is less than what you can glean in an hour on the Internet yourself, by visiting a few competent estate agents' websites.

The Department of Industry took High Court action recently, to close down six such schemes following an avalanche of complaints from dissatisfied clients who felt that they had been duped. The more reputable players have called on the Financial Services Authority to regulate the sector. Wait until they do!

Narrowing down your choice

These and many other factors will determine whether a particular country will both help you to achieve a high growth in property capital value and rental yield and be a pleasure to live in, visit or own. The next step is to run through each of the countries you are considering, with reference to Table 12.2, and see how they stack up against these criteria.

Table 12.2 Country appraisal checklist

Factor	Score out of 10 for Country or Area A	Score out of 10 for Country or Area B
Amount of inward investment. 0 = little; 10 = lots		
Growth in the economy 0 = much lower than developed economies; 10 = much higher than developed economies		
Level of unemployment High and staying high = 0; low and getting lower = 10		
Amount of tourism Not much and of poor quality = 0; lots and the infrastructure is improving = 10		
Political stability Always changing government = 0; regular elections but governments last their term = 10		
Local mortgage market None to speak of = 0; well developed, lots of providers, keen interest rates = 10		
Cost of living About the same as developed economies = 0; a fraction of that in developed economies = 10		
Property and income taxes Higher than your home country = 0; much lower than your home country = 10		
Access to country One airline and one airport = 0several budget airlines and several airports = 10		
Lifestyle and amenities Still Third World-like = 0; almost like home – good cinemas, theatre, restaurants and healthcare = 10		
Total out of 100		

Anything over about 60 should make you a reasonable return and be pleasurable. Above 80 and you are onto a winner.

But these are not neccessarily all the factors that can apply. There may be some dormant factors which have not yet appeared on the horizon but whichyou need to build into your thinking when assessing the potential for a particular country.

PART 3

Buying into a Country

Once you have worked your way through the first two parts of this book and made a few tentative visits to foreign fields, you should have narrowed your choice down to a handful of countries – perhaps even a handful of locations within a particular country. Only now can you begin the serious task of looking at individual properties, making offers and going through the buying process.

Visiting countries can be a time-consuming and expensive activity. The detailed 'due diligence' study essential to making an informed decision, though not costly (most of the data sources recommended here are freely available to anyone), will typically take even more time than the country visits. It follows, therefore, that serious property investors should limit their detailed country research, as far as is practicable, to a handful of areas. Unless you have visited the country on your shortlist before – perhaps several times – it may be prudent to consider renting or staying long-term in a hotel before committing to buying a property: doing that will certainly give a more rounded experience of what the country really has to offer.

There are plenty of people who have the detailed country-specific information needed to reassure you that your buying decision will be soundly based. Estate agents, lawyers, surveyors and translators abound in every country. The rub is to find reliable, ethical, competent people who ideally are members of a recognised professional body.

These chapters explore these issues and more, as well as signposting the organisations and publications who can help find the best advice.

CHAPTER 13

Using an Estate Agent–Broker–Realtor

In this chapter:

- Finding the best real estate brokers.
- Checking out international broker qualifications.
- Using house hunters.
- Stepping away from introducers.
- Monitoring developers' achievements.

Almost certainly, one of the first people you will come across in your property quest will be an estate agent, broker or realtor (as those who sell property are known in the USA). They play a pivotal role in matching supply and demand. Despite appearing to sit between buyers and sellers in the housing supply chain, estate agents are in fact appointed by the seller to look after their interests. Not only are they chosen by sellers, they are often, though not always, paid by them too, by way of a percentage of the price realised on the property.

So, far from being in *your* team, the estate agent is in *someone else's* team and they are rewarded more for getting you to part with as much money as possible. Right? Wrong. Estate agents are, above all, realists. They know it takes two to tango and, as the person with the cash, you are going to lead the dance. Until a property is sold, the estate agent is out of pocket for their services. They need a buyer so that they can get paid. So, while sellers are nominally paying them, they are actually really busy working to find you the property you are after. They have hundreds of villas, apartments and plots of land on their books. They also have links with dozens of other estate agents who in turn have hundreds more properties for sale. If they end up selling a property on the books of another estate agent, they split the sales commission with them.

A really attractive aspect of all this is that, if you handle it properly, the estate agents can be working for you in your team, while being on the payroll of someone else. In other words, you have a free resource and if you handle them well, they can take much of the sweat out of the job.

Getting an estate agent on your side will require that you follow some, or ideally all, of the following steps:

- Contact an estate agent only once you have done some initial spadework and have established a firm idea of what sort of property you're looking for. Unless you appear serious, there is little chance they will take you seriously.
- Stay in regular contact with the agent, so that you keep yourself at the forefront of their mind. The more contact you have with them, the more likely they are to think of you if something suitable comes on the market.
- Keep a record of your dealings with the estate agent. Record details of any telephone conversations that you have with them, including who you spoke to, on what date and what was said. This will demonstrate your professionalism and so keep them on their toes. It might also help to avoid any disputes further down the line if something that you had thought was agreed is later denied.
- Try to have the money in place before you start to look. Estate agents will take you more seriously if they know that you are a cash buyer or at least have a 'decision in principle' from your lender that you will be able to borrow the sum required. It might also give you the edge over other potential buyers.

- Ask lots of questions. Far from being an irritation, this will only serve to reinforce your interest in doing the deal. The questions closest to an estate agent's heart will those related to how quickly the sale could be wrapped up. So, ask at the outset how quickly the seller wants to sell, or how soon they can vacate the place. Make sure this fits in with your timing, but generally anything that speeds up the process and moves money into the agent's coffers more quickly will endear you to them.

Every property you see advertised already has a commission payable to the estate agent built in, with anything from 5% to 10% being the norm. So you can expect the best estate agents to work for their money, though how much work they do will depend on how successful you are at getting them to put you towards the top of their priorities. The sorts of tasks it is reasonable to expect them to perform include:

- Sending you details of all suitable properties on at least a weekly basis. Don't be too disappointed if they take poetic licence with your idea of a suitable property. The chances are that they will pitch anything within your price band and 10% above in your direction, in the off-chance that something might strike a chord.
- Arrange viewing trips, with the most professional fixing up everything including flights, hotels and taxis.
- Advise you on the key facilities, schools, hospitals, shops, transport and so forth in the area.
- Pass any offer you make to their client promptly and keep you fully informed of the negotiation as it develops.
- Help you find a surveyor or local builder.

Avoid introducers

These people hang around estate agents' offices, banks, hotels and bars, watching and listening, searching for foreign people who are obviously in Spain on a property-hunting visit. They latch on until an opportunity arises to introduce themselves; a obliging English speaker who just happens to know of a special, bargain dream house that is not known to the market at large. No one works for nothing, so these people will have an arrangement with an estate agent who can 'load' the deal to pay off the introducer.

There is absolutely nothing an introducer can do that you can't do yourself by diligently ploughing round the estate agents in your chosen area. No vendor in their right mind is likely to surround the sale of their property in a veil of secrecy.

Although the vendor pays estate agents, as soon as you show any serious interest in a property you will be asked to put your hand in your pocket.

As soon as you have seen a property, or perhaps even before, you may be asked to put down a deposit to secure the property. You may be pressured by such statements as: 'Property is selling so quickly that it is pointless viewing unless you can get here this week. Your best option is to put down a reservation deposit so we can keep the property for yo'. Or 'prices are being raised on this development next week/month'.

There is one rule that applies to anything involving contracts and money: ALWAYS take legal advice. An estate agent may tell you that if the transaction is fairly straightforward they can save you the 1–1.5% of legal fees by undertaking the contracting themselves. You won't know how straightforward the transaction really is until you come to sell the property. It is only at that stage that the real problems as to title, boundaries and access will show up. This is especially the case if you are buying a property from someone with several adjoining properties to sell, as they have no interest in paying legal fees to put these matters in good order.

Looking for qualifications

Surprisingly, the advent of the EU and globalisation has made life harder in some respects for the international property buyer. For example, under the law of Spain, the country where perhaps the most property has been sold into foreign ownership, it was illegal for anyone to sell property or real estate unless he or she had qualified as an estate agent and belonged to the association of real estate agents in Spain. Only university graduates who had taken the appropriate course, or other professional people such as lawyers or architects, were able to join this privileged body of recognised specialists. In addition, they all had to pass an exam in order to receive their diploma. These elite professionals were known as APIs (API = *Agente de la Propiedad Inmobiliaria*) After a while, a new type of property agents appeared who had only attended a short but comprehensive private diploma course. They were usually not graduates or qualified in any other way, unlike API members. These agents were known as GIPEs (GIPE = *Gestoria Inmobiliaria Propiedad España*).

APIs were reluctant to give up their monopoly of the Spanish property easily, so they fought a long and bitter war through the courts, getting most of the GIPEs' offices closed down and a few individuals jailed for contravening the law that constrained anyone other than APIs from selling property in Spain.

As Spain gradually became fully integrated into the European Community and more foreigners arrived from other parts of Europe, pressure was brought to bear in the European courts until eventually the law restricting the market to APIs alone was abolished. Since 2000, anyone can be an estate agent. Since the deregulation of the real estate industry in Spain, thousands of agencies have sprung up and fewer than 20% are licensed or are in any professional way qualified for the job. This same phenomenon has been replicated in other property markets around the world and very few brokers are professionally qualified: a situation that still prevails in the UK.

Few foreign property brokers are bonded with professional indemnity insurance or carry malpractice insurance. Those who do limit their insurance cover to a few hundred euros, so, to be prudent, limit your relationship with estate agents to introducing you to the deal and let your lawyer do the rest of the work.

In finding an estate agent/broker realtor there are three primary options:

UK property professional associations

In the UK you will find that a lot of people have jumped on the overseas property bandwagon, some with little or no previous experience of dealing in property. It would be prudent to deal, as far as possible, only with established estate agents with a strong UK track record or who are members of a recognised professional body or trade association such as:

Federation of Overseas Property Developers, Agents and Consults

(www.fopdac.com)

Established in 1973, the Federation unites agents, developers and specialist consultants active in the international property markets who have the experience and professional expertise to meet the criteria set out in its Code of Ethics. Where Federation members accept clients' monies for payment for land or property, they must maintain a legally separate clients' account which must be properly conducted. While this falls short of carrying any insurance or bonding to guarantee the protection of clients' money, it is at least a measure of protection. There is a full A–Z listing of members on the website.

The National Association of Estate Agents (NAEA)

(www.naea.co.uk)

The NAEA is the UK's leading professional body for estate agency personnel, with over 10,000 members who practise across all aspects of property services both in the UK and overseas. These include residential and commercial sales and lettings, property management, business transfer and auctioneering. Its aim as a professional body is to reassure clients that by dealing with an NAEA member they are working with someone who is bound by a vigorously enforced code of practice and adheres to professional rules of conduct. This thread (www.naea.co.uk>agents>international.asp) takes you to country directories of NAEA-regulated members. There you have the option of selecting either a UK-based member who specialises in a particular country or an NAEA member in a particular country.

International property professional associations and major brokerages

A number of federations and associations act as general trade associations for brokers operating in particular countries. All these associations have directories of their members listed by country and/or city and usually have details of their qualifications and whether or not they are bonded.

The Europe Real Estate Directory

(www.europerealestatedirectory.net)

This is a directory system with the stated aim of helping brokers to reach a targeted real estate audience. The site offers cross-linking with all the sites listed in the directory. The goal is for the directory to be the single best source for real estate agency information. The site has country databases for some 50 countries, taking an elastic definition for 'Europe'. Select a country from the list on the home page; ignore the top few listings which are mostly advertising of vaguely related subjects such as cheap airline tickets, hotels and phone companies. At the bottom of the country page (designated by a large yellow star) are links to the country's real estate brokers. The covering is not massive, but certainly sufficient. Albania has 5 brokers listed; the Faro Islands 3; Serbia 18; and Hungary 60.

The International Real Estate Portal

(www.internationalrealestateportal.net)

This is closely related to the European Real Estate Directory, but stretches its coverage to over 120 countries. For much of the world, the coverage is at best patchy and seems to be more 'under construction' that delivering real value. But if it reaches the coverage of the European portal, it will be worth persisting with.

International Real Estate Directory (IRED) (`www.ired.com`)

IRED is not so much an association as an information directory. It provides a comprehensive database of real estate-related information. On the home page there is a world map under the heading 'The Directories'. By selecting a continent you will be taken to a country-by-country web link, such as that shown in Table 13.1 for Europe.

Selecting 'Greece' in the Europe Directory, for example, provides the web address of the Hellenic Association of Realtors, the local professional association, which in turn has a directory of local member firms. Also under 'Greece' there are direct links to a dozen or so local property brokers' websites and other related associations.

Table 13.1 European countries with real estate broker networks covered by IRED

Austria	Hungary	Romania
Belgium	Iceland	Russia
Bulgaria	Italy	Serbia/Montenegro
Croatia	Latvia	Slovakia
Cyprus	Liechtenstein	Slovenia
Czech Republic	Lithuania	Spain
Denmark	Luxembourg	Gibraltar
Estonia	Malta	Sweden
Finland	Moldova	Switzerland
France	Monaco	Turkey
Germany	Netherlands	Ukraine
Greece	Norway	United Kingdom
Greenland	Poland	Yugoslavia
	Portugal	

The International Real Estate Federation (FIABCI) (www.fiabci.com)

Founded in the 1950s, the FIABCI, as the International Real Estate Federation is known, has built up to having 50 Chapters throughout the world. There are also around 100 professional associations in membership, making a total membership approaching 1.5 million practitioners. Select 'The FIABCI Research Zone' to access the Federation's database of brokers, surveyors, lawyers and tax accountants, listed by country.

The National Association of Realtors (NAR) (www.realtor.org)

Founded as the National Association of Real Estate Exchanges on 12 May 1908 in Chicago, the association is the driving force behind the 'Certified International Property Specialist Network' (CIPS). This comprises 1,500 real estate professionals focused specifically on the 'international' market. Through NAR's alliances with 70 national and regional co-operating associations around the globe, you can locate a CIPS Network member almost anywhere. Through the online directory, the search features can be used to locate someone with specific business, location and/or language specialities. This site includes information about NAR's co-operating associations, market profiles of more than 40 international markets, US international local councils, CIPS Network membership, information and resources and more. The majority of this site is open to the public, but there are a few pages available only to NAR members. From the home page, select 'Directories' in the top horizontal menu bar, followed by 'International property specialists' from the vertical menu bar headed 'Find a specialist to help you'.

International Property Directory
(www.internationalpropertydirectory.com)

In any search for 'international property' in MSN or Google, the directory provider claims that you will find this site on page 1, 2 or 3 – placing it in the first 30 results worldwide out of millions. It has a

Google rank of 4 for its home page and high rankings for many more pages within the site.

There are three directories on the site: 'Property'; 'Realtors (Brokers/ estate agents)'; and 'Builders (Developers)'. The first is a limited listing of properties for sale or rent; the second a rather wider listing of brokers; the third is perhaps the most valuable listing, bypassing brokers and taking readers to a listing of property developers.

Central European Real Estate Associations Network (CEREAN) (`www.cerean.com`)

CEREAN is a non governmental, not-for-profit organisation, concerned with the development of ethical and professional real estate markets in the member countries. It works closely with international and European organisations operating in the real estate market and towards establishing a common European business platform for professionals operating in this field. Founded in 1990 by a small group of brokers from Poland, Slovakia, the Czech Republic and Bulgaria, the association now has 13 member countries and a host of ancillary affiliations with related organisations such as the Ukrainian Association of Valuers and the Real Estate University in Poland. From the top horizontal menu bar, select 'Country' and then the country of your choice from the pull-down menu. On the country page, you will find the web address of the local professional association and, from there, the individual country members. For example, in Armenia you will find the web link, address and phone numbers for the National Association of Realtors and Appraisers (NARA). Once in the site, the 'Members' link takes you to a directory of contact details for 43 real estate firms.

Worldwide Tax (`www.worldwide-tax.com`)

This site is a very comprehensive one, dealing with a host of taxation and financial subjects for some 70 countries. From the left-hand vertical menu on the home page, under the heading 'Directories', select

'Real Estate', where you will be offered links to real estate brokers in around 27 countries.

The World Real Estate Directory
(www.worldrealestatedirectory.com)

This is a directory in the RealEstateAdvertise.com stable – a web development company focusing on designing, developing and marketing premier real estate web directories and sites. Basically, it produces websites listing links in categorised pages. This one lists links to brokers by country.

Confédération Européenne de l'Immobilier (www.webcei.com)

This is one of Europe's largest professional organisations of estate agents, now counting well over 45,000 members from hundreds of cities in 13 European countries (Austria, France, Germany, Greece, Hungary, Ireland, Italy, the Netherlands, Portugal, Romania, Spain, the United Kingdom and the Slovak Republic). This represents an overall total of 60,000 operators in real estate, all of whom have subscribed to the CEI's strict code of contact. (You can see the code in the 'About CEI' link, accessed from the horizontal menu at the bottom of the page. From the left-hand vertical menu, select 'CEI members' and from there search by name of agency, country or city.)

International Real Estate Directory
(www.internationalrealestatedirectory.com)

The site is designed to be a one-stop destination for anything you can think of that is about or related to international real estate and its mission is to be 'the leading provider of quality e-business, advertising and information services for International Real Estate market'. The home page has direct links to over 123 countries listed in A–Z format. Each country has upwards of half a dozen brokers listed, with direct links to their websites.

International real estate companies

These are businesses dealing almost exclusively with those wanting to buy property in a foreign country. They usually have strong legal and tax networks so if those are areas of particular concern, they are worth seeking out.

Colliers (www.colliers.com)

This is a global affiliation of independently owned real estate services firms with 9,327 employees in 241 offices in 54 countries. They are able to provide expert local real estate advice wherever their clients need it. Until recently, the company has concentrated on commercial properties, but that is changing and residential is fast being included both for sale and for rent. You can search the country and city database of properties either by selecting 'Jump to an office' labelled at the very top of the home page, or by clicking on 'Find a property' in the options on the right-hand side. The company also produces comprehensive reports on property market conditions for around 100 countries and cities. Selecting 'Market Reports' in the left-top of the home page can access these.

Hamptons International (www.hamptons.co.uk/int _ index.asp)

This has offices selling developments and properties in some of the more exotic locations around the world, such as Marrakech, Mauritius and Grenada. Office locations and properties can be accessed from the vertical menu bar on the left of the screen.

Sotheby's International Realty (www.sothebysrealty.com)

This organisation was founded in 1976 as a real estate service for clients of Sotheby's auction house. Since then it has developed into a global organisation selling fine properties in all price ranges in 34 countries, concentrating at or near the top end of the market Its property database can be searched by country or by category, such as historic buildings, waterfront developments, resorts or land, or by a combination of country and category.

Knight Frank (www.knightfrank.com)

Knight Frank has over 140 offices in over 30 countries across five continents, with over 4,500 brokers. From this screen you can access a database of properties in each country.

Checking out brokers' (and developers') performance

Some property brokerages are large concerns and others are a one-man band. Size is not much of a guide as to competence. You should check to make sure anyone you are dealing with is properly registered, as any errors in the buying process can have far-reaching consequences. As you will be dealing for much of the time in a foreign language and with translations of legal documents, it is doubly important that you seek the reassurance that membership of a professional body will bring. At least with members of the professional bodies who are properly licensed, you have some hope of obtaining redress if anything goes wrong. Aside from establishing whether a broker is qualified, bonded or a member of a recognised association or trade body, you can see how they are rated by clients such as yourself.

Sources of information concerning developers and broker performance

Holiday Truths (www.holidaytruths.co.uk)

This is a moderated blog, which is cleaned up to keep it respectable, but no effort is made to check the veracity of the information. In the 'Specialised Topics' section on the left-hand vertical menu bar, select 'Ex-pats and Owners Abroad'. In here you will be able to get the low-down on how brokers perform in respect of managing inspection trips, returning deposits and so forth. This is a typical discussion forum thread: 'I would like to invite any people who have had problems as I have had with XXX Properties. I think people should be aware so they are not ending up losing money and being promised things which cannot be delivered. These include . . . no-one getting back with customer service, selling developments with no building licences, charging crazy agency fees, charging extra on developments i.e. penthouses and corner plots. and generally lots of problems with customers. I am aware that a lot of people have been waiting months to get refunds back from developments that did not have licences on. XXX Properties do not tell anyone about this before they purchase. It would be interesting to see if other people have had bad experiences.'

There are over 19,000 comments on some 1,300 different topics running in this forum area, so expect to find something on almost any country, anywhere.

Eyes on the World (www.eyeonworldwide.com)

This is not strictly for keeping track of brokers, rather it is a site to help keep tabs on how off-plan developments are progressing. However, as off-plan properties are the main products that brokers sell overseas, and their ability to select on market successful developments is fundamental to buyer satisfaction, monitoring the clients' satisfaction with a development is vital. Eye on Worldwide was conceived following the success of the Eye on Spain website, run by an independent company with no links to any developers or promoters.

Using Eye enables property buyers, both actual and prospective, to communicate with fellow buyers from the development into which you are buying, anywhere in the world.

The service is free of charge but you first need to register. Once on the website, select the country in which you have bought or are considering buying a property from the list on the right, and then select your new development from the country list in alphabetical order. Then you can communicate with fellow off-plan buyers via the message boards and share construction photos of your future holiday home or investment.

Working with a house hunter

If you can't spend much time travelling around the world, you may consider employing the services of a person or organisation to do some of the legwork for you. 'House hunter' seems to be the common descriptive term for this sort of service. A house hunter doesn't replace the estate agent; rather, their work is complementary. House hunters can be affiliated with a specific estate agent, or not. You want a house hunter who works with *every* estate agent so that you can be sure of getting unbiased help.

Usually, house hunters ask you to fill in detailed questionnaires designed to capture your needs precisely. They then set to the task of finding properties in the area you want, at your price, and those that they believe correspond to your needs. They personally visit properties, take detailed notes and photos, and send information to you for viewing before you make the trip to visit their selections.

After you're in the country, they set up viewing appointments and even accompany you on visits. If you decide to buy one of the properties, you deal directly with the estate agent. The fee structure depends on the type and level of service you decide on, but the following gives you an approximate idea of the cost range of house-hunting services:

- Retainer fee: **between** €1,500 and £2,000 (£1,030 and £1,370) to search for a property to purchase or rent. You can deduct this fee from the final completion fee, if your search is successful. This fee retains services for a period of usually 13 weeks.
- Completion/success fee: Between 1 and 2% of the final purchase price, with a minimum fee of between €7,000 and €10,000 (£4,800 and £6,800).

- Search for rented accommodation: Typically, one month's rental fee.
- Orientation tours: Beginning at €1,000 (£860). This service involves taking you around a chosen region, highlighting important factors such as roads, schools, building projects or anything that may make an area more or less attractive.
- Area review report: Around €400 (£275). If you can't visit an area or want an overview of several areas, house hunters can write you a report that covers much the same ground as an orientation tour provides.

Useful websites for locating house hunters

WNM International Property Search (www.wnm-int.com)

This organisation claims to work worldwide. It searches the property market at all price levels, for properties fitting their clients' requirements, covering East and West Europe, Asia, the Americas, Australasia, Africa and the Orient.

Elite and VIP (www.eliteandvip.com)

This offers a range of specialist skills which include property experience, legal expertise and foreign languages, making it possible for its clients to buy with confidence. Case examples on the website include clients for whom it has found properties in Canada, New England, France, Italy and Spain.

CHAPTER 14

Finding a Property Yourself

In this chapter:

- Checking out papers and magazines.
- Searching websites.
- Using local tourist offices.
- Getting the low-down on property auctions.

In is undoubtedly true that the vast majority of overseas property buyers use an agent or broker to find a property. But brokers' services come at a cost. Every person who places themselves between a property for sale and the ultimate buyer adds cost – and that cost is invariably added to the final price. Some costs are inescapable, such as local property costs and notary and legal fees. But some are optional, in that, with some leg-work, buyers can take on the work themselves (See Figure 14.1.) While this may not be a realistic option for everyone, it is certainly worth at least exploring ways of proceeding that could result in savings of 30%.

Reading papers and magazines

Almost all the British Sunday newspapers, and many of the dailies, have overseas property sections. The newspapers also carry articles on most aspects of living abroad, ranging from getting medical cover to pension rights and finding a mortgage. From time to tine, you can also find detailed coverage of particular regions in a country. On a recent

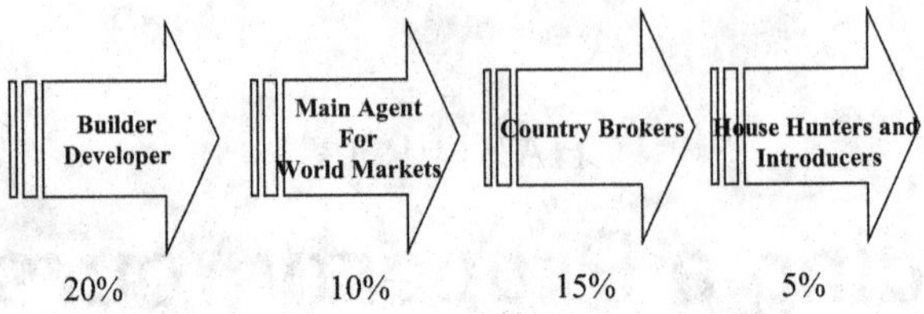

Figure 14.1 Savings by getting down the chain

count, more than 1,000 overseas properties were for sale in British newspapers and magazines per month, in most months. You can also find a number of glossy magazines tending to feature new resorts, often adjacent to ski resorts, golf courses or marinas.

Listing of UK newspapers and magazines with international properties

Make the following papers and magazines part of your regular reading list while researching the property market:

Dalton's Weekly (www.daltonsholidays.com)

This is available as a hard-copy version, as well as a new website. Both carry advertisements for properties in Eastern and Central Europe.

Homes Overseas (www.homesoverseas.co.uk)

This is a monthly worldwide magazine and website with extensive property listings. This link (www.homesoverseas.co.uk/propertyforsale/map.aspx) takes you directly to it's a–Z country listing of properties.

International Homes and *International Luxury Homes* (www.international-homes.com)

These are two glossy monthlies published by International Property (P Pass Ltd). They cover property and lifestyle in the UK and abroad and are distributed in supermarkets and newsagents across the UK and Europe. The publisher claims that 'These magazines have proven so popular that British Airways take 40 tons of each issue to distribute freely to their passengers at departure gates.' The publisher also organises annual International Property Awards, the results of which are published in an annual, *The World's Best Developers & Estate Agents.*

Overseas Property TV Magazine (www.optv-magazine.com)

This is a subscription-only magazine, costing £36 for the year's 12 issues. The first 3 issues are free, so you can taste before you buy. Each issue has around 100 pages of property information, lifestyle guides and details of the latest developments. The TV programme (www.overseaspropertytv.com) is on Satellite Channel 287. On the TV website there are some basic fact files on a number of countries and areas: Cyprus, Florida, Bahamas, Cape Verde, Morocco, Portugal, Romania, the Dominican Republic and Bulgaria. Clicking on 'Fact Files' in the left-hand vertical menu bar, headed up 'Home', accesses these. Rather irritatingly, the country fact files are revealed in random order, so you have no idea which countries will be shown where. The TV programme covers an extensive range of topics, including: 'Property Kings', where successful people talk about how they made their millions in property; seminars on topics such as 'Buying into Brazil', 'Dealing with Tax', 'Retiring Abroad'; and discussion with various experts.

Property Mart Overseas (www.propertymartoverseas.com)

This is a monthly that started life as *Property Mart Spain* in May 2004, before expanding to a global market a year later. It has over 90 country guides, a collection of buying guides and numerous useful articles, as well as an in-depth look at the world's leading property exhibitions. Its Frequently Asked Questions section covers a range of the most usual topics as well as containing the answers to the most common readers' questions for the preceding 4 months.

The *Daily Telegraph* and *Sunday Telegraph* (www.telegraph.co.uk)

Both these papers have 'property for sale' sections. From the website, select 'Sunday Telegraph' and then ' Expat' takes you to articles on life for Brits abroad.

The Financial Times (www.ft.com/home/uk)

On Saturdays, the FT has a section listing overseas properties and developments for sale. The website has articles, but no properties. The only way to find relevant articles seems to be by entering a term such as 'overseas property' in the search pane.

The Sunday Times (http://property.timesonline.co.uk)

The paper has an extensive international property section with both listings and helpful and informative articles. The website only has the articles. From this link, select 'Overseas' from the left-hand menu.

World of Property (ww.outboundpublishing.com)

This is a bi-monthly publication covering international locations; it features periodic sections on specific countries.

A growing number of English-language papers and news-sheets are published and distributed in many of the countries popular with UK buyers. These publications target both the expat communities and property buyers in general. See, in Part 4, 'Finding local English language media' for how to locate these papers. Also search:

Magforum.com (www.magforum.com/buyingproperty.htm)

This lists all magazines published in the UK, together with circulation figures and some pithy comments on reliability. The site is put together by hand and the editor, Tony Quinn, funded by donations from readers, processes everything. As well as UK magazines there are links to sources of information on magazine publishing world-wide. This link goes straight to the property magazine list.

Trawling the Internet

The Internet can be a great way to find out a little about the property market in a particular area relatively quickly – and from the comfort of your own home. Hundreds of websites offer (or claim to offer) comprehensive details on property in every corner of the globe. While the Internet is a useful starting point for your research, do not consider it to be the end of your process.

As you search online, you're sure to encounter many sites promoting properties 'off plan', which means that building work may well not even have started and a completed apartment or villa may be years away. Often, off-plan internet sites show a convincing computer image of the property on offer and invite you to 'reserve' your villa or apartment for a mere £500, usually payable online using your credit card. You must understand that you are getting *absolutely nothing concrete* for your money and that you have little chance of recovering any investment if the property is not completed for years or, worse, never completed. (See Holiday Truths (`www.holidaytruths.co.uk`) and Eyes on the World (`www.eyeonworldwide.com, listed earlier`) for ways to keep track of a developer's progress.)

You can start your research by typing your specific needs into a search engine such as Google: 'three-bed villa Croatia', for example. But don't be surprised if these key words result in apartments in Florida, farmhouses in the Dordogne and watermills in Tuscany. Advertisers have now mastered the art of planting key words into their search engine listings, so that the search flags up everything with even a tangential connection to what you are looking for. Persevere, refine your search, and keep at it. The hours on the Internet are a whole lot less and a whole lot cheaper than wasted trips to Poland or Turkey – however pleasurable in their own right – if you have nothing worthwhile to view when you get there.

Directory of major Internet international property websites

The following Internet property sites cover most of the world and between them claim to list over 200,000 properties in 150 overseas countries. However, this is not an exhaustive list: sites come and go all the time.

`www.castles.glo-con.com`

This is a separate listing in Glo-Con's website (see below), listing castles from around the world (including Poland, Italy, India, France, Spain and Croatia), at prices from €120,000 upwards.

`www.findaproperty.com`

Launched in 1997, FindaProperty.com now publishes the details of over 257,654 properties to buy or rent from over 5,177 different agent offices around the UK and the rest of the world. From the horizontal menu bar across the top of the home page, select 'Overseas'. From there, you will find a continent-by-continent directory of countries covered. There are also some useful 'how to' guides and general property news on the site.

`www.glo-con.com`

Claims among its 28,689 properties listed that 4,492 are in Italy, 2,037 in Germany, 906 in France, 1,052 in Spain, 381 in Russia, 68 in Hungary, 76 in Greece and 660 in Portugal. It has one of the largest international property listings on the Internet.

`www.oliproperties.com/oliproperties`

This site accepts registration from any individual or agent who has property to sell or let, both residential and commercial. The site lists more then 9,000 properties, in countries including Bulgaria, Croatia, Cyprus, Czech Republic, Hungary, Malta and Turkey.

`www.primelocation.com/international-property`

This site was launched in 2001 by a consortium of more than 200 leading independent estate agents across the United Kingdom who wanted to be in the vanguard of online property marketing. In 2006, the company was bought by Daily Mail & General Holdings Ltd as part of its further expansion into the online business sector. The site's international section carries more than 50,000 properties from estate agents in more than 40 countries, including Cyprus, Croatia and Bulgaria. It has a search engine for filtering property by country, by price and by for sale or for rent.

`www.propertiesabroad.com`

Not to be confused with the similar but smaller offering from www.property-abroad.com, this site has strong listings, primarily in Brazil, Cyprus, Dubai, Egypt, Florida, France, Morocco, Portugal, Spain and Turkey and its scope is extending fast.

`www.property-abroad.com`

This is a family-run business set up by Les Calvert and features more than 28,000 properties in more than 42 countries, including Bulgaria, Croatia, Cyprus, the Czech Republic, Hungary, Malta, Poland and Turkey.

`www.propertyfinder.com/property/international`

This site has links to 270,000 properties for sale or rent, covering around 100 countries. Once in the country pages, you can search for properties by price, by number of bedrooms and by type of property (e.g. 'villa', 'apartment' and so forth)

www.remax.com

This is a franchised estate agent network with 5,400 offices in more than 50 countries, between them covering properties in 150 countries. The link to international properties is in an almost insignificant pull-down menu at the bottom-left of the home page, headed 'Remax Worldwide'. Within each country section you can search by region, by price range and by property category such as 'residential', 'commercial', 'farm' and so forth.

www.sunandskihomes.co.uk

This site lists properties to suit all budgets, from €15,000 to €1 million plus. Its portfolio of properties includes exclusive homes, apartments, villas, farmhouses and golf courses throughout many countries including Bulgaria, Croatia, Spain, Greece, Portugal, Italy, Malta, Turkey, Cyprus, Thailand and Brazil. It also has a section (accessed from the horizontal menu bar at the top of the screen) on private islands, with listings starting at €111,000.

www.themovechannel.com

Founded in 1999 by Dan Johnson, this site started life as a simple guide to the buying procedures for residential properties in the United Kingdom. Now with over 200 partners, it covers buying guides and property listings for nearly 100 countries. The site has an amazing filter allowing you to pre-select properties to view by a host of specialised criteria, including 'ski property', 'golf property', 'renovation projects' and 'commercial property'.

www.viviun.com

This currently has more than 6,300 properties listed in over 50 countries including Brazil, Bulgaria, Canada, Costa Rica, Croatia, the

Czech Republic, Estonia, Hungary, Lithuania, Panama, Philippines, Poland, Slovenia, Turkey and Ukraine.

www.worldrealtynews.com

This site carries 700 properties including those from Bulgaria, Croatia, Cyprus, the Czech Republic, Jamaica, Hungary, Malta and Turkey.

Tackling the tourist office

You may be one of those travellers who avoid tourist offices like the plague. Backpackers often do clog up these offices, pocketing leaflets by the dozen. All worthy people, no doubt, but not exactly entrepreneurial types bent on adventure and property acquisition. While you may be right in this assessment of the clientele, the people behind the counter are made of sterner stuff. For a start, they all speak English – an invaluable asset when you are seeking out useful information in a foreign land. Also, a tourist office is a reassuring indication that you may well have a holiday rental market for the property you plump for.

Following here are a few subjects to probe those in the tourist office about, to help you decide whether an area is worthy of your attention:

- **Transportation.** This is a topic on which tourist office personnel are well geared up. First, find out the routes, frequency and rates of buses and trains. These answers give you a feel for how easily you can live in the area without a car, as well as how likely you are to attract potential business or holiday renters.
- **Accommodation.** Tourist offices usually maintain a database of local hotels, guesthouses and private landlords willing to put you up. These recommendations are almost certain to be more inexpensive than the places you find being plugged on the Internet or by travel agents.
- **Local attractions.** The more leaflets on display, the larger the office and the more staff at work, the more certain you can be that the

area is popular for visitors: a fact that you can't be quite so confident about just by reading a guide book or searching the internet. After you know just how popular an area is, you are more able to build a forecast of likely rental income.

- **Quality assessment.** Many tourist offices rate local properties using a star or other measurement system. Understanding how an area's tourist office assesses quality is the key to knowing how to pitch a rental for any property you may buy.

Tourism Offices Worldwide Directory (www.towd.com)

This is a guide to official tourist information sources: government tourism offices, convention and visitors bureaus; chambers of commerce; and similar organisations providing free, accurate and unbiased travel information to the public. Businesses such as travel agents, tour operators and hotels are not included. The directory has been operating since 1994 and, as of October 2006, contains 1,421 entries.

From the A–Z pull-down menu bar 'Tourism offices for countries other than the USA', select the countries in which you are interested.

Attending auctions

As you travel around your chosen area, you are sure to come across property auctions. You can find out a good deal about property prices and values in an area by attending a few auctions. In particular, one benefit of auctions is that the final selling price is transparent, as are the bids. You don't have to rely on estate agent 'hype' for figures.

Auctions operate much the same the world over. If you intend to do anything more than observe, you need to do all your research beforehand, take your legal representative with you to the auction and have your cash ready, in the country, to finance the transaction.

The following are some tips for winning at auctions:

- Set an **outside limit** on how much you can spend – and never exceed it. You can all too easily get carried away with auction fever.
- Do a '**dummy run**'. Auctions are usually advertised 6–8 weeks in advance, so go to one or two to get to know the ropes.
- Do the usual **homework**. You need to complete all the inspections and checks *before* you bid because, after the hammer goes down, the sale is final. In Chapter 16, we cover the things you need to look out for.
- Be prepared to make a **deposit**. You will be asked to put in a bidding deposit of 10%, refundable if you do not win the auction. You need to check out how you need to make that deposit and you must have the funds for that available on the day of the auction.
- Have the **balance of payments** ready. Not the subject that worries the Chancellor of the Exchequer, but you must have the full funds ready to complete the purchase – usually within 28 days.
- **Call ahead** to double-check that the house you are after is still in the auction. Properties can be, and are, sold prior to auction by smart – or desperate – buyers 'knobbling' the vendor.
- Have your **insurance** in place. After the gavel comes down, the property – and the risk – are all yours.
- Send your lawyer the **auction details** beforehand. Doing so ensures that you don't make any mistakes. Consider giving your lawyer power of attorney (this is covered this in Chapter 15), then he or she can bid for you and keep you within your budget.

Sources of information on international property auctions

The Move Channel (`www.investment-property.themovechannel.com/Websites/Property/Sales/Auctions/world`)

This site is an offshoot of the Move Channel website described above. It lists information on current property auctions around the world. At the time of writing, 40 auctions were listed, from as far afield as New Zealand and India, as well as Spain and the Canary Islands.

Property Abroad
(www.property-abroad.com/spain/shop/auctions.html)

This site is an offshoot of the Property Abroad website described above. It lists property auction details around Spain and Tenerife, at present with plans for a wider listing of countries.

World of Property (www.worldofproperty.co.uk/Visitors.htm)

This site is owned by Outbound Media & Exhibitions, a division of Johnston Press plc. It runs live property auctions at some of its UK exhibitions. The one listed at the time of writing was for property in Turkey, in 23 lots ranging in price from €40,000 to €110,000.

CHAPTER 15

Finding a Lawyer

In this chapter:

- Seeing why you always need a lawyer.
- Understanding the role of notaries.
- Appreciating the essence of title.
- Locating the right lawyer for the task.
- Knowing about power of attorney.

It is estimated that over three-quarters of foreign buyers don't take independent legal advice when they buy a property abroad. Often, buyers only rush out to find a lawyer when they hit some snags after they have paid a deposit or – worse still– signed a contract. Sometimes the serious problems only become apparent when the property is to be sold on. That is especially true if, as is often the case, the sale is to a local of the country in question. Their lawyer will almost certainly be well versed in local issues, boundaries, planning rules, new roads and so forth. It will be their job to uncover any weakness in the title (ownership) document. They get a double benefit when they are successful – first, there is professional satisfaction; second they open up the prospects of a protracted set of negotiations and hence increase their fees.

You need a lawyer to look after *your* interests in the transaction, as little in the property world ever works as smoothly as you would like. Ideally, they should operate within 50 km of the property you are buying, speak good English and be versed in any matters relating to foreigners buying property in their country.

Your lawyer performs a n umber of vital functions, including the following:

Paying deposits

Your lawyer will draw up the initial pre-sale contract and handle the payment of the customary 10% deposit. Your lawyer is the only party to the sale who is likely to carry liability insurance to protect your deposit money in the event that things go wrong. You will be invited, early in the buying process, to demonstrate your commitment by putting down some hard cash. Reservation deposits and any payments made to an agent, whether licensed or not, are not legally binding on the vendor. It is only when a sale and purchase contact has been agreed and signed by both parties and 10% paid that the vendor is legally bound to sell you the property, so there is no point in paying any reservation deposits to an agent.

Reservation deposits for new developments should be made direct to the developer; any and all payments should be made by or under the supervision of an independent lawyer. Only in this way will your interests and your money always be protected. You will also be sure that the sale and purchase contract is in your name and not in the name of the agency. This may be convenient for the agency, as it allows them to control the sales process and speed things up, especially if you are out of the country, but you will have no legal claim on the property. If you pay money to an agency and the deal falls through, the only way you may get your deposit back is to stick with that agent until they find you another property you like and can afford. Also, be sure to take care that any deposit you make goes into an escrow account, which is only accessible when the sale goes through.

Power of attorney

If you are not going to be in the county in which you are buying during all, or even some of, the purchase process, or you would like to be sheltered from the mind-numbing bureaucratic process that so often prevails, you would be well advised to give your lawyer power of attorney. This document authorises the person appointed – in this case your lawyer – to act on your behalf in certain prescribed matters, as though they were you. In effect, they assume the full responsibility for making your decisions and committing you irrevocably to certain matters by signing documents on your behalf. Granting the power means signing in front of a notary, either in the country or it may be possible to do so in the UK embassy of the country in question. Setting up power of attorney (sometimes also known as a letter of attorney) will cost between €10 and €50. Even if you grant power of attorney, if you are in the country at the final gasp – when the final document transferring ownership is signed – you can turn up and sign yourself. As well as being an experience in itself, you can have a last look around the property to make sure everything you thought was included in the sale is actually present and correct.

Price declaration – the ever present problem

Your lawyer will also advise on the ramifications of under-declaring the selling price. In many parts of the world there is a practice which involves paying some of the purchase price 'under the table'. In effect, you are being asked by the vendor to pay some of the purchase price in cash, undeclared to the authorities, and the balance in the normal, visible manner. There are attractions to this strategy for both parties. Both you and the vendor will lower their property sales tax bills, to some extent, and the charges by professionals (being based on the declared selling price) will be lower too. So, in theory, only the government, a lawyer or two and the estate agent are the losers.

However, there are a few snags with under-declaring, especially if the proportion of the total selling price under-declared is large. For a start, it is illegal in many countries and where it *is* illegal there are often severe penalties. The practice could also leave you with a larger capital gains tax bill when you sell up than you would otherwise have, unless you can persuade your buyer in turn to under-declare by the same proportion. You may also find it rather difficult – with anti-money laundering regulations being so prevalent – to make a large sum of cash just disappear.

It is highly likely, especially in rural areas where you are buying a property which has been in the same hands for a long time, that you will be pressurised into agreeing to some level of under-declaring. The reason for this is simple. The vendor could have a large capital gains tax liability, which in effect is taking a big slice of the money they hope to get from the sale of the property concerned.

Overseas estate agents indicate that, at present, sellers are seeking somewhere between 20% and 50% as the under-declared amount. Informally, this is considered 'acceptable', much as doing 75 mph on the motorway is – though, of course, strictly, you would still be breaking the law. In this area, more than any other, you need to seek sound legal advice and follow it.

Proving title

According to a prominent estate agent selling property in many overseas markets, out of every 30 properties they see, barely 10 will be properly documented and ready for sale. The only way you can be absolutely certain of who owns a property is by examining its title deed as registered in the country's property registry. The title deed provides a description of the property, the details of the owner and details of any mortgages or other charges against the property.

But two issues make this more difficult in these markets than in, say, the UK. In the first place, some of the countries (Croatia and Cyprus being prime examples) there has been a civil war raging. The land, homes and other possessions of the 'losers' of this conflict were widely regarded as part of the 'spoils of war' by the victors, who in any event were bent on ethnically cleansing parts of the country. To secure lasting peace. property had to be restored to its rightful owners and this has not always been achieved successfully. Second, many Central European countries are grappling with the fundamental issues of restoring the concept of private ownership of land and property after decades of state ownership and the confiscation of estates. Many are struggling to re-create their land registry – a vital first step in proving title – and, after more than 40 years of neglect, this is proving to be both complex, expensive and time-consuming. In Ukraine, for example, where the land is registered separately from the building, the difficulty of the process is doubled.

It is not only in developing countries that title can prove problematic. In October 2006 residents of Dartmouth Square in Dublin found, when trying to buy out the ground rent from a new landlord who claimed to have bought the square, that they may not actually own the houses they thought they had bought. They have been told that the Irish land registry has no record of the square changing hands, so, while those who bought their homes from the previous landlord can rely on title granted by the previous owner, newer owners are in 'limbo' and cannot take full possession. Therefore, while they can continue to live in their houses, they can make no alterations nor can they rent or sell them.

On average, the countries examined take 180 days to accomplish the whole procedure of checking the property title and registering a new owner. The fastest is 3 days and the slowest 956 days. A number of countries speed up registration by offering a fast-track procedure. For example, by paying 25% more in Lithuania, a buyer can cut the time down from 29 days to 3. In Croatia and Slovenia, court backlogs can cause delays of over a year. It is often possible to obtain a provisional title on application – a process favoured by many brokers – but you won't know for certain that you own the property until you get the final title.

It is your lawyer's job to make sure that the title is correct and transferred to you on completion of the sale. You do need to ask for evidence of their professional liability insurance. In some countries you may be offered insurance against a 'defective' title. You should consider this carefully and discuss it with your lawyer.

Sources of further information on property title issues

Doing Business (www.doingbusiness.org)

Provided as a collaborative venture by the World Bank Group in co-operation with the Lex Mundi Association of law firms and the International Bar Association, the Doing Business database assesses and measures business regulations and their enforcement across 155 countries. From the left-hand menu bar, select 'Registering Property', where you can see the bureaucratic and legal hurdles you are likely to encounter. The columns in the centre of this page give a summary of the position in each country and, by selecting a particular country, you can see more detailed information. Using the database, you can see, for example, that buying property in Poland takes 197 days but in Lithuania only 3 days.

The World Bank
(http://rru.worldbank.org/PapersLinks/Open.aspx?id53598)

The Bank publishes a paper on *Registering Property Rights*, reviewing countries' successes and failures as they update their land registries and procedures. Reading this will give you an idea as to how complex, lengthy and risky the process of proving title will be.

The role of the notary

In most of the countries covered it is usual to have a 'notary' involved in the deal. Where that is the case, you will absolutely have to use one as, under the country's laws, only deeds of sale witnessed and authorised by a notary can be registered at the land registry. Without such registration, no ownership transfer is complete. It doesn't matter much who you choose, for one simple reason: they won't be working for you. Unlike your own lawyer, who you expect to be looking after your interest, the notary is neutral. They carry out some checks on the property and make sure that all the paperwork is in precisely the correct order for smooth processing by the land registry so that registration can take place. They also have a responsibility to make sure that the appropriate property transfer taxes are paid on time. The convention is usually that the buyer chooses the notary.

Finding a lawyer

Aside from knowing the law of the land in question, you need a lawyer who is competent and who speaks English. So, how do you find such a paragon? Well, you should start by trying to find someone you respect and trust who has used a lawyer in that country before. Not always an easy task, but if you stretch that definition a bit to include someone you know who knows someone then you might have more success. Otherwise, use the following resources to ensure that you find someone competent and trustworthy.

International lawyer network organisations and other referral sources

The Martindale-Hubbell Lawyer Locator
`(www.martindale-hubbell.co.uk/)`

Generations of lawyers have relied on Martindale-Hubbell as the authoritative resource for information on the worldwide legal profession. With a history spanning more than 138 years, the Martindale-Hubbell Legal Network is currently in a database of over one million lawyers and law firms in 160 countries. On the left of the home page, in the horizontal menu bar headed 'Martindale-Hubbell Lawyer Locator', select the country, then the practice area ('Real Estate') followed by the firm size ('1–10'; '11–25'; '26–50'; and 'over 500'). Few developing countries will have law practices in the larger of these size bands and, in any event, for a single property transaction you ideally want a small law firm based in or close to the town in question, as they will know local circumstances best. For most countries this search will throw up a good choice of property lawyers. For Trinidad and Tobago, for example, over 100 lawyers are listed, while for Thailand the score was over 200 and for China 100. Just occasionally, you will draw a blank. Zimbabwe lists no lawyers, and such cases must be a clear signal that buying property there is not a good idea.

International Law Office (`www.internationallawoffice.com`)

Launched in February 1998, the International Law Office delivers global analysis to lawyers worldwide via e-mail, on a free subscription basis. It provides legal developments from around the world, a comprehensive directory of firms and partners, a database of the world's major deals and the legal advisers involved, as well as a global news round-up. Select ' Law Directory' from the horizontal menu bar at the top of the home page. From here you can search out lawyers by country, by work area and by languages spoken. You can also find in this database lawyers practising as notaries.

Waterlow Legal (`www.waterlowlegal.com/indexinternational.htm`)

Waterlow, established in 1844, is a professional publisher specialising in legal reference information and directories. This link is to its online directory of lawyers on a country-by-country basis. Checking out 'Egypt', for example, yielded four lawyers: one based in London, two in Cairo and a final one in Giza.

Worldwide-Tax (www.worldwide-tax.com)

This website is a very comprehensive one, dealing with a host of taxation and financial subjects for some 70 countries. From the left-hand vertical menu bar headed 'World Directories', select 'Lawyers', from which you are directed to a country-by-country list of lawyers who have usually been pre-qualified as having English-language websites and whose partners have a good command of English.

British Embassies (www.fco.gov.uk)

From this website, in the shortcut pull-down menu bar at the top of the page, headed 'Most popular sections', go to 'UK Embassies Overseas', select the country in which you are interested in buying a property and follow the threads through to the UK embassy. Once in that country's UK embassy website, select 'Services' from the left-hand menu, then you should find a heading: 'English speaking lawyers'.

The Federation of Overseas Property Developers, Agents and Consultants (www.fopdac.com)

The Federation of Overseas Property Developers, Agents and Consultants was established in 1973 to unite those agents, developers and specialist consultants active in the international property markets whose common aim is to conduct their activities in a manner which seeks to protect the interests of those who have decided to purchase or sell a property overseas. From the horizontal menu bar across the top of the page, select 'A–Z List of Members' where you will find a vertical menu bar containing a number of options one of which is 'International Lawyers and Advisors'.

CHAPTER 16

Undertaking Surveys

In this chapter:

- Understanding the value of surveys.
- Undertaking preliminary checks yourself.
- Recognising the different types of survey.
- Finding a local surveyor.

It is neither usual nor a legal requirement to have property surveys done in many overseas countries. Unlike in England, where offers subject to survey are allowed, in most countries you are expected to 'get your ducks in a row' before you 'shoot'. The vendor will expect you either to take the risk or to have the property surveyed before putting in an offer.

You may well find that the seller claims that the property has been 'surveyed' – often the case where a developer is offering properties with mortgage finance included. This 'survey' probably will have been carried out by an estate agent and will be confined to comparing the price of the property similar ones nearby. But if you have done your research thoroughly, you should know better than anyone how much comparable properties cost. The lender, however, wants to ensure that the amount you are borrowing is less than the value of the property. Any mortgage offered to you will be based largely on the results of this assessment.

In practice, this 'survey' is almost valueless, as far as the new owner is concerned. While a mortgage valuation survey should highlight any glaring catastrophes waiting to happen, you will have no comeback through it if you should have subsequent problems.

Types of survey

The term 'survey' covers a number of related – sometimes even overlapping activities. These are categories most commonly encountered when overseas properties are surveyed. What you survey will depend to some extent on what you need the survey for. If you're after complete peace of mind and want to be reasonably confident that the property is sound and no large bills are looming on the near horizon, then nothing short of a full survey will do. But if you just want to keep the bank happy for lending purposes, a simple valuation may suffice.

Full structural survey

This provides a full picture of the construction and condition of a property and is the most thorough and detailed report on the condition of a property that you can buy. It is most likely to be needed if the property is of unusual construction, dilapidated or has been extensively altered – or where a major conversion or renovation is planned.

The surveyor will check for structural problems concerning the roof, dampness, timber decay, roof spaces, walls, floors, woodworm and gutters and identify any significant structural defects and items of disrepair in a property. You should also ask them to check that the electricity and water supply will be sufficient for your needs, including extra bathrooms, a swimming pool and air-conditioning. Some developments have been set up so quickly and extensively that the water supply is insufficient for a bath, so only showers can be used in the entire resort – a fact not mentioned in any of the property details.

The surveyor's report, up to 30 pages long, will include a table of costs for rectifying the major defects and problems. It will also suggest the order in which work should be carried out and how long the works should take, in sufficient detail to allow you to put together your own budget. With this survey you will know, with a reasonable degree of certainty, how much it is going to cost over and above the asking price to make the property habitable and secure. Armed with this information, you could go back to the negotiating table and hammer away at the vendor's aspirations.

A valuation is not normally included but can be provided at a modest additional charge.

What you get from seeking the opinion of a trained professional for parting with your hard-earned cash is peace of mind. If anything later crops up that the surveyor did not spot and draw to your attention, then you can hit them with the bill for rectifying the problem. That is why they carry professional indemnity insurance.

Buyer survey

This is intended for conventional residential property that appears to be in reasonable condition. Delivered in a standard, template-based format, the report focuses on urgent and significant defects affecting the value of the property. The survey is designed to assist the prospective buyer in making an informed judgement on whether to proceed with a purchase.

Valuation survey

This is designed to provide valuations for mortgage purposes, divorce proceedings, probate (when estates have to be wound up and taxes paid) and company audits. This later case applies when a company is used to buy either the property or the land in question. Valuation surveys pay scant regard to the condition of the property. The most important consideration will be how much similar properties in the same area and broadly the same condition have sold for in the preceding 6 months. In some cases such surveys are done without even inspecting the property itself.

Doing your own pre-survey

If you are planning to see and seriously consider buying a number of properties, you are unlikely to want to go to the expense and trouble of having surveys done on every likely candidate. Unlike in the UK, where an offer to buy can be made subject to survey, in most overseas markets you are not afforded such protection. It makes good business sense, therefore, for those taking their property investment activity seriously to arm themselves with sufficient skills and knowledge to make a first appraisal themselves.

These are some things you can check for yourself and so rule in or out on any property you may be considering:

- **Roofs, joists and guttering**. Hard to see from the ground but this area can be the most expensive to remedy and until these areas are put in good order, nothing much else can be done. Look out for missing or slipped tiles, damp patches on ceilings and walls and any sign of rot in the timbers. Check that the gutters are there and functioning.
- **Floors**. Fortunately, (unlike in the UK) you will probably not encounter any carpet, so you should be able to inspect both on and below the surface of the flooring. Check the joist for rot; make sure that there is some effective form of ventilation.
- **Windows and doors**. Check for obvious signs of rot. Do they open and close easily and do the catches and locks work? Look out for signs of condensation which could mean poor ventilation, which in turn can lead to rot.
- **Electrical, gas and plumbing**. Most holiday homes have a power rating of 3.3 kW to keep costs down. But that will not be sufficient if you plan to live there full time, so you need to check the capacity of the power supply and ensure it can be increased without undue cost. Check the wiring and fuse box, which will give some idea how old the wiring is. Make sure there are sufficient plug points. Gas will almost certainly be bottled. Check that the tank is in a secure place and that a back-up valve is in place. Check out the water

supply and establish whether it is reliable and whether you have a back-up water tank. Check drainage to see if it is through a septic tank and, if so, what condition it is in.

- **Heating and air-conditioning**. How is the house heated in winter and kept cool in the summer? Wood stoves may be economical, but will you be able or bothered to keep them stocked up with wood? Also, this form of heating is impossible to have 'turned on' before you arrive, so you will always have a cold start. Will the house be cool in the summer heat? This will be a factor of which direction the main rooms are facing (towards the mid-day sun will make them harder to keep cool); whether the floors are stone flagging; and whether or not the windows have shutters.
- Check whether the **description** of the property and the **plan** correspond to the property itself. Estate agents and vendors can be less than rigorous when it comes to both measurements and descriptions, so you need to make sure that you are not being short-changed. This will also be important if you plan any changes yourself, as the planning consents will be made on the basis of the plans on file.
- **Access roads and paths**. How do you get to and from the property, who owns the right of way and who is responsible for the upkeep of them? A 500-metre drive may guarantee privacy and in the summer add a certain charm. But in the winter it may be impossible to use except with a 4-wheel drive vehicle and it may cost more than the house to keep in good order.
- **Common areas**. Are there any areas that you have to share with neighbours? In an apartment this could include lifts, gardens and swimming pools. In the country it may include garden walls, fences and paths. You need to check out their condition, see when work was last carried out, what might need to be done soon, how much any work might cost and how those costs are to be shared.
- **Swimming pool, outbuildings and gardens**. These can be a bonus or a burden, depending on their condition. If the pool is old, or does not have adequate safety features to stop people (children, in particular) stumbling into it, then you may have some big bills arriving soon.

Overseas property is sold by the square metre. A 100 sq. m apartment in a new block will include;

- 15 sq. m of common parts (stairs, corridor etc)
- 8 sq m of space occupied by walls
- 10 sq. m of balconies.

Leaving just 67 sq. m of real living space.

So a nominal price of €500 a sq. m for a 100 sq. m apartment is a real cost of €756. This is the figure you should use when comparing prices.

Figure 16.1 Vanishing space

Everything to do with swimming pools is expensive. The theory is that if you have one, you must be rich so you can afford it. Outbuildings may look charming, but if they are in disrepair and dangerous you could have a large unwanted bill on your hands just to stop them falling down. Remember: even when you are not there, gardens and pools need attention.

- **Disputes and defects**. You need to check that there are no disputes with neighbours over common ground, access and services such as water, power, telephone and drainage running across your or their property. Also, check that all equipment being left behind is in good working order, outstanding defects have been made good and details of any guarantees and warranties have been provided.
- **Size**. It is usual to sell property overseas by the square metre. But not all square metres are equally valuable. (See Figure 16.1.)

Organisations to help in finding surveyors and carrying out survey estimates

Royal Institution of Chartered Surveyors (RICS) (www.rics.org)

This is the UK's premier professional association for those involved in almost every aspect of property, other than selling it. It has 120,000 members around the world and affiliations with scores of the professional surveying associations in overseas countries. From the left-hand menu vertical menu bar headed 'Quick links', select 'Find a surveyor'. You will then be offered a pull-down country menu bar. You should be able to find at least one RICS member in

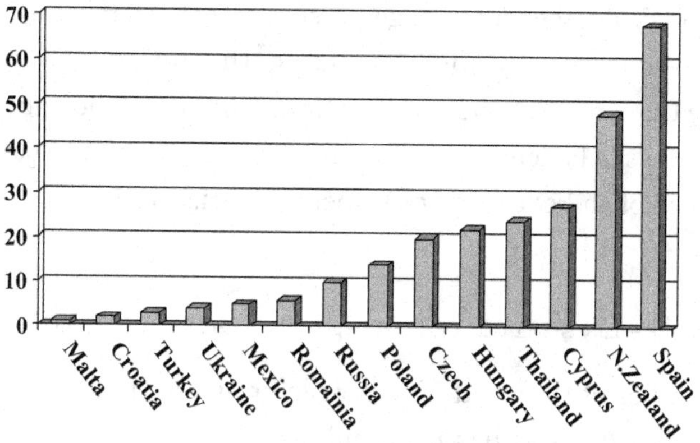

Figure 16.2 Royal Institution of Chartered Surveyors Members in various countries

most countries around the world. Figure 16.2 shows the numbers for a selection of countries.

World Association of Valuation Organisations (WAVO)
(www.wavo.org/wavo)

WAVO is the body which brings together professional property valuation organisations representing valuers and related property consultants employed in private practice, business and industry, the public sector and education, as well as some specialised groups interfacing frequently with the profession. Member country associations include API (Australia); AIC (Canada); CAS (China); HKIS (Hong Kong); KAB (Korea); ANEVAR (Romania); PFVA (Poland); SISV (Singapore); AI (United States); and RICS (United Kingdom). This is a new association, whose first conference was held in Singapore in November 2006. The members list accessed from the top horizontal menu bar was under construction at the time of writing.

The European Group of Valuers' Associations (TEGoVA)
(www.tegova.org)

TEGoVA represents the interests of qualified valuers of some 42 professional bodies from 26 countries, including such organisations as the

UK's RICS. From the home-page screen, select 'Members' to find a country-by-country directory, including the unfortunately named Degerleme Uzmanlari Dernegi (DUD) from Turkey and the impossible to pronounce Polska Federcja Stowarzyszen Rzeczoznawców Majatkowych (PFVA) (the Polish Federation of Valuers' Associations).

Kelly (www.kellysearch.com/qz-product-194000.html)

Now a member of the Reed Elsevier plc group, Kelly was established in the UK in 1799 and has been published ever since. Kelly has become synonymous with high-quality industrial product and service information and it now offers a global database of companies to users and even more opportunities to companies around the world who want to promote their services. This link takes you straight to a listing of approximately 300 property surveyors in countries around the world. You can also use the country pull-down list in the horizontal menu bar at the top of the screen, headed 'Suppliers', to narrow down your search.

The Move Channel (www.investment-property.themovechannel.com/Websites/7/Services/Property/Surveyors/World)

Founded in November 1999 by Dan Johnson, The Move Channel straddles the world with information of use to overseas property buyers. This slightly torturous web address will take you straight to 112 surveyors in countries ranging from Australia to Spain, by way of Cyprus and Italy.

Holiday Lettings UK (www.holidaylettings.co.uk/p-services/sc _ id.12.architect-surveyor-services)

Established in 1999 by Ross Elder and Andrew Firth, Holiday Lettings aims to provide holiday home owners with the means to promote their properties to the widest possible audience while also helping holidaymakers find suitable holiday destinations. Among the general services offered on the site is a modest but growing directory of overseas property surveyors, within a slightly larger section dedicated to architectural activities in general. Currently, only France, Spain, Italy and the USA are listed but countries are being added as the service extends its reach.

Bricks and Brass
(`www.bricksandbrass.co.uk/buying/survintro.htm`)

This organisation has been running since 1999, beginning as 'The London House'.

For the web visitor, its aim is to provide comprehensive information on the architecture, design and history of houses in England, Scotland, Wales and Northern Ireland. Sections cover architectural styles (classical, Gothic, Arts and Crafts, Art Nouveau etc.); external and internal features (walls, roof, windows, rooms etc.); period house maintenance; and a directory of companies offering products and services, books and events. From this link, select ' Personal Survey' from the left-hand vertical menu bar. There you will find five checklists for do-it-yourself surveys covering, general matters, exterior, interior, garden and garage. There are also useful guides on what to expect of different types of survey and how to go about choosing a surveyor.

Yellow Pages World
(`www.yellowpagesworld.com/international.htm`)

This is an international directory of online *Yellow Pages* and *White Pages* whose goal is to make it easy to find an online directory provider in the country in which you want to search. Currently, 31 countries are covered. Select the country you want, and you will be taken to a link showing the nearest equivalent the country has to a *Yellow Pages*. Usually the directory will be in English. For example, choosing 'South Africa' takes you to `www.yellowpages.co.za`. There you will see a search pane into which you can put your request. The word 'surveyor' produces a listing of 928, categorised into such groupings as 'quantity', 'land', 'building', 'marine' and so forth, as well as by province within South Africa.

Yellow.com (`www.yellow.com/international.html`)

This site is affiliated to `goClick.com`, whose business is persuading companies to list their sites in its search engine and so receive targeted traffic. The *White Pages* horizontal menu bar across the top of the home page has links to *Yellow Pages* and directories around the world. They are not always the ones you may be used to; for example, in Kenya you are directed to the website of the Nairobi Business Directory and for China the link is to `chinapages.com`. But, on the plus side, the links are usually to English-language sites and almost every country is covered. In each country you find either a sub-directory of types of organisation to choose from, or a search pane into which to put the word 'surveyor'. For the United Arab Emirates, for example, you will be taken to the website of AME Info, owned by Emap Communications. This site covers all business matters in the region, with separate listings for each country from Bahrain to Yemen. Putting 'surveyor' into the regional search pane produces links to 250 surveyors.

CHAPTER 17

Renting Before You Buy and Other Non-Ownership Options

In this chapter:

- Checking out hotels.
- Taking an apartment.
- Caring for property.
- Going in for a house exchange.
- Making sure of the fine print.

Buying a property anywhere can be a time-consuming business – and buying abroad often adds a further layer of complexity, with almost inevitable additional delays. You may not know exactly where in your chosen country you want to buy. You may even be less than certain about the country itself. Renting or finding some other way of staying in a country for a few weeks or months is one option that can help, while you gather sufficient information to make informed decisions as you look for your dream house.

Renting is not an option that is in itself free of risks and complexity. It will, almost inevitably, have tax and legal implications. In this chapter we review the pros and cons of renting in your chosen country so that you can decide whether that is the right course of action for your needs.

Reasons for trying before you buy

The most compelling reason for renting, living in a hotel or adopting any such course of action before buying is that it gives you the opportunity to truly get a 'feel' for the country and the area before you commit to purchasing a property. If, even after careful research, you find that the region, country or even the type of property you thought was right for you turned out to be less than ideal, then at least if you are in temporary rented accommodation you can move out with relatively little pain or cost. Once you have bought a property, the costs and timescales become higher and longer respectively, should you decide to change your mind.

If you take short-term rentals, or even just holidays, in the different countries on your shortlist of desirable locations, you will have the chance to compare and contrast. In that way, you can be more certain that the area in which you choose to buy will be a better long-term bet. An even better approach is to come back at different times of the year. The highly desirable country location, bustling with people in the summer, may turn into a very lonely place in winter when the visitors have gone and the restaurants and bars have shut down.

A further big advantage of living in the area temporarily while looking for a property to buy is that you will have a better chance of widening your network of contacts in the housing market. You can spread the word that you are looking for a particular type of property and, in no time, the owner of your favourite restaurant will have turned amateur broker and be taking you round the properties his friends and relatives are thinking of putting on the market.

The principal disadvantage of renting really only comes into play if you are operating in a sharply rising market or one in which there is a great scarcity of the type of property you are looking for.

You don't have to wait until you get to your chosen country to hunt out a place to rent in the short or long term. You can use any or all of the newspapers, magazines and websites you use to find a property to buy in order to find one to rent. These are described in Chapters 6 and 14.

If you think it may take you months rather than weeks to find a property to buy, then you need to think carefully about your 'creature comforts'. You don't want your first experience of living in a new country to be soured by renting an unseen place that could turn out to be a disaster. It may make more sense to take a hotel room or holiday apartment for a week or two while you look around for somewhere to rent in the longer term. Properties for rent are advertised in the local papers and in estate agents' windows. Also check out small ads in shop windows and notice boards in supermarkets, colleges and universities.

Living in a hotel

If you want to see and experience a number of different areas of a country or countries before you settle down to the serious business of buying a property, then you could always stay in a hotel. All the countries listed are awash with inexpensive places to stay for a few days, weeks or months, without having to commit yourself to renting an apartment or villa for months at a time.

At the lower end of the scale, staying in a room in a private house can cost as little as €5 a night or in a 2-star hotel with half board between €15 and €35 a night. You could knock as much as 40% off those figures for a stay of a week or over, outside the high season.

Bargain hotel breaks

There are dozens of highly efficient websites providing information and direct online booking for hotels of every category around the globe. There are also some newer search engines claiming to be even more efficient at sniffing out bargain hotel rooms, operating on the principle 'search with us – book with them'.

Websites for making efficient hotel (and travel) reservations

Lastminute.com (www.lastminute.com)

One of the few survivers of the 'DotCom' bubble, Lastminute.com has as its mission 'To become the number one European e-commerce lifestyle player by delighting our customers with great-value inspiration and solutions'. It searches 80,000 hotels, in 871 cities, in 72 countries. While that leaves a lot of countries and, for that matter, cities out of its remit, to be fair: it does include most of those that are desirable for the discerningoverseas property buyer. A quick trawl at the time of writing produced accomodation in Fiji from £25 a night, in Croatia from £40 and in New Zealand from £34. It was less successful at finding accomodation in more out of the way places such as Vietnam, which may not be high on most property searchers' list in any event.

Travelocity.com (www.travelocity.com)

Travelocity and its joint venture partners have 13 websites in major countries throughout the world, operating in 9 languages and searching 45,000 hotels at 230 chains. (One of its newer 'partners' is Lastminute.com.) Its promise is that when you book with Travelocity, 'you'll never roam alone'. On checking at the time of writing, all the usual destinations were easily covered and a search for Vietnam threw up 20 hotels, starting from $19 a night in the interestingly named 'TinTin Hotel' in Hanoi.

Expedia.com (www.expedia.com)

Founded in 1995 within Microsoft and then spun out in 1996, Expedia, Inc. first went public in 1999. In 2001, USA Networks – now InterActiveCorp led by Barry Diller – bought a controlling stake in it. Diller's company bought the remaining stake in 2002. Expedia delivers consumers everything they need for researching, planning and purchasing a whole trip. The company provides direct access to one of the broadest selections of travel products and services through its North American website, localised versions throughout Europe and extensive partnerships in Asia. Expedia comfortably passed the 'Vietnam test' applied above, yielding the 'Funky Monkey Hotel' at just $18 a night.

Kayak.com (`www.kayak.com`)

In 2003, founders of three big online travel agencies (Orbitz, Travelocity and Expedia) decided over a dinner meeting to join forces and tackle the industry's number one problem: consumers were visiting three to four websites before making a purchase because they didn't believe that any one site had all the best deals. Research also revealed that the majority of consumers who searched prices and availability online ended up booking direct with the hotel. Kayak.com, the joint business the founders set up, searches over a hundred travel sites and 105,000 hotels to provide the widest possible choice. It makes money when people click onto advertising on its website and when people click on the results from their travel partners: a revenue model similar to that of Google.

Mobisso.com (`www.mobisso.com`)

Mobissimo is the brainchild of three young entrepreneurs, including a professor of computer science at the University of Chicago who originally collaborated with the founders of Google when at Stanford. Frustrated with the quality of travel information, they believed that there should be a better way to search for travel prices and availability, so, with venture capital funding, they created Mobissimo with a philosophy encapsulated in the slogan 'We search, you travel'. It claims to search 140 hotel search engine websites.

SideStep.com (`www.sidestep.com`)

SideStep was founded in 1999 when its six original team members, holed up in an apartment in Palo Alto, California, wanted to work up the idea of creating a search engine that was fundamentally different to 'general-purpose' engines such as Google. The team aimed to tackle a single vertical market in depth, in a sector that traditional engines couldn't serve well. Travel quickly emerged as an ideal target market. The success of companies such as Expedia and Travelocity had proven that consumers would buy travel products online. Yet the information these online agencies offered was incomplete. Moreover, generic search engines such as Yahoo couldn't fill the consumer information gap, as their 'search and store' model simply didn't work for travel – an industry in which information on pricing and availability is continually changing. With $17 million in funding from Trident Capital and $2 million from private investors, the business has forged alliances with leading travel marketers including British Airways, easyJet, Hilton International and eBookers, searching multiple sites in one click. In the 'Vietnam test' while it did deliver, the rate for the lowest-cost hotel offered for the same dates was £65.

TripAdvisor (www.tripadvisor.com)

This claims to be the largest travel community in the world, with more than 5 million unbiased reviews and opinions, covering 160,000 hotels. The website allows millions of travellers to view, contribute to and edit the freshest travel 'guide books' available on more than 24,000 destinations worldwide. Its 'Hotel Popularity Index' is the first index of its kind dynamically to rank hotels worldwide, based on the popularity of a given hotel, as measured by both the quantity and quality of content written about it on TripAdvisor and across the web. This is certainly worth using before you check into an obscure hotel in an unknown country. A few comments like this (on a far from cheap Bangkok hotel) might give pause for thought: 'It's a place to rest your head, but it's not a place I'd want to spend more than a night'.

Cutting a long-term hotel deal

For the money you spend crouching by a radiator this winter, you could be keeping warm under the sun in an exotic overseas location, while searching out a house to buy. Spending anywhere between 3 weeks and 3 months in a holiday resort can be cheaper than staying at home for the coldest months of the year. Staying in a hotel may seem like an expensive option. But as you cut out all the costs of taking out a lease, putting down a deposit and sorting out telephone, heating and local rates, it may actually be cheaper than renting a villa or apartment. As winter heating bills can easily hit €300 plus per month, you could actually be saving money while researching your market.

Doing the maths shows that renting a small apartment costs €500 a month; and the rates, legal costs and other charges will come to around €200. So, 3 months in an apartment will set you back €1,700 and you still have to feed yourself after that.

Both the Thomson and Direct Holidays winter sun deals will cost less than that figure and feed you into the bargain. Plus you have none of the hassle of renting. The maths will, of course, change if there are more than one or two of you.

Organisations arranging long-term hotel stays

Biz-Stay.com (www.biz-stay.com)

This organisation provides information based on its own research, including comparison of features and amenities at extended-stay hotel chains; a weekly discount-rate survey for over 1,300 extended-stay hotels; and global first-hand suite-hotel reviews. The 'Visitor' section in each of the 1,000 or so cities around the world contained in the database gives details of where to eat, how to get around and what to see. It claims to have over 18,000 listings in 136 countries.

Direct Holidays (www.directholidays.co.uk)

This offers long-stay hotel accommodation (from 21 to 84 nights) – currently in Spain, Portugal, Cyprus and Tunisia, but these are being added to. Half-board for a couple starts at around €35 per night. It may be easier to phone them on 0870 238 7700, as searching their database for long-term accommodation is far from simple.

Thomson Direct (www.Thomson.co.uk)

On this website you can book up to 99 days in a hotel – with or without air travel. The half-board hotel deals in a 3-star hotel start at €45 per night for two people, but the rooms can squeeze another person in.

Extended Stay Hotels (www.extendedstayhotels.com)

The purpose of an extended-stay hotel is to make long-term hotel living affordable and to provide hotel accommodations that creates a home-like experience. There is more space in which to live and work, as well as amenities specifically designed with long-term business, leisure or relocation travellers in mind – two of these conveniences include a kitchen and 24-hour guest laundry facilities. Instead of simply getting a room, you have a studio suite that is larger than most typical rooms and can be more economical when compared with corporate apartments or other extended-stay options. Currently, this organisation has 680 hotels in the USA and Canada, but the concept could well be rolled out beyond that continent.

Hostelling

If you hope to see property in several countries as well as visiting a number of different locations in each country at different times of the year, you could run up a hefty accommodation bill before you actually start paying out for the property itself. That expense will be compounded if you stay a week or two in each area in order to get a good flavour of the environment and fully research the market. One way to square this circle is to stay in a hostel, where average costs can be as low as €7 a night. Hostelling, as one organising group aptly describes it, is 'travelling cheaply with an adventurous spirit'.

Decades ago, hostels offered dormitory-style accommodation with bunk beds; sharing bathroom facilities with up to 30 fellow noisy guests was the norm; and you had to be in by midnight. Today, many hostels are more like budget hotels but a whole lot cheaper. En-suite rooms; small dormitories for four or so people; bars and restaurants; 24-hour opening; self-catering kitchens; and Internet cafés are all features that have been added to the basic model. But don't expect luxury, as it is rarely either offered or required by travellers on a budget. Sometimes you will have to join an 'association' to be able to book accommodation, but mostly you can turn up or book online with no formalities. There are tens of thousands of hostels across almost every town of any size or place of particular interest almost anywhere.

Help with finding a hostel

Hostels (www.hostels.com)

Web Reservations International Ltd (WRI), a leading provider of online reservations technology to the budget youth and independent travel market, owns Hostels.com. It has one of the most comprehensive selection of hostels on the Internet, with almost 7,000 listed. It is continually developing the site to meet customer needs, particularly by enabling online confirmed reservations at a growing number of its properties. There is also comprehensive content of interest to the budget and independent traveller, including travel stories, a travel newsletter and FAQ on hostelling and backpacking. Other products available for purchase on the site include travel insurance and rail passes.

From the horizontal menu bar at the top of the screen, select 'Hostels Worldwide' where you will find links to hostels by continent and then by country. Alternatively, if you know the town or area in which you want accommodation, you can put that into a search pane.

Hostel World (www.hostelworld.com)

This organisation was founded in 1999 by Tom Kennedy and Ray Nolan, winners of the Ernst & Young Emerging Entrepreneur of the Year Award. The company employs 70 people and has offices in Dublin, Ireland; Sydney, Australia and San Mateo, California. It prides itself on connecting customers with hostels for the lowest commission levels in the industry. Select 'Hostels' from the horizontal menu bar across the top of the page. There you will find, on a single page, a full listing of countries served, continent by continent. There is comprehensive coverage of most countries. For example, Argentina has 60 towns with hostels listed, some with several individual hostels. Also listed are a handful of smaller hotels, some campsites, guesthouses and apartments.

Hostelling International (HI) (www.hihostels.com)

This is a membership organisation; members receive benefits in addition to staying in HI hostels. Ideally, you should join before you leave home. Non-members may stay at hostels if they purchase an international membership on arrival at the hostel or pay a small supplement. Applying for membership directs you to the home page of your country's national association: for England, this is the Youth Hostel Association. The fee you pay depends on where you join.

Renting an apartment or house

You may believe that a property is unfurnished just because there are no beds, linen or crockery there. In many countries, 'unfurnished' can mean 'completely naked' – literally, bare walls and a door or two. Such niceties as light fittings, a cooker or a fridge may well be missing. 'Furnished' apartments, on the other hand, can come complete with every conceivable luxury (such as a dish-washer or a fridge with water and juice coolers) – in short, everything designed to give tourists a great holiday.

The local English-language magazines (see Chapter 14) are a good place to start looking for an apartment. Prices can vary from as little as €150 a month in developing countries (for somewhere with reasonable sanitation and to a standard above that generally acceptable to the local population) to the stratospheric prices in London, Tokyo and New York.

Help with finding apartments and houses to rent

Apartments2book (www.apartments2book.com)

Martyn Lawson, who cut his teeth owning and managing his own central London property consisting of 73 serviced apartments, runs this organisation. He now has on his books apartments in Australia, Canada, the USA, Dubai, Singapore and most major European cities.

CasaSwop (www.casaswap.com)

This is a free international housing network, where you can rent, sublet and swap accommodation with others from all over the world. You can find a place to stay, get a room-mate and exchange your own room, apartment or house. Also, you can sublet your own property. CasaSwap was launched in 2004 by some Danish students after they had experienced considerable difficulty in finding somewhere to rent while studying abroad. It is primarily intended for young people, students and academics but anyone, including private landlords, can join. And you do have to register to be able to access the site.

Clickflatshare (www.clickflatshare.co.uk)

This offers a free service for anyone searching for or wanting to rent out a flat or share a flat or just a single room. It covers UK, Eire and much of the rest of Europe, as well as Australasia. The coverage is patchy: a dozen flats on offer in Berlin; 20 across the whole of Portugal; and just three in Tokyo. But coverage and volume look set to grow.

Relocation Apartments (www.relocationapartments.com)

Relocation Apartments was formed in 1997 to provide a quick and easy way to find apartments for rent and relocation/moving companies anywhere in the world. The site has expanded rapidly over the years and now claims to have the largest apartment database on the Internet, with nearly 100 countries covered. A quick check at the time of writing showed 30 apartments in Thailand, 15 in China and 12 in Hungary.

Slow Travel (www.slowtrav.com)

This is an online community and a resource for finding longer-term holiday rentals. They are not travel agents but offer a message board where 'Slow Travellers' exchange information. The site has information on villas, houses, cottages, apartments and farms, in the countryside, in villages or in cities throughout Europe, North America and, increasingly, other parts of the globe, which you can rent by the week. They are not hotels or B&Bs, but properties with kitchens that let you live comfortably for a longer stay.

Sublet (www.sublet.com)

This is an international rental marketplace where tenants and landlords match their housing needs. On the site you can find: apartments for rent; room-mates sought; subleases; and houses for rent directly from owners, cutting out agencies. Leases for periods from one day to one decade are on offer, either furnished or unfurnished, with pets and without pets and at every price range. A quick check at the time of writing showed over 70 apartments to rent in Mexico, six in Croatia and six in Russia.

Holiday Rentals on the Web (www.holidayrentalontheweb.com)

This is the site of a Costa del Sol rental organisation offering long-term accommodation too. This link (www.holidayrentalontheweb.com/long-rental.asp) takes you to its long-term section, which at present covers only Spain.

Unique Home Stays (www.uniquehomestays.com/long-lets.asp)

Run by Sarah Stanley from her base in Cornwall, Unique Home Stays has a selection of superior private houses (including castles, priories, rectories, windmills, water mills, townhouses, coastal homes and luxury cottages) to rent in the long term. It operates in 14 countries, including the UK, the USA, Spain, South Africa, Portugal, New Zealand, Italy, India, Greece, Germany and France.

House sitting

House sitting involves the home-owner arranging for someone (perhaps you?) to live in their home while they are away. In exchange for free accommodation, the house sitter will perform specified duties to care for the home, garden, pool and pets. The home-owner gets the benefits of having an occupied (and hence safer) home. Also, the consistent maintenance of lawns, gardens and pools keeps a valuable asset in top condition. You would get free accommodation while you search for your home, for little more effort than you would have had to make in any case had you been in a house of your own.

The home-owner will expect you to:

- Accept total responsibility for caring for their home, pets, gardens and pool areas.
- Maintain the same standard of care for their home and pets as you would for your own. To this end, they will need to satisfy themselves as to your suitability.

- Take all reasonable steps to ensure the safety and security of their home, premises and contents at all times.
- Carry out some or all of these tasks: gardening; lawn-mowing; rubbish disposal; pool maintenance; forwarding mail, faxes and important documents; and pet care (including vet visits and necessary medications).

You will usually be expected to pay for the utilities (electricity, gas, phone etc.) during your stay. Other recurring bills (such as local or property taxes) usually remain the responsibility of the owner.

House sitting organisations offer various levels of service to put you in contact with property owners looking for house sitters. They are subscription-based services, so take care to establish that they have clients in the country in which you are interested before you sign up and commit any money. The fees are usually fairly modest – up to €100 being the norm.

Organisations arranging house sitting

House Sit Worldwide (www.housesitworld.com)

This claims to have had successful sitters from South Africa to Scotland, Canada to Australia, New Zealand to England, Germany to the USA, Brazil to Belgium and many in between. Its website has Italian, Spanish, French and German versions as well as the English one.

House Carers (www.housecarers.com)

In the 'Guide' section, accessed from the top horizontal menu bar, you can find out all you ever wanted to know about house sitting, and perhaps a bit more. There were 232 house-sitting assignments on offer at the time this section was researched, in countries such as Ireland, Australia, the USA, Italy, New Zealand, Spain and the Dominican Republic, lasting between 5 days and 6 months.

Caretaker (www.caretaker.org)

This organisation has been operating since 1983 and fills over 1,000 house-sitting assignments each year around the world. At the time of writing, it was advertising for a couple or single person enthusiastic about life in the jungle to look after a property in Hawaii; a naturalist for Belize; and adventurous retirees for Mexico, Costa Rica and Jamaica.

Swapping homes

The idea of home exchange holidays was developed in the 1950s when Dutch and Swiss teachers began to exchange homes during the long summer holidays, although an American firm (Intervac) lays claim to starting the idea as a business in 1953. The Internet has given the concept an enormous boost and now you can find literally hundreds of businesses in the field. Today, there are an estimated 100,000 house swaps a year worldwide: a figure that is growing exponentially.

Home exchanges generally operate as membership clubs run by agencies with a network of properties around the world. Some, such as Intervac, have staff in over 30 countries who can assist you over the telephone, in person or online.

Each member submits a brief description and photograph of their house, and usually a line on where they would like to visit and when. There is no limit to the length of stay but in practice it is usually anything from a few weeks to several months, but some listings are for a year or more. The details are then placed on a website which non-members are free to view, but cannot contact.

Rather like a dating agency, the success of these schemes is based on having a very large database of people with homes to swap and who want to do so. In theory, by charging a membership fee (usually somewhere between €50 and €100), only reasonably serious people sign up, so there should be few time-wasters. Most house swappers are fairly flexible about where they end up. A month in your UK home may be just as acceptable as a similar period for a home-owner in Cyprus or Malta, whereas you might find fewer takers from, say, Ukraine or Croatia, where there may be visa restrictions on inward travel to the UK. Having a single end destination in mind probably means you will need to join several networks to be sure of finding a suitable range of properties from which to chose.

Once you have found a suitable partner with whom to exchange houses, you should follow up with e-mails or phone calls and sufficient information for both sides feel to feel happy. When both are ready, they need to exchange a formal signed agreement, usually on a standard form which will be supplied by the agency Domestic bills are usually paid on a reciprocal basis (though this needs to be confirmed in writing), as is insurance cover. You will have to inform your household insurers but generally they accept that a home is at less risk of burglary when occupied and so will not charge extra. You are unlikely to want to swap cars, as motor insurance is a very personal matter, but this too is a possibility in the house swap arena.

Organisations arranging house swapping

Dialanexchange (www.dialanexchange.com)

Dialan exchange is an independent exchange company working for the individual timeshare and holiday property owner. It started in Australia in 1995, extending to Europe in 1999, when a business was opened in the UK.

It operates a 'bank' of weeks for properties. Members deposit weeks into the 'bank' that they do not wish to use themselves. In return, they receive a 'credit', valid for 3 years from the date of deposit, which can be used to 'withdraw' any week out of the system, on payment of the exchange fee. These withdrawn weeks can be used for members' own holidays or given to family and friends. The majority of members are owners of timeshare apartments. However, the owners of managed holiday properties (cottages, gîtes, villas, condos, townhouses and apartments) can now benefit from the same exchange service that has been available to timeshare owners for many years.

Intervac (www.intervac.co.uk)

This organisation arranges house swaps in Austria, Australia, Barbados, Canada, the Caribbean, Finland, France, Greece, Iceland, Italy, Morocco, Spain, Sweden, Switzerland, the UK, the US and a host of other less usual destinations. Founded in 1953, this is one of the 'granddaddies' of the industry.

Exchange Homes (www.exchangehomes.com)

This is currently offering a beach house in California; an apartment in Paris or London; a villa in Italy; a cattle ranch in the Colorado Rockies; and family homes in Australia or New Zealand. It also includes yacht swaps, either for other yachts or for homes.

Swap House (www.swaphouse.org/eng)

This site claims to have 5,000 members and currently has house swaps in the following continents: Africa (62); Asia (46); Caribbean and Central America (45); Europe (3,281); North America (578); Oceania (384); and South America (46).

Legal and paperwork issues involved in using other people's properties

What ever arrangements you are making, when it come to staying in someone else's property in the longer term, you will need to consider a couple of factors that don't come into play when staying in a hotel or, for that matter, when buying a property. However, neither of these is an insurmountable hurdle and both could even be considered a 'dummy run' in the event of your going into the property-renting business at a later stage.

Checking the agreement

You will find guidelines and standared agreements for these transactions on the websites of the organisations listed in the relevant sections above. For private properties, the rental agreements vary from country to country but for the most part are standardised legal documents. If there is anything you are uncertain about in the contract, have it checked out by a lawyer before signing it.

The contract should contain:

- The landlord's and tenant's names, addresses and other contact details.
- A description of the property, including an inventory of contents.
- The contract term, stating start and finish dates.
- The amount of rent, payment terms and if, when and how the rent can be increased.
- Details of who is responsible for local taxes and utility bills.
- Any other legal provisions that the parties agree, such as subletting, access etc.
- The rental contract can usually be rescinded by the landlord if the tenant:
  - Fails to pay the rent or deposit.
  - Sublets without the landlord's consent.
  - Causes damage to the property.
  - Alters the property in any way without the landlord's consent.
  - Causes serious nuisance to the neighbours.
- The tenant can usually rescind the rental contract when the landlord:
  - Fails to keep the property in a habitable condition.
  - Fails to repair or remedy defects.
  - Does anything that makes it difficult for the tenant to 'enjoy' the property (that is, use all the normal facilities).

Taking the inventory

Whether swapping, sitting or renting in or out, it is important that you take a full inventory, noting the condition of key items. The renter will be expected to put up a deposit as a guarantee against damages, so it is in both the landlord's and the tenant's interest to ensure that these matters are dealt with comprehensively. Have the inventory signed and dated by both parties and keep it safely, along with the rental contract.

Taking the inventory is part of the usual services provided by the estate agent handling the property. They will make a small charge for the work (usually around €40–€60) both on moving in and on moving out.

A suggested form for an inventory is shown in Table 17.1.

Table 17.1 Form of inventory

	Inventory		
	Tenant's name(s) ________________		
	Property address. ________________		
Item	Condition on arrival	Condition on departure	Cost of repair or replacement
Linen			
Cutlery			
Furniture			
Etc etc			
	Inventory taken on move IN on ______ at ______		
	Signed by ______ (Tenant) and ______ (Landlord)		
	Inventory taken on move OUT on ______ at ______		
	Signed by ______ (Tenant) and ______ (Landlord)		

Organisations helping with inventory matters

Lawpack (`www.lawpack.co.uk`)

This company sells downloadable inventory templates.

Macleod-Lorway. (www.macleod-lorway.com/inventory.htm)

This is an insurance company which, among other useful property tips, has a free inventory template on its website.

Safeco (www.safeco.com)

This is an American general insurance company, with an extensive range of useful information on protecting your personal assets on the website. This link in the 'Consumer Tips' section (www.safeco.com/safeco/for_you_or_your_family/consumer_Tips/pdfs/home_inventory.pdf) will allow you to download a 20-page inventory template with supporting guidance notes.

CHAPTER 18

Climate Matters

In this chapter:

- Seeing the effect of weather on cash flow and profits.
- Checking out the climate.
- Exploring the coastal atmosphere.
- Finding the facts on winter snow.

At one level, the climate in a country or a specific location is an interesting by-product of geography. However, for most overseas property buyers, particularly those from the UK and other countries with fairly middle-of-the-road weather, climate is the single biggest attraction in making a purchase decision. By 'middle-of-the-road' is meant a climate that is neither particularly and reliably warm and sunny in the summer months nor cold and snowy in the winter. Those two features (reliable sun and snow) are what make a country attractive to live in – if you like beach life and ski-ing, that is. But, more important than the benefit to owners is the attraction to holidaymakers. It is important to keep in mind that what ultimately drives property prices is the certainly of a particular rental yield. The more money a potential buyer can see coming their way from renting out a property (whether or not they actually want to take on tenants), the more they will be prepared to pay. (The other main rental market is incoming business people, arriving from more developed counties – an aspect covered in Chapter 6.)

Climate and its effect on rental income and capital value

Figure 18.1 shows the effect of climate on rental yields in two broadly similar developing countries in Europe. On Odessa's Black Sea coast, you can rely on only 12 weeks of weather hot and sunny enough to command good prospects of attracting holidaymakers. Croatia's coast, in contrast, has a further 8 weeks of summer season, making 20 in all. To keep the maths simple, let's assume that the weekly rental is the same (which was true at the time of writing); that you could buy similar properties for €100,000 (which was not true, but more on that in the next paragraph); and that neither property could be rented to tourists out of the summer season (broadly true at the time of writing). This means that the rental yields (before expenses and tax) are 4.2% and 7% respectively. That makes the Croatian property the more attractive proposition, from an investment perspective.

However, Croatia's coastal property is more expensive at present than property on Ukraine's Black Sea coast. But to be sure of having equally attractive investment returns, just how much more could you pay for the Croatian property? Were you to pay €200,000 in Croatia, the rental yield would drop to 3.5% (7,000/200,000 x 100) which is lower than the 4.2% obtainable in Odessa. In fact, as the yield in

12 ωεεκσ at €350
=€4,200

Town / Country	Jan	Feb	Mar	Apr	May	Jun	Jul	Aug	Sep	Oct	Nov
Odessa, Ukrainian Black Sea Coast											
Average Temperature (Centigrade)	-1	0	3	10	15	20	23	21	16	11	5
Average Rainy Days	6	5	8	8	8	6	5	5	6	5	8
Zadar on Croatian Dalamation Coast											
Average Temperature (Centigrade)	7	7	11	13	19	23	25	25	20	17	12
Average Rainy Days	4	3	3	3	2	1	2	0	2	3	5

20 weeks at €350
=€7,000

Source: www.climate-zone.com

Figure 18.1 Great climate equals great cash flow

Croatia as a direct result of having a longer summer season is 66.67% higher than in Odessa (4.2% versus 7%), an investor can afford to pay that much more for a similar property there. So an investor could pay a price of €166,670 for a property in Croatia that could be bought in Odessa for €100,000 and still have an equally attractive investment.

The same calculation can be made for ski resorts and indeed any area in which weather plays an important part in its attractiveness or otherwise. Even some cities are not immune from the influence of weather on their attractiveness. For example, some Polish cities have extensive rainy periods in the summer and autumn, as well as plenty of cold snowy days in winter, without that being mitigated by having somewhere to ski near at hand. An important factor to keep in mind is that even if the sun and snow are not primary considerations for you as a buyer, when you come to sell up the same rules may not apply. It is near certain that the market for buyers will be bigger and better if you get the climate equation right.

Finding the facts about the sun, snow and general weather conditions

It is unlikely that anyone involved in selling a property will have done more than the most cursory amount of work on establishing the real climate conditions near any location you plan to buy in. But there is no reason why you should remain in ignorance. The following are the organisations providing the most reliable factual information concerning snowfall, rain, temperature and daily hours of sunshine. The information is kept up to date each year, so you see only the latest facts as measured by meteorological stations.

Sources of information on general weather conditions

Climate Zone (www.climate-zone.com)

Based in part on information in the *CIA Fact Book*, this website contains details of the average temperature, rainfall and snowfall for every country in the world, on a city-by-city and/or regional basis.

The information is displayed in tabulated form based on the latest 8–10 years of historical weather readings. The data is shown month by month throughout the year, and temperatures can be displayed either in Fahrenheit or in Centigrade.

There is also a general summary of the climate for each country as well as basic data on the geography and terrain and links to weather-related readings.

CNN Weather (`www.cnn.com/WEATHER`)

This is among the world's leaders in online news and information delivery. Staffed 24 hours a day, 7 days a week, it is based in CNN's world headquarters in Atlanta, Georgia, and in bureaus worldwide. Its global team of almost 4,000 news professionals keeps the latest information on its website.

From the vertical menu bar in the centre of this page, select 'Find Weather Around the World'. From there you are invited to select a continent, then a country and finally a city within that country where you will find a 5-day weather forecast.

BBC Weather (`www.bbc.co.uk/weather/world`)

The information here is broadly similar to that obtainable from CNN. One useful additional feature on this site is the regional weather map, selected from the menu boxes in the centre of the page (East Europe; Central Europe etc.). There you can see a current overview of weather conditions across a thousand miles or so of neighbouring terrain. Useful if you are looking for somewhere nearby with better weather than you are expecting.

World Metrological Organisation (`www.worldweather.org`)

This site contains the official weather observations, weather forecasts and climate information as supplied by National Meteorological &

Hydrological Services (NMHSs) worldwide. The NMHSs make official weather observations in their respective countries and from this site you will find links to their official weather service sites and tourism boards/organisations are also provided whenever available. Weather icons are shown alongside the text, to make the information more accessible. At the time of writing, 113 members were supplying official weather forecasts for 1,112 cities.

Alongside the latest weather forecast for each city are the average daily temperature and rainfall, month by month throughout the year.

Researching beaches and surf

While knowing the temperature, hours of sunshine and average rainfall is useful, for some people only being well informed about the state of the surf is enough to be certain that a beach is worth visiting. The condition of the beach as rated by international agencies such as Blue Flag (see below) is helpful but not sufficient to guarantee full enjoyment – for that, you need to know the average wave height and the likelihood of running into sharks or the similarly unappealing Portuguese Man-of-War.

Websites for tracking beach and surf conditions

Surf Line (www.surfline.com)

Surf Line has compiled close to half a million words and 1,500 images and video clips, organised so that content is easy to get at. Its goal is to 'pin you to your chair at the same time that we inspire you to get out of it'. On this site you can get a precise reading on what the waves are doing at nearly 100 surf spots around the globe, from Hawaii to Peru, by way of Newquay (Cornwall) and Zarautz (Spain). Each page features detailed tide charts, wind data, water temperatures and whatever additional information is needed to describe exactly what the surf and conditions are like right now, as well as a forecast 5 days out.

Bugbog (www.bugbog.com)

Bugbog, so the founders of this eclectic website claim, is an abbreviation of the last words of King George V who, while dying, heard one of his Ministers attempting to encourage him by saying 'Cheer up, your Majesty, you'll soon be at Bognor again'.

The King groaned 'Bugger Bognor!' and promptly died. Bugbog is an independent, impartial travel advice website run by a group of experienced world travellers whose watchwords are: 'download speed, clarity, simplicity and utility – with a hint of humour to ease the techno-pain'. It is primarily designed as a destination-finder and travel resource to help potential holidaymakers quickly and efficiently choose the best worldwide holiday spot according to their needs and holiday date.

Wanderlust magazine Travel Awards ranked Bugbog 6th out of 500 travel websites in a satisfaction league table. (Lonely Planet was first.)

From the horizontal menu bar across the top of the page, select 'Beaches', on the extreme right. There you will find detailed information on everything about every beach worthy of the title 'best'. The country links direct you to the most useful directory for that area. So, searching for the best beaches in the UK, for example, will take you to the Good Beach site (www.goodbeachguide.co.uk) where you can find detailed information on 1,200 beaches.

Information on the beaches around the world stretches to warnings on such factors as:

- **Winds**: High winds can make the water murky with drifting sand, so making snorkelling difficult. It will also cause choppy seas, making fishing trips or any other small boat travel unpleasant. Windsurfing or sailing may be impractical, unless you are very experienced.
- **Clouds**: Unvarying clouds reduce sunbathing prospects and even make photos look drab.
- **Humidity**: In areas where the humidity is excessive, places without air-conditioning will be damp and dank.

- **Dangers**: Warnings are given on such dangers as jellyfish, Irukandji, Portuguese Men-of-War and sharks and what to do to protect yourself or how to deal with an attack.
- **Skin cancer**: Signposts the places where the danger is greatest and provides tips on how to protect yourself.

Blue Flag (`www.blueflag.org`)

The Blue Flag is an exclusive eco-label awarded to over 3,100 beaches and marinas in 36 countries across Europe, South Africa, Morocco, New Zealand, Canada and the Caribbean. The Blue Flag Programme is owned and run by the independent non-profit organisation Foundation for Environmental Education (FEE): a non-governmental organisation consisting of national member organisations representing 44 countries. The Blue Flag works towards sustainable development at beaches and marinas through strict criteria dealing with water quality; environmental education and information; environmental management; safety; and other services.

From the left-hand vertical menu bar, select 'Blue Flag Beaches and Marinas'. Here you will find a table showing how many Blue Flag-rated beaches each country has, ranging from Estonia, Poland and Iceland (with 2 each) to Greece and Spain (with over 400). The stark differences between some countries that are sometimes considered to be broadly similar in attractiveness can be seen in their relative beach ratings. For example, Bulgaria has just 6 Blue Flag beaches while Romania has 8 on a much shorter coastline. Montenegro has 15 and Croatia a staggering 103, with 19 marinas thrown in for good measure.

On the right-hand side of this screen is a list of countries covered in the scheme. Selecting a country takes you to a map with the beaches indicated by blue half-circles. Click on that to be taken to an individual listing of beaches and marinas in each country and from there you can find information on each beach, including pictures.

Marinas.com (www.marinas.com)

This claims to be the world's most extensive marine website. It list s709 marinas in France, 266 in Spain, 691 in Italy and 15 in Guadeloupe and has information on marinas in over 80 other countries at this link (http://marinas.com/search/). The basic data is free, including low-altitude, high-resolution aerial photographs of marinas and an interactive mapping database showing key inlets, harbours, bridges, restaurants and marina facilities. There is a link to each marina's office so that you can reserve a berth. There is certainly enough information to establish whether or not the general sailing conditions would merit buying a property in the area.

Scuba Travel (www.scubatravel.co.uk/topdiveslong.html)

This site provides information on dive sites and centres around the world, as well as personal views written from experience. This link is to its listing of the world's 100 best dive sites.

Evaluating ski resources

Having a good reliable snowfall is obviously a pre-requisite for ski-ing, but on its own it is not sufficient information. The facilities at the resort – in terms of ski runs, gondolas, lifts, hire facilities, hotels and restaurants – all contribute to making an area a desirable resort. Building new ski facilities is one of the world's fastest-growing activities. The countries of Eastern Europe are upgrading resorts to international standards at the rate of two per year. It is now possible to ski in India, Turkey, Japan, China and Turkistan, among many new ski destinations.

Organisations and publications informing on ski-ing matters

Go Ski (www.goski.com)

GoSki is a member of the RSN Web Network, RSN being a US national television network specialising in creating and distributing outdoor content for premier holiday resorts. This site provides coverage of over

2,000 ski resorts in 58 countries from Algeria to Tajikistan, including over 800 resorts in the USA. From the top horizontal menu bar, select either 'US Resorts' or 'Global Resorts', to be taken to a listing of either individual US resorts or a country-by-country web link. For example, investigating Uzbekistan will reveal Baldersoi ('a fun mountain with a steep 500' vertical above tree-line rope tow and a rickety 2100' vertical double chair') as the country's only ski resort. There is information on costs ('you pay by the ride, about €1 for the chair and 50 cents for the rope tow, though some days all skiers can negotiate a set price for unlimited rides') and on dangers ('Stray to the left and there are armed soldiers guarding a hotel (with a good bar for Uzbekistan) and too far to the right and you'll end up in a creek'). The site also has information on restaurants, hotels and access and a 3-day weather forecast.

Skimaps (`www.skimaps.com`)

Skimaps.com is the largest collection of ski maps and ski area data on the web. Online since the mid-1990s, it is owned by the Tristar Media Group which in turn is the licensee of Skimaps.com from the University of Maryland through its office of Technology Commercialization (www.otc.umd.edu).

Select 'Ski maps' from the horizontal menu bar across the to of the page to be taken to a state-by-state listing for the US and country listing for the rest of the world. Once on the country page, there is a list of ski resorts from which you will be directed to a ski run guide and other resort information on height, number of runs, lifts and gondolas. The results are a little patchy, but omissions are compensated for to some extent by a healthy correspondence from users giving links to more current maps and general ski information.

Ski Club of Great Britain (`www.skiclub.co.uk`)

This is the UK biggest ski club. Its 30,000 members get information of ski resorts worldwide, reports on tour companies and discounts on holidays and equipment. For the property buyer, perhaps the most useful information is contained in the Historical Snow Reports where you find out the average weekly snow depths from the last 13 ski seasons. You need to register on the site (free) in order to access this data. Information is presented in an easy-to-interpret chart where you can see at a glance how many weeks of skiing is likely at each resort, at upper, lower and (where appropriate) intermediate slopes. Follow this thread (www.skiclub.co.uk>reports>historical) then select your resort.

ABC of Skiing (`www.abc-of-skiing.com`)

This is a website provided by MaxLifestyle.net, a fast network of life-style and lifestyle improvement websites. It aims to cover the complete scope of lifestyle, ranging from extreme sports (such as snowboarding, sking and rock climbing) to hobbies and games (such as golf, tennis and fishing) and even personal development subjects (such as meditation and yoga). The ski site covers an extensive range of subjects about the sport, including; techniques, disciplines and the necessary pieces of gear and equipment. There is an information section; a news desk; gear and equipment shop; holidays and travel services portal; and a ski and snowboarding community. On the home page you can select a region from a map towards the bottom of the page and from there go to a country and resort destination map.

OECD Report Climate Change in the European Alps: Adapting Winter Tourism and Natural Hazards Management (`www.oecd.org`)

This report reviews the likely effect of global warming on European ski resorts. In summary, seasons will be shorter and more artificial snow will be needed (pushing prices of ski passes up sharply) and there will be greater pressure on other world ski-ing areas. To find a free summary of the report, enter its title in the search pane.

PART 4

Settling In

Both in concluding your negotiations to buy a property and when settling into a country, you may, unless you are yourself a speaker of the local language, come face to face with a major problem: how to communicate with the various parties of importance to your new life. While you may or may not decide to learn the language, there remain a myriad of tasks to undertake in order to make life comfortable and profitable. You will certainly have to find out about how to build up local networks, perhaps to improve your understanding of medical provision, schooling, local transport systems and more prosaic matters such as how to find the best places to shop, and how to steer clear of dangerous areas. Speaking – or at least having an appreciation of the basics of – the language will certainly smooth your path in these areas, as it will if you become involved in any building work such as renovations or adding a swimming pool or hot tub.

You will also need to consider whether to ship your furniture and fixtures out or to start again with new items. There are pros and cons to both strategies and in practice most people buying property overseas end up adopting a mixture of both . There are significant cost implications in furnishing a property and in moving fixtures and fittings around the world and these will have an immediate impact on both cash flow and the profitability of any property venture.

Perhaps the most important area for investors is to establish your options for renting out your properties at home and overseas. Mistakes in finding the wrong tenants, misunderstanding the costs involved (and hence the profits) and failing to keep good records are among the most common reasons for those new to buying property overseas to be disappointed in their investments.

CHAPTER 19

Language Matters

In this chapter:

- Appreciating the importance of language.
- Finding translators and interpreters.
- Figuring out the costs.
- Working out ways to learn the language.

There are basically two options when it comes to dealing with a foreign language. You either learn it yourself or you hire in expertise to help with the critical areas. In fact, unless you are fluent you should always get someone to translate crucial documents concerning property matters such as purchase, improvement or renting out.

Engaging a translator

All the people you will enlist into your team are in their own way 'professionals' and all have their own language, supplemented liberally with the jargon of their trade. As if this isn't hard enough to handle, all this communication (every part of which could be conveying vital information that could influence your decisions) is being conducted in a foreign language. In vast swathes of the world, especially in developing countries and even in the rural areas of developed countries, you are unlikely to find a notary or lawyer who speaks sufficient English to explain very much of the buying process to you. There are important matters concerning such matters as inheritance on which you will almost certainly want advice, so, without a common language, you will miss out on some vital advice.

Translating conversations

Estate agents can help if they speak good English, but they are hardly a source of unbiased advice nor are they necessarily very knowledgeable when it comes to law. Even in cases where a notary does speak good English, it is almost certain that they will know little or nothing of the international dimensions of the transaction, for example on matters such as UK taxation.

Even if you or your partner speak the language, you may not feel up to handling multiple conversations going on simultaneously, as will undoubtedly happen when you come to signing the deeds. By this stage there should be quite a crowd of you in the notary's office. Aside from the notary and their clerk, yourself and perhaps a partner, there will be: the vendor and perhaps their partner; your lawyer; the estate agent; and perhaps someone from your mortgage provider. You should insist on a translator being present so that you know exactly what you are getting into and are confident that you are not straying into a minefield.

Deciphering documents

Documents such as your surveyor's reports (if you use a local surveyor); the contracts; the building certificates; the planning consents; and the property registration documents all need translating. Your lawyer may be able and prepared to summarise in a letter the areas that he or she thinks are important, or even have translated any areas of potential concern. But unless your lawyer or the person on whom they rely for translation is reasonably competent in the technical aspects of surveying or building work, much vital information can be lost.

The translation industry is unusual in that its customers, by definition, can't understand the product they are buying. This can make you think of language as simply a commodity which anyone with a command of the language can handle. However, the quality of the resulting translation is just as much a function of the translator's familiarity with the subject-matter being translated and their level of experience as it is of their language skills.

To produce a good translation, the translator must be able to understand the document thoroughly, not just produce a verbatim copy. So, how can you be sure you are getting a suitable translator? Start by looking for formal qualifications such a Diploma in Translation (Dip.Trans.) issued by the Institute of Linguists. Then look for the translator's relevant experience, and membership of a professional body. This will give you some comfort as to their skills and the assurance that they carry professional indemnity insurance if things go wrong.

Translating and interpreting are different skill sets: The best way to remember the difference is that translators work with written words while interpreters work with spoken words. Translators translate documents, web pages, e-mails and other correspondence and usually work alone, at their own pace. Interpreters work with other people and always under time pressure. Just because someone is fluent in Spanish and a good interpreter won't necessarily make him or her a great translator of legal documents, for example.

Translators can only work with the material they have been given. If the original Spanish document is poorly drafted, badly structured and perhaps even erroneous, there is nothing that translating it will do to make it better.

Assessing the costs of translations

Translating documents will cost anything between €100 and €200 per thousand words, depending on such factors as the complexity of the work and where the work has to be done. Fortunately, most translation work does not involve travel, so expect usually to be paying the lower end of those figures.

London Translations Ltd (www.london-translations.co.uk) has a useful online 'quick quote' service. This will give you an estimate of the cost of translating any document and an idea of when it will be ready.

Interpreters will charge out at between €500 and €800 per day, plus VAT and travel and subsistence expenses. Taking someone out from the UK could prove an expensive option. Alternatives are to hire an interpreter in the local country, where rates may be significantly lower and travel costs should be minimal. Another alternative is to use a telephone translation service. This works by setting up a conference call using a telephone with a loudspeaker at an agreed time. This service costs around €75 per hour.

Organisations for help and advice with translations

These organisations can provide you with someone to translate technical documents or provide a translator for crucial meetings

Association of Translation Companies (ATC) (www.atc.org.uk)

The ATC claims to be one of oldest professional groups representing the interests of translation companies in the world. It is dedicated not only to representing the interests of translation companies, but also to serving the needs of translation purchasers. Founded in 1976, it vets members before admission and all are required to carry full professional indemnity insurance cover to safeguard the interests of the translation purchaser. There is a members directory on its website as well as a quotation request form, or you can call its Languageline on: + 44 (0)20 7930 2200.

To access the membership list, select 'Members List' from the horizontal pull-down menu at the top of the screen entitled 'Members' Details'.

Association of International Conference Interpreters (AIIC) (www.aiic.net)

AIIC is the only worldwide association for conference interpreters. Founded in 1953, it has on its books more than 2,695 professional conference interpreters in over 80 countries who it claims can work in any language, anywhere. Its members work outside the conference field, in any area where language and languages are at the heart of an international communication. This web link (www.aiic.net/hire) will take you directly to the Directory of AIIC Consultant Interpreters where you can select the region where your transaction will take place.

The Institute of Linguists (www.iol.org.uk)

The Chartered Institute of Linguists serves the interests of professional linguists throughout the world and acts as a language assessment and accredited awarding body. Founded in 1910, it now has around 6,500 Fellows, Members and Associate Members. It aims to:

- Promote the learning and use of modern languages.
- Improve the status of all professional linguists.
- Establish and maintain high standards of work.
- Serve the interests of all linguists.
- Ensure professional standards among language practitioners through its Code of Conduct.

There is a directory of members which can be accessed from the left-hand vertical menu bar by selecting 'Find a Linguist'. From here you will be offered three directory choices: 'Interpreter', 'Translator' or 'Language Tutor'. Once in a directory, you will be asked to refine your search further before being offered potential candidates. For example, when seeking to find an interpreter you are asked to answer the following questions before executing the search:

1. Specify the type of interpreting you require.
2. Specify which languages you wish to interpret between.
3. Specify which industry type or category your interpretation involves, or leave blank to find a general interpreter.
4. Specify the location in which you would like the interpreter to be based.

Institute of Translation & Interpreting (www.iti.org.uk)

The Institute of Translation & Interpreting was founded in 1986 as an independent professional association of practising translators and interpreters in the United Kingdom. It is now one of the primary sources of information on these services to government, industry, the media and the general public. Its aim is promoting the highest standards in the profession. From the left-hand vertical menu bar, select 'Directory' where you can find three categories of members: freelance translators; freelance interpreters; and corporate members (companies providing these services). Select the category you need and follow the instructions. Your search will generate a list of qualified linguists matching your selection criteria. The more closely you define your criteria in terms of languages required, geographic location and subject, the more likely you are to find the right candidate for the task.

Learning the language

In some countries (Malaysia, Malta, the Carribean and Cyprus, for example, and in much of Africa), English is widely spoken. But in most of the other countries, few people outside the cities and main tourist areas speak much English. From buying your property, where being able to negotiate (or at least follow a discussion) is an added advantage, through to making new friends (where you will find your relationships limited to other expats if your don't), learning even the basics of the language of your chosen country will prove rewarding.

Some parts of the world have other dominant languages knowledge of which may be as useful as learning the local language itself. In Eastern Europe, some 300 million people in 18 countries (including Ukraine, Belarus, Poland, the Czech Republic, Bulgaria, Serbia and, of course, Russia itself) all have languages similar to Russian. Indeed, many of the citizens of these countries speak Russian as their second language. French is widely spoken in the parts of Africa which don't speak English; Morocco; Algeria; Equatorial Guinea; Haiti; the Québec province of Canada; and Egypt) and it is even used extensively in two areas in the USA (Louisiana and New England). But of course there is no real substitute for a local language and until you have a reasonable command of that, you will be restricted as to how far you can integrate into a country, for either social or business reasons.

Language teaching organisations and associations

There are plenty of colleges and other institutions, both public and private, offering foreign-language tuition. No one institution in the UK (or elsewhere, for that matter) offers tuition or teaching resources and aids in all languages. The teaching comes in a variety of formats, ranging from classroom-based programmes through to various forms of distance learning such as audio and video discs, books, online tutorials and telephone conversation practice sessions. These programmes are rarely cheap: a 1-week crash course may cost around €2,500 and a total immersion week costs €3,800. You may strike lucky and find a local college offering the language in which you are interested, in which case the costs will be around a tenth of these figures, though the teaching materials and support are unlikely to be of a similar standard.

Organisations and websites to help with learning languages

Grant and Cutler (www.grantandcutler.com)

Established in 1936 and now claims to be the largest foreign-language bookseller in the UK, stocking more than 55,000 books, DVDs, CDs, cassettes and software packages in more than 150 languages. It specialises in the major Western European languages and Russian, but prides itself on covering all living languages, from Afrikaans to Zulu. It has a useful pull-down search menu on the right of the screen, from which you can search all the material available in any given language. Once on a country page, you will be offered five further subdivisions of learning material: 'Courses'; 'Grammars'; 'Phrasebooks'; 'Dictionaries'; and 'Literature & fiction'.

Inlingua (www.inlingua-cheltenham.co.uk)

Inlingua Cheltenham opened in 1990 and is a member of Inlingua International (founded in 1968), the largest association of privately owned language centres in the world. Around 300 centres in more than 22 countries share both the name and the teaching materials and methods. It has a range of over 30 languages on offer, as well as an online assessment centre where your level of a ability can be gauged so that you can start your learning from the appropriate level.

Cactus Language (www.cactuslanguage.com)

Offers a range of languages from Arabic to Turkish at all levels and for all purposes – business and leisure. It offers evening and daytime courses and incorporates holidays and family-based learning into its programmes.

Association of Language Travel Organisations (ALTO) (www.altonet.org)

ALTO was established in 1998, under the auspices of FIYTO, the Federation of International Youth Travel Organisations. It has grown into an association of buyers and sellers of language travel programmes and national language travel associations, with 183 member organisations in over 40 countries. Its mission is to encourage 'in-country' learning of foreign languages among people throughout the world. From the vertical menu bar on the left of the home screen, select 'List of members'. From there you can choose a country and the type of organisation in which you are interested, e.g. agents, schools, associations or suppliers of teaching materials.

How to Learn Any Language
(http://how-to-learn-any-language.com)

Francois Micheloud, a Swiss entrepreneur, started this quirky website. Here you will get an introduction to all the languages and links to various learning resources. This site is made for people who love languages, is totally independent and is based on Miceloud's personal experiences with languages and on the site's discussion forum.

Transparent Language (www.transparent.com)

This organisation provides language-learning teaching materials for over 100 languages, available direct from its website and through Amazon. Self-study programmes start from as little as £8 for a basic book up to £200 or so for a complete set of CDs or DVDs.

Language Learning (www.language-learning.net)
and Language Course (www.languagecourse.net)

From the online databases of these two organisations you can find 10,000 language schools covering 88 languages in 115 countries, searchable by up to 80 criteria including length of course; location; accommodation; age group; and the additional leisure, cultural and social activities on offer. All offer a range of classes at various hours of the day and evening, catering for absolute beginners upwards.

The most popular courses run for 20 hours a week (for between 1 and 4 weeks), at a cost of around €100–€300 per week.

Foreign language dictionaries

These websites (www.yourdictionary.com; www.foreignword.com, www.word2word.com; and www.englishpage.com) provide links to thousands of online foreign dictionaries as well as information on books, videos, CDs, DVDs and language-translation software.

Translation software

Translation Experts (www.tranexp.com) and Systran Soft (www.systransoft.com) offer translation software which can be used for e-mails, letters and websites. Between them, these companies offer translation software in 36 language pairs. Lingvosoft (www.lingvosoft.com) has a range of dictionaries and translation packages covering the countries of Central and Eastern Europe which can be downloaded onto a PDA (personal digital assistant). Babel Fish (http://babelfish.altavista.com), powered by Systran's software, is a free basic translation package with 30 pairs of languages for translation online.

Using the immersion technique

You can pick up quite a smattering of a new language just by listening, watching and reading. TV programmes in foreign countries, though universally disappointing for anyone not mad about football or old American soaps, are a great way to soak up vocabulary and pronunciation. Children, in particular – just by watching cartoons – can pick up most of the 200 or so words needed for a basic grasp of any new language. For the first 6 months abroad, don't ration your TV viewing. Watch anything and everything, and let the kids watch too. You will be amazed at how much of a language oozes into your subconsciousness almost effortlessly.

You can listen to radio stations as you drive on viewing trips. The weather forecasts and traffic reports are particularly rewarding to listen to as you can quickly find out if you really understand what you are hearing. Many of the headline stories in the press abroad cover much the same world events as elsewhere so while you are reading, you will have at least a basic idea of what is being covered.

It is unlikely that you will become expert in a language by immersion alone. You need to reinforce your learning with a language course such as those described above, or by taking private lessons. You can take private lessons both in the UK before you go and once you get abroad. This is an expensive option unless you can find someone who wants to do a language exchange: you give your teacher English lessons or just conversation practice and they teach you their language. The same local papers you will be reading in your hunt for a property will probably carry advertisements for language tutors (see Chapter 14). Also, the local town hall will have a number of people on file worth contacting; or search for adverts in local newspapers and on notice boards in shopping centres, supermarkets and language colleges. Anyone else you come across who has learned the language recently may know a good teacher. Expect to pay up to around €10 an hour for private lessons.

You don't have to wait until you get to a country to start immersing yourself in the language. The websites listed in Chapter 24 will connect you with radio and TV stations anywhere in the world.

CHAPTER 20

Getting Around the Country

In this chapter:

- Finding out about the rules of the road.
- Taking public surface transport.
- Checking out metros.
- Tracking down sea routes.
- Pursuing flying options.

While getting to and from the country where your overseas property is located is indubitably a key factor in evaluating desirability, it is equally important to consider how you and others will travel around the country once there. The effectiveness of internal travel will be important considerations both for tourists who want to get around and see the sights and for businesses locating in the country who want access to a wide labour pool and to be able to move their products and supplies around.

Some countries have a good range of internal travel methods. France and, to a lesser extent, Germany are well covered by air travel, coaches and motorways as well as having fast train services. The TGV, for example, connects Paris, in the north of France, to Marseilles on the Mediterranean coast, covering the 500 miles in just over 3 hours at a cost of around £60. Travelling the same distance in the UK, for example going from London to Aberdeen, would take 8 hours and cost over £100.

Even less-developed countries can have an extensive internal travel network, though it is often based almost exclusively on buses and planes of dubious quality. At the micro level, particularly in cities, the availability and prospects of good connecting transport, such as subway systems, trams and express road links, are all factors favouring one location over another, in terms of rental prospects and the potential for increases in capital values.

Driving yourself

The rules of the road vary significantly from country to country, as do the conditions of the roads themselves and the approach taken by drivers. Spaniards, Italians and most South Americans tend to drive as though the entire country is one big race track but, in fact, speed limits do exist, though they are routinely ignored. In parts of Eastern Europe, Bulgaria and Albania, for example, late at night there is at least a sporting chance that if a 'policeman' stops you while driving, you are being car-napped (at worst) or perhaps just being robbed. Even when stationary, 'driving' can be a confusing business; parking your car facing oncoming traffic is illegal in some countries, while the direction is irrelevant in most.

Roads in most developing and Third World countries are generally narrow, badly lit, frequently under repair (especially in the summer months), and often also used by pedestrians and animals, which all contributes to making driving, especially after dark, a hazardous affair. It is salutary to note that 3,000 people die each day on the world's roads – 85% of them in developing countries.

Alcohol consumption, frequently a contributing factor in accidents, is effectively prohibited in many countries: For example, Polish law restricts blood-alcohol levels to below 0.05. Penalties for drunk driving include a fine and probation or imprisonment for up to 2 years. Even those drivers involved in accidents can expect severe penalties and in accidents causing injury or death, the penalty can be imprisonment from 6 months up to 8 years.

Local driving regulations and road conditions – helpful organisations

The Back Packers Ultimate Guide (www.bug.co.uk)

This website supports Tim Uden's BUG Travel Publishing venture, whose guidebook series covering Australia, New Zealand, Europe and shortly the rest of the world focuses solely on the needs of the backpacking traveller. Budget travel is what these guides are all about. 'No flash hotels and fancy banquets – just the most comprehensive information on backpackers' hostels and enjoying your trip without blowing the budget' is the publisher's claim. The site has a colossal amount of invaluable information for the international traveller.

From the home page you are presented with a map of the world from which to select a destination. Under each continental zone is a vertical menu bar with these options: 'Essentials', 'Transport', 'Destinations', 'Hostel Reviews' and 'Forums'. All are worthy of exploration, but start with 'Transport'. Within this, you will find 'Air Travel', 'Bus Travel', Train Travel' and 'Car Travel'. Within 'Car Travel' you will find information on speed limits, road conditions, fuel, toll charges and any other matters of concern to drivers. In Turkey, for example, it is useful to know that a sign reading 'Park Yapilmaz' means no parking and in Australia you should watch out for road trains (50-metre-long semi-trailers) if you're driving in the outback. There will also be links to the local motoring association's website, where more detailed information can be obtained.

US Department of State (www.state.gov)

This web link (http://usembassy.state.gov) takes you directly to the State Department's directory of US Embassies abroad. Select the embassy of the country you are interested in exploring. From the horizontal menu bar across the top of the page, select 'US Citizens Services' then from the vertical menu bar on the left of the page, click on 'Country Information Sheet'. In the section headed 'Traffic System and Road Conditions' you will find all you need to know in order to be legal when driving – or alternatively to stay off the road, if that is what prudence dictates. In the Côte d'Ivoire the US Embassy includes a warning about carjacking, among many others. The embassy's advice is: don't resist, stay calm and give them what they want – always. It goes on to advise that it is not uncommon for carjackers to take an occupant (usually a woman or child) as hostage to ensure their safe escape; the hostage is usually released unharmed. The advice is that this is 'a very difficult situation, so use your best judgment at the time to decide your course of action'.

Fédération Internationale de L'automobile (FIA) (www.fia.com)

Founded in 1904, the FIA brings together 213 motoring associations in 125 countries, between them representing over 100 million motorists. From the horizontal drop-down menu bar at the top of the page, headed 'The FIA', select 'Member Clubs'. From there you are invited to choose a continent and then a country within that continent. From the country pages you are given the web address of the country's motoring association(s). The Automobile Association of Malaysia, Touring y Automovil Club del Peru (TACP), Macedonia's Avto-Moto Sojuz na Nakedonija (AMSM) and so forth. The motoring associations' websites contain advice on motoring in the countries and how to get help and assistance when problems arise.

Buses and taxis

Statistically, travel by bus and taxi is the next safest way to travel after flying. It is a close-run thing when comparing these modes of transport with the train, as you are dealing with differences of two or three places of decimals when comparing billions of miles travelled. But in much of the world, particularly the developing countries, travel options within a country can be severely limited. Train systems are expensive to establish and run, and where they exist they were established by the empire-building European nations a century ago, and barely maintained yet alone improved on since.

Buses of various shapes and sizes are the transport method of choice for most people in most parts of the world, where cost and convenience are major considerations. Turkey's bus network is a good example of what can be expected. While there are a dozen bus companies there, only two offer a comprehensive service covering the whole country. The major regional transport hubs are all interconnected, with regular day or night services from which you get onto smaller buses until you reach your destination in an outlying region. Tickets are sold via websites often using English; bus stations; offices around towns and cities; and travel agencies.

There is usually a service (in Turkey this is called a Dolmus) which consists of minibuses running set routes within towns and cities, and between cities and nearby towns and villages. These are very cheap– 50p or so – and plentiful. Dozens of routes are covered. They have their destination written on the front. They pack as many people in as they can, so don't expect much comfort!

You may also find within larger countries oddball bus systems worth considering if money is tight and you want to scoot around as much of the country as possible in order to get an overview before settling on a region to look at in greater detail. In Turkey, Fez (www.feztravel.com) runs such a service. Fez operates a 'hop-on, hop-off' bus, pitched at budget travellers and backpackers, with coaches covering virtually the whole country every second day in an anti-clockwise direction from Istanbul. You buy a pass that is valid from 25 April until 27 October for around £129. You can start anywhere you like around the circuit. Just let them know where you want to start your travel and they'll be there to pick you up, as long as it coincides with their schedule. Fez buses are fully air-conditioned, non-smoking, 15–46 seater coaches, with onboard PA systems and stereos. There is an English-speaking 'guide' on each coach who can fill you in on information as you go along. Booking accommodation along the way is down to you.

Taxis are, at best, a variable service in many countries, where you can easily be taken for a ride in every sense of the word. Drivers rarely speak English, or admit to doing so, and often abuse their local knowledge to maximise the distance travelled. Many set the charge clock to a higher rate for foreigners, where a clock is used at all.

Bus and taxi travel options – helpful organisations

Bus Station Net (www.busstation.net)

This guide to bus, coach, tram, trolley and transit-related links all over the world was started in 1997 by Steve Annells, from Oxfordshire, because he found it frustrating trying to find bus and transit sites through the major search engines. From this page, select the continent from the left-hand vertical menu bar, then the country. Once there, you will find links to the organisations running bus and related services in and around that country. Malaysia, for example, has 20 or so links, including a direction to NADICORP Holdings (www.nadi.com.my/transportation _ home.asp), who run 1,000 coaches using an e-ticketing system. For Vietnam, there are links to Hanoi's city bus service and a brief guide to buses throughout the country –all provided by a local enthusiast.

World Travel Guides (www.worldtravelguide.net/country)

Columbus Travel Publishing Ltd. has been producing the *World Travel Guide* book for over a quarter of a century and has published the basic data online since 1996. It has a team of 20 researchers and a worldwide network of freelance journalists and travel writers who between them produce four publications of value to overseas property buyers, though they are written primarily with tourists in mind.

From this page, select the country you are interested in and once there select 'Getting Around' from the right-hand vertical menu bar. There you will find general information on the bus services you can expect to find and the names, though rarely the web addresses, of the main bus companies. There is also quite a hefty amount of advertising on this site, often related to property matters.

Pongü's Travel Guides (www.pmgeiser.ch)

This website started out as the FAQ (Frequently Answered Questions) section of this German-based travel guide service. It now has a life of its own and, after 11 years on the web, has expanded to cover much of the world. Select a country from the list on this page. Once there, select 'Transport' from the bottom of the left-hand vertical menu bar. A further vertical menu bar will now open, offering 'Bicycle', 'Boat', 'Bus', 'Plane' and 'Train' as options. The coverage is general in nature, but does provide a flavour of the system operating in the country and offers near-ubiquitously applicable advice on being prepared against pickpockets on overcrowded buses.

Info Taxi (www.infotaxi.org)

This is an online resource for immediate information on taxi companies and taxi phone numbers worldwide. If you're planning a trip, if you're new to town or if you just need to know which taxi services are available in a particular location, you can use this directory. It currently lists 10,094 taxi services in 5,029 towns in 283 countries. Enter the city or town from the home page and you are taken to a listing of taxi service providers by name, address, phone and web link. At the bottom of the screen is a star user rating system for the various taxi services, together with comments by customers.

Holiday Taxis (www.holidaytaxis.com)

Paul Stanyer, who previously held senior management positions with some of the large UK tour operators, including Inspirations and, most recently, Thomas Cook, set up Holiday Taxis in 2002. Its goal is to meet the burgeoning demand for customers to be able quickly and effectively to book taxis from overseas airports to their hotels, timeshares or private accommodation. From the home screen you are offered 46 destination countries. Once a country is chosen, you are offered a choice of the country's main airports, then a selection of hotels, resorts or just 'city centre' as your final destination. This would certainly be a useful way of keeping out of the clutches of 'inspection trip' operators or for an initial settling-down trip to a country.

Urban mass transport (subway, underground, urban rail and tram networks)

Almost nothing makes a city more attractive to live in (either as a tourist or as a resident) or makes property more desirable and profitable as an investment than if it has an excellent and inexpensive transport system. London, New York, Paris, Tokyo, Madrid and Moscow all have excellent subway systems, as do Santiago in Chile, Mumbai and Delhi in India, Cairo in Egypt and Hong Kong in China, albeit to a rather lesser extent.

Finding out about the urban mass transport system for any country in which you plan to live or buy property would certainly be prudent; as would tracking what plans are in place to introduce, extend or improve such systems.

Urban mass transport systems – helpful organisations

UrbanRail.Net (www.urbanrail.net)

This site was initiated and is maintained by Robert Schwandl, an Austrian who, in his own words, is 'a mere metro fan not related in any way to any metro operating company or the rail industry'. Although he has done the biggest part in setting it up through the years since 1995 when the project was initiated, this site would not be possible without the help of hundreds of often anonymous helpers all around the world who contribute in many different ways: by sending the latest information from their city, providing photographs, correcting inevitable mistakes, suggesting new details and advising on developments.

The definition of what Schwandl understands by 'urban transport' – and consequently what information is on the site – is: 1. an urban electric mass rail transport system (i.e. one primarily used to move within the city); 2. totally independent from other traffic, rail or street traffic; 3. high-frequency service (maximum interval approximately 10 minutes during normal daytime service).

The site has details on urban transport in over 250 cities around the world. From the home page, select first the continent you are interested in, then select the city (either from the map at the top of the screen or from the alphabetical city list below the map). At the bottom of the screen, for each continent there is a section headed 'Metro or metro-tram networks planned or under construction'. Looking at Serbia, for example, you will see that the following significant activities are underway whichcould have an important bearing on property prices (and desirability) in Belgrade (Beograd), the capital of Serbia.

1. Line 1 – Centralna (2008) – will link Novi Beograd on the left bank of the Sava river to the city centre and the eastern suburbs. Planned stations are: Tvornièka Ulica – Stari Merkator – Opština Novi Beograd [Line 3] – Palata Federacije – Šest Kaplara (near Hyatt Hotel) [Sava] – Saborna Crkva – Trg Republike – Trg Nikole Pašiæa – Pravni Fakultet (Law School) [Line 2] – Vukov Spomenik [Beovoz] – Deram – Cvetkova Mehana – Kluz – Ustanièka Ulica.
2. The system called BELAM (Beograd Laki Metro) will be carried out by Yuginus and the Spanish company Ineco. Construction started in 2006and is due for completion in 2012.

For serious subway buffs, Schwandl has a link at the bottom of the page to his own online bookshop site where you can find a selection of books, including *Metro Maps of the World* and *World Metro Systems* – useful if you want an easy-access overview of the world as a prelude to choosing a country in which to buy investment property.

World Travel Guides (`www.worldtravelguide.net/country`)

Columbus Travel Publishing Ltd has been producing the *World Travel Guide* book for over a quarter of a century and has published the basic data online since 1996. From this page, in the 'Quick Jump' vertical menu bar on the top right of the screen, select the country and city in which you are interested. Once at the city page, select 'Getting around' from the long vertical menu bar on the right-hand side of the screen. There you will see detailed information on transport in the city: how it operates; how much tickets cost; how to buy them; how to get maps of the transport system; and what penalties are in force for travelling without a ticket. The entry for Barcelona, for example, includes this information: 'Apart from during the rush hour (0730–0930 and 1800–2030), when it becomes very crowded, the metro (M) is the most efficient means of transport in the city. Metro lines are all identified by a number and a colour – the direction is shown by the name of the line terminus. A single ticket (billet senzill) costs €1.10 and must be validated in a machine on the platform before boarding and carried at all times to avoid the €40 penalty.'

Urban Transport Fact Book (`www.publicpurpose.com`)

This site is sponsored by The Public Purpose as an experimental e-mail discussion list on the subject of transport policy around the world. There is a 'single' rule (according to the site's moderator): 'ad hominem (personal) attacks and questioning of the motives of participants is not permitted'. That this constitutes two rules seems to have escaped the author's notice. Wendell Cox Consultancy, established in 1985 and specialising in international public policy, demographics, economics and transport, is the sponsor behind the *Fact Book*. Its stated aim is

'To facilitate the ideal of government as the servant of the people by identifying and implementing strategies to achieve public purposes at a cost that is no higher than necessary'. There are valuable links, on a country-by-country basis, to papers and government proposals on urban transport; these may provide valuable clues as to future developments. For example, you can find discussion papers on plans to extend the Congestion Charge areas in London and the statistics for usage and government subsidies for the Tokyo Metro and Monorails. Both these papers contain facts that may directly affect property values in the areas concerned.

Boats and helicopter travel

In some countries, what are considered to be alternative or even merely leisure methods of transport are important contributors to the economy in so far as they facilitate more effective movement of goods and people, often commuters. Monitoring and tracking such services, rather as with the presence of an efficient mass urban transport system, can give early warning of potential property price movements as well as helping newcomers to 'enjoy' more fully their life in a new country overseas.

The most common of these alternative transport methods are: by boat (using inland waterways, rivers, lakes and canals); and by helicopter (usually over short sea crossings connecting far-flung parts of a country, and so integrating them with the main transport infrastructure). Examples include the river transport in New York, London, Paris and Stockholm; and the helicopter service linking Gozo (which has no international travel connection) with Malta (which has); and, similarly, the Scilly Isles with Penzance.

Sea and helicopter travel – helpful organisations

World Canals (`www.worldcanals.com`)

This website is the output of the Inland Waterways International (IWI), an organisation established in 1994 to bring together establishments, groups and individuals who share an interest in and feel a duty of care for inland waterways wherever they exist and whatever their present condition. IWI aims to increase understanding of the importance of inland waterways for commercial, leisure and historical value, and to encourage their greater use and appreciation. From the home page, first select a language, then click on 'Waterway Networks Worldwide' from the left-hand vertical menu. There you are invited to select a continent and then a country. Once on the country page, you will see an overview of the current inland waterway system, plans for future development and links to the country's main bodies overseeing that system. Selecting 'Russia', for example, reveals how surprisingly important internal water transport is to connecting up this sprawling giant land mass. The navigable waterways in the European part alone of the Russian Federation cover a total of 72,000 km, of which 18,000 km are canals or canalised rivers and 10,000 km are channels in natural lakes. This network provides routes across the continent linking five seas: the Baltic Sea; the White Sea; the Caspian Sea; the Sea of Azov; and the Black Sea.

PIANC (`www.pianc-aipcn.org`)

'Navigation, Ports and Waterways' is PIANC's strapline. This organisation was founded in 1885 and is the oldest international association concerned with the technical aspects of navigation. It is a worldwide, non-political and non-profit technical and scientific organisation of national governments, corporations and private individuals. Its objective is to promote both inland and maritime navigation by fostering progress in the planning, design, construction, improvement, maintenance and operation of inland and maritime waterways and ports and of coastal areas for general use in industrialised and industrialising countries. From the bottom of the home page, select 'Sailing Ahead' to receive a free copy of the association's newsletter and so kept informed on new developments in the field.

World Travel Guides (`www.worldtravelguide.net/country`)

Columbus Travel Publishing Ltd has been producing the *World Travel Guide* book for over a quarter of a century and has published the basic data online since 1996. From this page, in the 'Quick Jump' vertical menu bar on the top-right of the screen, select the country and city in which you are interested. Once at the city page, select 'Getting around' from the long vertical menu bar on the right-hand side of the screen. There you will find a section headed 'Getting Around by Water'. Selecting 'Thailand' will reveal that, depending on the season, there are up to 1,600 km (1,000 miles) of navigable inland waterway. Services operate between Thanon Tok and Nonthaburi, using long-tailed motorboats and taxi-boat ferries. Strong competition on all of the major routes ensures that fares are kept low. Services also operate along the east coast, the Andaman coast and the Gulf coast.

Helicopter Association International (HAI) (`www.rotor.com`)

Regarded throughout the world as the voice of the helicopter industry, the HAI, founded in 1948, is a not-for-profit, professional trade association of 1,450-plus member organisations in more than 68 countries. Primarily, it is a membership organisation with services directly benefiting its operations and advancing the civil helicopter industry by 'providing programs that enhance safety, encourage professionalism and promote the unique contributions made by helicopters to society'. From the drop-down menu under the heading 'Homepage', select 'Search'. Enter 'Heliport Database Search' into the search pane. That will take you to the web link for the Helicopter Association International's Heliport Directory on-line which provides heliport information on all permanent approved helicopter landing facilities. The database includes information on all Stolport, heliport, airport, balloonport, gliderport, seaplane base or ultralight airport facilities in the United States, Puerto Rico and the Virgin Islands. The database is being expanded to provide world coverage. You need to register on to the site in order to access this database: however, registration is free.

CIA World Fact Book (`https://www.cia.gov/cia/publications/factbook/fields/2019.html`)

This is the master site for all the facts gleaned by the CIA on every country in the world: a veritable goldmine of information. This link will take you directly to a country-by-country listing of the world's 2,021 heliports. Once on the country page, scroll down to the 'Transportation' section where you will find heliports listed just below the 'Airports with unpaved runways'.

Internal airlines

Poland and Romania have two internal airlines covering most cities and regions; Turkey even has a budget airline on the internal routes. Ukraine's internal airline is effective, except in the savage winter months when the service can become too unreliable and travellers have to fall back on a fairly primitive rail network. But Cyprus, Slovenia and Hungary have, as yet, no internal air travel and getting around can be torturously slow, as in many African and Asian countries.

The Federal Aviation Authority states that 'there currently is no evidence in accident data that would support the ranking of individual airlines based on their safety records. While there may be apparent differences in carrier safety records at any particular time, due largely to the infrequent but catastrophic nature of an air accident, there is no evidence that such distinctions persist nor that they are predictive of future safety performance. Rankings of airlines based on past accident records therefore provide no information to consumers seeking to make safety-enhancing comparisons for current or future travel choices'. I'm not sure what comfort that gives when you see that certain African, Russian and Chinese airlines have an accident every year or so, while others go for 30 to 40 years without incident. If you don't share the FAA's view of air safety, you can find out about the reliability and safety of local airlines using the sources provided below, as well as checking out the routes and airline choices.

Internal air travel - helpful organisations

SkyScanner (www.skyscanner.net)

This is one of the few search engines allowing you to search for cheap flights within a country as opposed to between countries. Just register the country in question in both the 'From' and 'To' pull-down menus, from which you will find the list of internal airport routes.

See also other low-cost airline route websites in Chapter 8: 'Keeping tabs on flying options'.

Expedia (www.expedia.co.uk)

This is one of a number of conventional travel websites covering all airlines flying within a country. See also Chapter 17: 'Websites for making efficient hotel (and travel) reservations'.

Airline Safety Records.Com (www.airline-safety-records.com)

This site allows you to compare each airline's history of accidents, incidents and near mid-air collisions and see for yourself how they measure up.

Just click on 'Five Year Average' or 'One Year Average' to compare the safety records of US airlines. Since good airlines can go bad, and bad airlines can improve, the site is regularly updated with the most accurate airline safety information available. All statistics are calculated from data provided by the FAA, the National Transportation Safety Board and the US Department of Transportation. Both the 'Five Year Average' and the 'One Year Average' are updated several times a year, to make sure that the information remains accurate and relevant.

Plane Crash Info. Com (www.planecrashinfo.com)

This site, maintained by Richard Kebabjian, contains statistical data on over 4,850 plane-related accidents. Reassuringly, Kebabjian states: 'Accidents are extremely rare, with the probability of a passenger being killed on a single flight at approximately eight million-to-one. If a passenger boarded a flight at random, once a day, everyday, it would be approximately 22,000 years before he or she would be killed'. However, China Airlines and Cubana both languish at the bottom of the accident tables in the statistics presented. You would be between 100 and 200 times more likely, statistically, to have an accident on the airline with the worst accident record than on the one with the best. Select 'Accident statistics' to find fatal accident causes by airline and 'Accident rates' for fatal accident causes by category, such as pilot error, weather, mechanical failure or sabotage.

International Air Transport Association (IATA)
(www.iata.org/ps/services/iosa/registry.htm)

IATA is the global trade organisation for the air transport industry. One option for looking at an airline's safety record could be through an interesting tool at this link on its website. Its programme called 'Operational Safety Audit' (IOSA) independently evaluates airlines, with checks on their safety records. Created in 2001, the programme has approved a total of nearly 75 airlines. In its examinations, the IATA sends aviation consultants who take a closer look at the airline's machines, management, cargo and cabin for 5 days. If the airline fails to meet the standards, it has 1 year to fix its problems. After that, if the airline has improved to a degree IATA deems acceptable, it will be publicly identified as meeting international standards; otherwise, it will be clear that it has not. By 2007, all 260 IATA members, who between them account for 94% of all air travel companies, will need to have successfully undergone the IOSA audit in order to achieve or maintain IATA membership.

Air Disaster.Com (www.airdisaster.com/statistics)

Started in 1996 as a small website dedicated to aviation safety information under the name 'The Aviation Accident Site', it was re-launched in 1998 under its new name. The tables at this link provide statistical information regarding the safety of selected aircraft types and the safety of selected airlines.

CHAPTER 21

Moving your Effects

In this chapter:

- Checking out options for moving, storing and hiring furniture.
- Getting pets into (and out of) the country.
- Moving vehicles abroad.
- Bringing in household effects.
- Transporting business assets.

In terms of sheer operational hassle, this subject is probably more time consuming and fraught with the potential for problems than any other aspect of buying property abroad. Yet, in theory at least, aside from drugs and guns, there is little that you can't take with you to your new life. In some of the countries in which it has become desirable and profitable to buy property there is already an over-supply of those two commodities. The big questions are: whether you want to take everything with you; and, if you do, what is the best way to get the move done so that you don't end up too much out of pocket or without your belongings for too long. The seemingly bureaucratic and inconsequential matter of moving effects can have the most profound effect on the profit (or loss) in any property investment. If you have a straight choice between investing more capital directly into a property which you hope will appreciate in value rather, incurring the cost of moving furniture around the world or buying new when existing equipment will do, the former option will always win hands down. Perhaps the only exception is where chattels have personal rather than intrinsic value.

Often it's the little things that cause big problems when you move. Check that you have spare bulbs for the refrigerator, as the fittings may be different. If any lamps you are bringing with you have bayonet fittings, bring spare bulbs as almost everywhere else in the world uses screw fittings. Also, you may find that the electrical supply system uses a different voltage and current and a converter is needed to make your current equipment usable. The plugs connecting your equipment may have to be replaced to fit in with local systems. Even your car may cause problems, as few countries drive on the same side of the road as the UK. Even global car brands are made differently for different markets, so getting spares may be difficult. Your furniture may not be ideal for the climate of your new country and taking it with you will make it impossible to keep and rent out your UK home – a sensible insurance policy in case your overseas investment proves unsatisfactory for any reason.

If all these factors put you off moving your own effects, don't worry too much, as there are plenty of options. Furnishing your new overseas property may be your biggest expense after the purchase cost, so you may be tempted – on economic grounds alone and leaving aside any sentimental attachments – to move your furniture with you.

Local furnishing options

You do have two other options when it comes to fitting out your new property, neither of which involves moving your own effects. Each has its own attractions and drawbacks.

- Buy a **furniture package**. If you are buying into a new development and either intend to let the property out, or think you may do so in the not too distant future, this is a good route to go down. These 'packages' include everything in terms of furniture, linen, cutlery etc. that holiday rental companies include as a must if they are to take your property onto their books. The developer you are buying from or the estate agent will be able to put you in contact with a supplier. Expect

Table 21.1 The economics of moving

Sell your house contents (which cost £20,000) for, say, £3,000.
Save on the removal costs (£6,000).
So you have £9,000 to put towards the cost of buying some new (and perhaps more appropriate) furniture abroad.

to pay from around €6,000 fully to equip a studio; and up to €12,000 for a two-bedroom apartment, including fitting out a kitchen.

- Buy **locally**. Many countries covered have their own specialised furniture-makers and a thriving second-hand market. Though you can expect to make a substantial saving over the cost of buying a furniture package, the quality and design will usually not be acceptable to renters. If you find furniture that meets your needs, however, then that's fine.

Most people use moving home as a great opportunity for a clear-out and there is certainly a case to be made for selling up everything apart from truly personal items. The maths is fairly simple:

Transporting furniture

You can find dozens of reliable firms to move your furniture from Aberdeen to Budapest or Beijing. You also have enormous flexibility as to exactly how much you take to your new home. You could go for a full load of your belongings or save some money with a part load. A part load can be quite substantial and, unless you are planning to sell up and move out permanently, this may suffice. Shipping fees are calculated in cubic metres, so taking the Aga or a giant freezer is less of a problem than you may think, even if it proves less useful than in your home country.

Moving the contents of the average family home to and from most of the countries in Europe costs between €6,000 and €12,000 (£4,150 and £8,300), depending on where exactly you are coming from and going to.

Once you start to travel between continents, the costs can escalate to double that figure, and perhaps more. Also, as neither you nor your furniture and effects can be in two places at once, you are going to have to plan to be separated from them for several days (on the most optimistic view) or several weeks (if you go down the 'part load' route or if you are shipping to the other side of the world). This will mean either camping out with friends or relatives or making arrangements to stay in the country to which you're moving. (See Chapter 17 for options on staying locally.) Use the checklist below to make sure you move only the essentials.

Table 21.2 Making your list

To begin planning your shipment, go through the following process:

1. **Go though your home and write an inventory of all the items you are thinking of taking with you.**
2. **Review the list and eliminate items which may be valuable but virtually useless in your new home.**
   - Carpets and heavy rugs, for example, are totally redundant in warmer climates.
3. **Carefully consider all bulky items on your list, determining whether they're truly worth shipping.**
   - Because you pay for shipping by the cubic metre, remove from your list items it may be cheaper simply to replace. Wardrobes and chests of drawers fit into this category, and many new properties have these items fitted as standard.
4. **Investigate thoroughly before shipping any electronics or appliances.**
   - Some items that you consider essential may turn out to be totally useless abroad. For example, British televisions operate on a system called PAL-1, while many countries in Europe are on PAL B/G. Unless you have a multi-standard television, it will not work in your new country. European washing machines are mostly cold-fill only, so check whether yours can work satisfactorily abroad before shipping it.
5. **Review your list again. If you have not cut it in half, go through the process again until you have.**

Finding a remover

The *Yellow Pages* is full of removal companies and you should also check out the property press where some of these firms advertise. (See Chapter 14.). Get at least three written quotations from reputable removal firms and make sure you are comparing like with like. That means ensuring that all quote for packing, moving, unpacking and re-assembling furniture in the right rooms, insuring and delivering to your schedule. If you would be content to use two or more of these firms, then it's time to negotiate in order to decide which one to choose. Aim to get between 5 and 10% off the quote. If you are successful, that's quite a chunk of cash saved and your decision is made for you.

The most experienced and trustworthy firms will be members of a trade association. Companies in these associations will carry bonds which give you a reasonable chance of redress if the firm fails to carry out the move on the terms agreed, or if your belongings are lost or damaged. Check that the removers' bond covers you for hotel accommodation if they fail to turn up on time with your belongings. If you are doing your own packing, check the insurance position in case of damage in transit, as the remover may not accept liability. Also, you will need to label each box or carton with the room for which it is destined. A basic floor plan will be sufficient for a competent remover to work from.

Organisations and websites to help with finding a remover

The British Association of Removers (www.removers.org.uk)

The association has been in existence since 1900. Its modern form was created in 1972 as a result of the unification of two older organisations: the National Association of Furniture Warehousemen and Removers (NAFWR) and the British Association of Overseas Furniture Removers (BAOFR).

The association's mission is 'to promote excellence in the Removals Industry for the benefit of its members and customers'. To that end, it carries out these four functions of potential benefit and reassurance to those using a member firm:

- Set professional standards for the industry by its criteria and Code of Practice.
- Provide professional training and support for the removal industry.
- Provide information and advice to removers and their customers.
- Provide a complaints and disputes resolution service.

From the horizontal menu across the top of the home page, select 'Moving with BAR', then click on 'Introduction to moving' from the left-hand vertical menu. There you will find a brief introduction to moving and a link to a more comprehensive pdf download: 'Guide to a Successful Move'. To find a UK-based removal firm, enter the postcode of the house you want to move furniture from into the search pane in the lower left of the home-page screen.

To find a removal firm based overseas, return to the 'Introduction to moving' section and select 'International associates' from that horizontal menu, then follow the on-screen instructions.

Fédération Internationale des Déménageurs Internationaux (FIDI)
(`www.fidi.com`)

Founded in 1950 to represent the interests of companies specialising in international removals, FIDI has evolved from a European to a major worldwide federation claiming to be the largest global alliance of independent, quality international removal companies. Its mission is to 'provide a forum for the advancement of integrity, quality, and mutual co-operation to those companies focused on the intercontinental movement of household effects and to carry out programs and studies designed to help promote affiliates' competitiveness within the international moving and storage marketplace'.

From the vertical menu on the left of the home page, select 'FIDI Network' which will in turn open a further vertical menu. From that, select 'Find a FIDI mover'. From the two options then offered, select 'Click here if you are a customer looking for a FIDI mover'. Then you are offered a country pull-down vertical menu. Selecting 'New Zealand' yielded seven accredited FIDI member removal firms and 'Vietnam' produced three.

The Overseas Moving Network International (OMNI)
(www.omnimoving.com)

OMNI represents 260 companies in 70 countries who are committed to providing 'the finest moving service available for its customers, through the closest possible co-operation between its members', according to its mission statement. All OMNI members work to the FAIM (FIDI Accredited International Mover) quality standard – the only international moving network to so do. FAIM is monitored and administered by Cap Gemini Ernst & Young to ensure that the top standards of service are adhered to at all times. It covers every aspect of the administration and performance of an international removal. OMNI companies are encouraged to achieve the standard of FAIMISO which combines the FAIM standard with ISO9000 accreditation.

All OMNI members will provide:

- Comprehensive international moving service for household goods, antiques, bric-a-brac, motor vehicles, boats, caravans, etc.
- Advice on moving abroad.
- Movement of goods between third countries (i.e. between two countries other than the country in which you are resident).
- Air freight services.
- Secure storage.
- Comprehensive insurance.

From the horizontal menu on the left of the home page, select 'Locate OMNI Member' and follow the on-screen instructions. For

Argentina, two firms were listed; for India four; and for Poland one firm.

Putting furniture into storage

As a short-term measure, you could put your furniture and other effects into storage until you know whether or not you want to take them overseas. If this is just a temporary measure to plug the gap between selling up in the UK and your new home abroad being ready to move into, this could make economic sense. In that case, the company you are using for the removal will be able to advise you. It may even have storage facilities that your could negotiate into the deal.

Longer-term storage is unlikely to be effective, with the possible exception of using a company which allows you to self-pack containers. These are similar in concept to rubbish skips, where a 10' or 20' steel storage unit is delivered to your home for you to load at your leisure. Once done, give the company a call and it will collect the unit and place it in its storage centre and deliver the unit to your new home when you are ready. Expect to pay from £6 a week for 10 cubic feet if using a self-store facility, while conventional storage will cost from £32 per week for the contents of a typical four-bedroom house.

Organisations to help with putting furniture into storage

Homestore Direct (www.homestore-direct.co.uk)

This company offers what it claims to be a unique system where a 10' or 20' steel secure storage unit is delivered to your home for you to load at your leisure and then lockup. Give it a call and they will pick it up at a convenient time and the unit is not entered or opened again until eventually it's delivered to your new home, wherever it is. This reduces the possibility of damage, as your home contents are only handled twice by an outside party – at loading and offloading. Conventional removers would handle four times. Homestore will store the contents of anything from a one-bedroom flat to an eight bedroom detached house. It will even store cars.

Admiral Storage (www.admiralstorage.co.uk)

This is a family-owned business where the directors have over 20 years' experience of domestic and commercial storage and removals. It provides clean, dry and secure purpose-built storage rooms suitable for household and business storage, at a size to suit your requirements. CCTV, sophisticated alarm systems and 24-hour security monitors protect their 26 modern, heated storage centres. Space can be hired for any length of time and you only pay for the days you have used, subject to a minimum charge period of 2 weeks. You have unlimited free and easy access to your private self-storage room with your own key.

Self Storage Association United Kingdom (www.ssauk.com)

This association is the recognised trade association for this relatively new industry. It is a membership organisation including those professional companies who operate self-storage centres and the suppliers who service the industry. Through this site you can find out all about the industry and locate the centres most local or convenient to you. From the vertical menu on the left of the home page, select 'self storage' to find out more about the types of service offered in the industry. Select 'locate a store', where you will find a directory searchable by name of business or by UK postcode.

From the right-hand vertical menu you can find out more about the industry in the section headed 'Publications'. The SSAUK Mintel survey of member companies is listed here. The first of these surveys was carried out in 2005, with 89 companies (representing 70% of the self-storage industry in the UK) taking part in the research. The study certainly provides an interesting snapshot of the industry and will inform any would-be user of self- storage.

Federation of European Self -Storage Association (FEDESSA) (www.fedessa.org)

FEDESSA was formed in March 2004 to provide a European focus for the growing self -storage industry throughout Europe. Its membership is open to any European national self-storage association and its current membership includes the national associations of Belgium, Denmark, Finland, France, Germany, Italy, Sweden, Switzerland, Spain, the Netherlands, the Czech Republic and the United Kingdom.

From the horizontal menu at the top of the home page, select 'MEMBERS OF FEDESSA' where there are contact details for all country members.

Self Storage Association (SSA) (www.selfstorage.org)

The SSA, established in 1975, has 3,000 direct members and more than 3,000 members of affiliated organisations, including international self-storage associations. International members come from 17 nations, including Canada, South Africa, the Netherlands, Australia and Japan,. This document download (www.selfstorage.org/downloads/consumertips2002.pdf) is a consumer guide to using self-store. The Facility Locator (www.selfstorage.org/search.aspx) has a number of panes allowing various criteria to be entered. To find a company abroad, insert the country name in the appropriate pane. (There is no country pull-down menu, so you just have to put in a country and see if there whether anyone operates there.)

Hiring furniture

Another option is to hire furniture rather than move your own. You can hire a furniture pack through a relocation specialist. These cost about €1,500 a month for a typical four-bedroom family house. When you see the quotes for moving your furniture overseas, this may not seem such an outrageous figure. If you intend to keep your house in the UK on for a few months while you settle into life abroad then renting could also be a worthwhile option to consider. These are the advantages of hiring furniture:

- Significantly lower cost than shipping.
- No damage to your goods in transit.
- Right style of furniture for your new overseas home.
- Tax-deductible expense if you are renting out either your overseas or your home property.
- Less stressful, as packing and moving goods take time and effort Renting eliminates issues associated with customs clearances, shipping delays and breakages in transit.
- Eliminates the need for serviced apartments or hotels for corporate relocations, saving money and a second relocation.
- No waiting, as furniture can be selected and installed before your arrival.
- Electrical products will be compatible with local standards.
- TVs etc tuned for local channels.
- There is a cash flow advantage to renting rather than purchasing, as costs can be spread over months and years, rather than paying for everything up front.
- You have complete flexibility, as the length of contract and choice of products can be amended easily.
- Prompt product maintenance included, so eliminating any repair costs.

Organisations and websites to help with hiring furniture

European Relocation Association (EuRA)
(www.eura-relocation.com)

Formed in 1998, EuRA has 400 member companies operating in 65 countries, in Europe and across the globe. It is the professional body for relocation service providers across Europe and worldwide. EuRA members are specialists in every aspect of the relocation process, from visa and immigration advice; partner support programmes; and home and school searches to area and cultural orientation services and furniture provision. From the home page, select 'Members' from the horizontal menu across the top to be taken to a country list.

Roomservice Group (`www.roomservicegroup.com`)

This company specialises in designing and furnishing commercial and residential property interiors. It has been creating and delivering high-quality, practical and stylish interiors for over 20 years and its client list is testimony to the consistency of its service. It works for every size of client, from developers and builders with hundred of homes to buy-to-let landlords and one-off private commissions. It can quote for furniture hire almost anywhere.

The International Furniture Rental Association (IFRA)
(`www.ifra.org`)

IFRA is a non-profit trade organization founded in 1967 and claims to be the only industry association devoted exclusively to furniture rental and leasing. From the left of the home page, select the icon labelled 'Find a rental service supplier'. That will take you to the IFRA Furniture Rental Service Locator which will help you find furniture rental professionals who subscribe to the IFRA Code of Ethics (you can see these from a link on the website).

The directory of international furniture rental companies follows on from the list of US states.

The Association of Relocation Specialists
(`www.relocationagents.com`)

This association was formed in 1986. Select 'Home' then, from the horizontal menu at the top of this page, click on 'Specialist Providers'. There you will find links to a whole range of firms including: career consultants; cleaning services; concierge services; educational consultants; financial services; furniture rental; housing cost disparity consultants; immigration consultants; independent mortgage brokers; information services; professional vehicle sourcing; public relations consultants; removals companies; schools; settling-in services; solicitors/lawyers; structural engineers and building services; and taxation consultants.

Selecting 'furniture rental' takes you to a directory of providers.

Taking pets abroad

If the thought of leaving a pet behind, be it a 'mere' cat or dog or something more exotic such as python or lizard, it may well be possible– if a little complicated. A few things are reasonably certain. For example, if the animal is not travelling with you, it must be shipped in a container built to IATA (International Air Transport Authority) specifications which requires that it be large enough for the animal to stand up without touching the top of the box, lie down comfortably and be able to turn round. There must also be a fixed water vessel inside the container, with a means of filling it from the outside (funnel). It is sometimes possible to take your pet as excess baggage, which would mean booking direct with passenger reservations. Although this is often a cheaper option, some airlines won't take livestock and there may be restrictions such as 'standby' status, depending on the airline and the route.

The regulations concerning taking animals vary from country to country: There is no quarantine for cats and dogs entering South Africa from the UK, as long as all the paperwork is completed correctly– if not, then animals are subject to 60 days' quarantine. Thai authorities appear relaxed about quarantine, as long as the animals are clinically healthy on entry and have the correct documentation. The same is true of the USA, though entry requirements vary from state to state, with some requiring that a rabies vaccination be administered on arrival if there is no documentary proof that this has already been given.

Throughout Europe, the position with regard to moving pets from country to county has been if not simplified, at least harmonised – which is in itself something. The Pet Travel Scheme (PETS), as the EU pet import/export process is now known, allows cats and dogs and an increasing array of other animals (including rabbits, ferrets and reptiles) to visit most other EU countries and countries outside the EU (60 countries in all) and return to their home country without the pain of sitting in quarantine for 6 months. PETS in effect eliminates the need to quarantine animals to prevent the transmission of disease, particularly rabies, provided that certain conditions are met.

- **Establish a good bill of health for your pet.**
  Dogs, cats, or ferrets under 3 months of age must stay at home until the powers that be consider them old enough to travel. Check with your veterinary adviser for details for your specific situation.
  Your pet must have an official veterinary certificate dated within 4 months of travel or up to the vaccine's expiry date, whichever comes sooner. Each certificate includes the following information:
  - Identification of the owner or person responsible for the animal.
  - Description and origin of the animal.
  - Microchip or tattoo number, location, and date of insertion.
  - Information on the rabies vaccine (the vaccine type must be inactive, and must comply with the standards of the OIE (the World Organisation for Animal Health).
- **Have your pet identified with a microchip or tattoo.**
  - As of 1 October 2004, all animals in the European Union PET Passport scheme must be identified with either a tattoo or a microchip compatible with standards ISO11784 or ISO11785. Check with your vet that your identification device complies. If an animal is identified with a non-compatible microchip, you must supply the appropriate reading equipment and be prepared for a bureaucratic nightmare at customs.
- **Prepare the transporting cage or carrier for your pet's travels.**

Label the cage or carrier with your name, your address in your new country and your contact phone number or that of the representative acting for you.

To use the PETS Passport system, you need to comply strictly with the letter of the law. This is not as easy as it may sound, as that letter keeps changing. The underlying regulations have been updated and extended every year since 2000, sometimes more frequently. Countries have been added and conditions altered in line with developments in technology. For the latest information on PETS, visit the Department for Food and Rural Affairs (DEFRA) website listed below.

Getting pets home again

If you want to take your pet back to Britain, you must comply with PETS as well as the European Union regulations in order for your pet to enter the United Kingdom without going into quarantine. If you are returning from a country not included in PETS, there will be similar, but often more rigorous, rules to follow. The Animal Health Divisional Office of DEFRA (see details below) gives specific advice on how to comply and a full list of offices throughout the United Kingdom.

If you want to take your pet back and forth to the United Kingdom, the rules are a little more complicated. You need the following documents to allow your pet to re-enter Britain without quarantine:

- **A PETS re-entry certificate.** Issued by a vet in the United Kingdom, this certificate states that your pet has been fitted with a microchip which meets an ISO specification; it has been vaccinated against rabies with an approved vaccine; and it has had booster vaccinations as recommended.
- **A certificate of treatment.** This document states that the animal is free of a potentially dangerous type of tapeworm and ticks. The treatment must be carried out by a vet 48 hours before re-entering the UK and must be done each time you enter the UK.

- **A declaration of residence.** This document confirms that your pet has not been outside any of the qualifying countries in the 6 months before entering the UK. This form is available from the transport company or from DEFRA.

Organisations and websites to help with and advice on moving pets around the world

Department of Agriculture and Food (DEFRA) (www.defra.gov.uk)

DEFRA is an attempt at 'joined-up government' in that just one department has brought together the interests of farmers and the countryside; the environment and the rural economy; and the food we eat, the air we breathe and the water we drink. Select 'Pet travel scheme' from the bottom left of the horizontal menu headed 'Quick Links'. Once in this section, you can find information on the latest rules applying to the scheme.

From this section, select 'Countries, routes and transport companies', where you can find which EU countries and those outside the EU are incorporated into the scheme. Select 'Fact sheets' from the same menu, where a there are a number of downloads in pdf format, covering in more detail the regulations applying to importing and exporting pets around the world.

Passport for Pets (www.passportforpets.co.uk)

Despite the official-sounding name, this are private air-supply shipping agents with 25 years of experience. They have moved everything to nearly everywhere: dogs and cats, of course, as well as animals as small as a spider and as big as a rhinoceros. Their service covers every aspect of the move and as well as actually shipping the pet, they sort out the minefield of paperwork for you. Select 'My Destination' from the horizontal menu at the top of the screen. From the vertical menu at bottom left, select the country to which you want to move your pet, where you will find the basic facts and regulations. Also, on the horizontal menu on the home page you will find the facility to 'Request a quote'. Getting a quote requires completing a form stating the type of animal, its height, width and length; where it is coming from and going to; and when it is planned to move it.

Pet Exports (www.petexports.co.uk/countries.html)

International relocation with pets is sometimes a minefield of legislation, veterinary requirements and logistics, as Pet Exports rightly claim. They are experienced professionals and conversant with exporting domestic animals. Their aim is to provide all the necessary advice and information in order to make this seemingly complicated process as simple as possible. At this link you will find, on a single table, the basic regulations for importing and exporting pets to most of the more usual non-EU countries including Australia, Canada, the USA, Thailand, the United Arab Emirates, New Zealand and South Africa.

Taking your car abroad

If you like adventure, then driving your car to your new home makes sense. If you think like an economist, skip taking the car: You can hire cars in most countries fairly inexpensively. For example, in Malta, a car hired long term costs around £8 a day. In Bulgaria, for little more, you get a driver thrown into the deal. In Thailand, you could get a local car and a driver on hand for a year or more for less than it would cost to move a car from Europe.

Bringing a motor vehicle from and to any European country is fairly easy, though keeping it there can prove more troublesome. In the first place, if you bring in a car you generally have to get used to driving on the right-hand side of the road, except in countries such as Malta, Cyprus, Malaysia and Australia. Right-hand and left-hand drive cars are often manufactured slightly differently, so you may have difficulty with servicing and spares if you stick with your UK model. You also stand out as a target for thieves, as foreigners everywhere are seen as easy targets.

You can bring in any EU-registered vehicle into other EU member nations for a continuous period of up to 180 days without formalities. You need to be the registered keeper or have his or her written authorisation to use the vehicle. After 180 days, you must go through the formalities of importing the car – something you do from the outset in the non-EU countries. Aside from being a seriously time-consuming chore everywhere, you may be responsible for a substantial import duty in non-EU countries.

Getting your car to your chosen country can cost between a few hundred pounds and a couple of days (to travel to Croatia, for example) to perhaps £1,000 or so and a week of driving (to get to Ukraine or Turkey). You can in many cases cover part of the journey by sea, but this adds significantly to the expense (see Chapter 7).

A further consideration will be motor insurance. Although a Green Card, as insurance cover for cars being driven overseas is known, is relatively inexpensive and easy to get, it is conditional on the vehicle in question being registered and normally kept in the country in question. So you may well need to consider taking out insurance cover in your new country if you take you car with you.

Organisations offering information and advice on moving vehicles abroad

Direct Gov (`www.direct.gov.uk`)

This site, produced by the Central Office of Information, brings together the widest range of public service information and services online. It also brings together an increasing number of online government services to make life easier – from booking a driving test and taxing your car to renewing a passport or applying for a student loan. From the home page, select 'Motoring' from the options listed in the centre; then click on 'Buying and selling a vehicle' from the left-hand vertical menu headed 'Motoring'. Once in that section, select 'Importing and exporting a vehicle' either from the left-hand vertical menu or from the bottom-right options box. There you can find the current regulations concerning either permanent or temporary export of motor vehicles.

Which side of the road do they drive on?

www.brianlucas.ca/roadside/#listofcountries

This is a one-man effort by Brian Lucas, showing which side of the road is used for motoring in all countries around the world. He provides a bit of history as to how everyone ended up on the side they drive on now; the driving populations in various places; and a small piece of information on road conditions around the world.

Foreign and Commonwealth Office (FCO) (www.fco.gov.uk)

Select 'Travel advice' from the top of the left-hand vertical menu. From there, click on FAQs near the bottom of this menu. Then, select 'Travelling & Living Overseas' from the options presented and from the right-hand vertical menu click on 'Driving abroad'. There you will find information on what you need to know when driving abroad and how to apply for an International Driving Permit (IDP) if required.

General rules on importing domestic items

In brief, the regulations governing the movement of goods, chattels (such as cars) and domestic pets are covered in the above sections. Apart from importing personal effects and furniture which has demonstrably been in use; or movements carried out between counties belonging to an economic block of which the person concerned is a citizen, such as the EU, there will often be import duty to pay. This duty is in effect a tax designed to protect the industries of a particular country. The UK, for example, along with the rest of the EU, has recently placed restrictions on the import of certain clothing products from China to prevent the market from being totally flooded with cheap imports.

The items on which duty is payable and the amount of that duty vary from item to item, time to time and country to country. Guatemala levels import duty even on used household goods and personal effects, while Peru is more relaxed as long as the items arrive within 120 days of their owner taking up residence in the country. Even the way in which the goods are packed and shipped can impact on their acceptability or otherwise. On 1 February 2006, Canada, the USA and Mexico instituted the Wood Packaging Import Regulation, covering all international shipments. Any package found to have infested wood packaging materials, or lacking an ISPM No. 15 mark or a phytosanitary certificate for entry to Canada will be refused entry, whether or not signs of pests have been detected.

An organisation providing customs information on transporting personal belongings overseas

The Overseas Moving Network International (OMNI)
(www.omnimoving.com)

OMNI represents 260 companies in 70 countries involved in transporting belongings around the world. From the left-hand vertical menu, select 'Customs Information' and then choose a country from the drop-down menu to view the customs details. In each country section there are full details of what duties are in force and the rates applied. There is also information on what items are exempt from duty and the documentation needed to secure that exemption. Cars; pets; and personal effects and furniture are all covered in these explanatory notes.

General rules on importing business items

If you are setting up in business overseas and intend to bring with you, or import later, various goods for resale then a different set of regulations and duties will apply to those prevailing for personal effects.

What constitutes 'business' as distinct from personal is often a fine line. But, for example, bringing half a dozen computers, twenty dogs or five bathroom suites will undoubtedly attract attention.

Organisations providing customs information on importing (and exporting) business assets. (See also Chapter 10.)

Simpler Trade Procedures Board (SITPRO) (www.sitpro.org.uk)

SITPRO, set up in 1970, is the UK's national trade facilitation agency. It is dedicated to encouraging and helping business trade more effectively and to simplifying the international trading process. Its field is within the procedures and documentation associated with international trade.

SITPRO offers a wide range of services, including advice, briefings, publications and checklists covering various international trading practices. It manages the UK-aligned system of export documents and licenses the printers and software suppliers who sell the forms, laser and export document software.

The One-Stop Internet Shop for Business (http://europa.eu.int/business/en)

If you need advice on how to do business in the European Internal Market, import/export regulations, how to certify your product, how to find a business partner in the EU, want to know about bidding for public contracts, or simply want a source of reliable information about the European Internal Market, then this site should prove useful.

It can help with these issues and many more because it brings together data, information and advice from many sources. It is part of the European Commission's 'Dialogue with Business', a service to help you to make the best of the Internal Market.

There is also information about European business news and trade shows and other practical information. The site is in all key European languages.

The Institute of Export (www.export.org.uk)

The Institute of Export is the UK's only national professional Awarding Body offering professional qualifications in international trade and graduate membership of the Institute of Export – MIEx (Grad). Courses of study leading to the qualification are offered nationally and globally.

Over 50 institutions of further and higher education and 12 universities throughout the UK provide a network of training supported by the Institute of Export. These offer tuition for the Institute's own examinations: the Advanced Certificate in International Trade (previously the Advanced Certificate in Overseas Trade) and the Diploma in International Trade (previously the Diploma in Export Management).

The Institute runs its own distance learning home study course, and is involved in the production of interactive computer-based learning materials. Almost 2,000 registered students are currently engaged in courses of study leading to the Institute's professional qualifications. The home study course is available internationally through online delivery.

Specialised training is available to both members and non-members through the Institute's seminar training programme. A comprehensive range of trade-related publications, including a series of standard texts, published by the Institute, covering the four modules of the Advanced Certificate, is offered to members and non-members.

The Institute keeps market information on all overseas countries trading with the UK and holds an extensive collection of regulatory, statistical, marketing and contact information as electronic resources.

HM Revenue and Customs Statistics and Analysis of Trade Unit (SATU) (www.uktradeinfo.com)

This government department has developed a free database that will allow you to build your own trade statistics tables. You can access the raw data directly on the import and export of nearly every good and service around the world and download them onto Excel files so that you can manipulate the data for your own purposes.

This website contains all you need to know about importing and exporting and the systems and procedures you need to follow, from high-level introductory guidance to in-depth information on everything from Intrastat to tariff quotas. You can now access most of the necessary systems and forms online.

CHAPTER 22

Renovating and Building

In this chapter:

- Searching our renovation and building projects.
- Checking out planning and building usage.
- Preparing a renovation budget and a contract.
- Commissioning an architect.
- Working with builders.

Even once you have chosen the ideal country in which to buy a property, you could still have a further difficulty to overcome. If, after an exhaustive property search, you have failed to find any property that quite meets your requirements, you needn't completely abandon the country in question as a prospective candidate. Many people find that – either because the house itself doesn't quite meet their needs or because it lacks the sort of view they want – they have to build their own house or carry out major renovations on what is, in essence, a wreck.

It would be misleading to pretend that this is an ideal option. Carrying out large-scale building work, even in your own country, is fraught with problems and dangers. Doing so with all the attendant problems of working in a foreign language, alien currency and probably having to operate at a distance, with only periodic site visits being possible, will not be easy. Added to that, as well as the people and organisations you have to deal with just to buy the house, there is a range of other professions whose names may not be all that familiar in a foreign tongue. Even in Portuguese (a fairly benign language), while the words for electrician (*eletricista*), architect (*arquiteto*) and builder (*construtor*) are recognisable, the word for plumber (*encanador*) is not such a familiar term.

The upside of building your own house is you do get the one you want, where you want it. You'll have a stream of lessons in the foreign language in question, with a crash course in the country's customs and practices thrown in for good measure. Many countries have excellent building materials and a wide range of architects. Portugal, for example, has nearly 9,000 architects registered with their *instituto*, and competent builders abound. So you can design in what you need in your home, as well as use the best materials and workmanship, rather than simply accepting what is on offer in the ready-built market. As you will probably have discovered by the time you have spent a few weeks going round the country looking at properties, a lot of people are building new houses. The message here is that it can be done, but it will undoubtedly be a lot more work – much of it frustrating, costly and time-consuming – than simply buying a house that is available now.

Plan to have your hands full for several months, dealing with the town hall, getting planning permission, and making sure that you can obtain the necessary building licences to cover the changes or designs you have in mind. Of course, there is always the option of hiring a project manager to supervise the renovation.

Finding a building plot or ruin

The basic process of searching for a building plot or ruin is much the same as for finding a property. This is covered in Part 3. However, there are a few extra channels to market, and a few more twists and turns on the way. Many locals – often farmers or farming families – have obtained planning permissions in the past, with the intention not of building themselves but of selling the plot together with the attendant permission to someone like you. The economics are quite straightforward: a plot of land with permission to build turns redundant agricultural land and buildings from dust into gold. However, many of the people who have obtained their planning permissions in this way have added an element to their marketing strategy. By making it relatively hard for you to find them, they know you are very keen to buy. You will see building plots in the local papers – usually the *very* local papers. You will also see a few in the estate agents' windows and on Internet sites. But, for the most part, you will have to rely on local contacts, discussions with the local notary (who depends on such transactions for their livelihood) and perhaps on architects and builders who also have something to gain once a plot or ruin is sold.

There are some unscrupulous operators at work in this sector, as there are in any country. People who will sell you land which has not the slightest chance of obtaining planning permission, hoping (in desperation or in the desire to save time and money) that you will bite on the bait they dangle. If you are offered land without planning permission, the big question you have to ask – both of yourself and of the vendor is: why?

After all, surely a local has the best chance of getting that permission and, if they do, the plot will be worth double or even treble the price. That is a lot of profit for filling in a few forms and arguing a case at the town hall.

You should also treat with caution builders offering plots and the associated building work as a package deal. Package deals always consist of jumbling products and services together so that the vendor makes more money than they would had the components been sold separately. The myth used in their marketing is that the package is cheaper because it is bundled. More convenient it may be, but cheaper: never. You should always try to 'unbundle' the deal and go for separate contracts on the land or ruin and the building work itself.

Websites to search for building plots and ruins

The Move Channel

(www.themovechannel.com/property/land/default.asp)

Founded in November 1999 by Dan Johnson, The Move Channel started life as a simple guide to the buying procedures for residential property purchase in the UK, coupled with a small directory of website reviews covering property sales and rentals, again primarily in the UK. This link will take you straight to 1,684 places with building plots in 58 countries. There is a 6-acre site where a planning application has been submitted but not yet approved on offer for £42,000: it is located in Kavarna, a charming small port town which has a broad outlet on the Black Sea, near two world-class golf courses under construction, just 6 miles from an airport. Before you reach for your chequebook, you should know that Kavarna is in Afghanistan. For about the same sum you could buy a 1,000-sq m plot in Maio, located in the south of the Cape Verde archipelago. Many of the building plots advertised on this site also include calculations giving estimates of likely building costs. While these figures are hardly likely to be unbiased, they will at least be a starting point.

Escape Artist (`www.escapeartist.com/International _ Real _ Estate/Lots _ Lands/Lots _ Lands.html`)

In operation since 1995, this website aims to show you how to re-start your life abroad. It has thousands of articles, contacts, resources, links and tools for finding overseas real estate, international employment, hidden enclaves, artists' havens, unique destinations, offshore investments and the requirements for living an international lifestyle. This link takes you straight to the building plot listing, featuring such offers as beachfront land in Fortim in north-east Brazil, claimed to be 'the most privileged beach with luxury end homes, making it the number one place to invest in'. Prices here start at $10,000. A 3-acre plot in San Juan Del Sur, Nicaragua, with ocean views in a 'solar powered community' is on offer for $40,000, while 1.5 acres of land is up for $35,000 in St Louis de Kent in Canada. It is difficult to see exactly how many lots are for sale on this site, as you have to scroll page by page, with around 10 lots to the page. But, at the time of writing, there were over 100, mostly in and around North and South America, Canada and the Caribbean. There were a few plots in Greece and in more exotic places such as French Polynesia.

See also the various organisations listed in Chapters 12 and 13.

Checking for planning permission and usage licence

This is the crucial first step before you waste time and money on further exploration.

Once upon a time, in the chaotic era before globalisation inspired a stronger legislative structure around almost every international transaction – property buying included – almost every property in a developing country came with a virtual guarantee of planning permission to extend, alter or improve. Local mayors typically wanted development, and builders, lawyers, and surveyors all wanted work, so planning went through virtually 'on the nod'. Today, however, you need to be very careful if you want to carry out major renovation work, as the rules have tightened up significantly – and not just throughout Europe.

Part of this process also will involve making sure that there are no rights of way, water-pipe routes or electricity pylon structures that will cause your plans to be restricted in any material way.

Aside from the strict legal aspects of planning and usage, there are a number of aspects of the plot or ruin that might render it uneconomic to proceed with. The most obvious, particularly in country areas, is the cost of providing usable water and, to a lesser extent power, sewage facilities and telephone. There may be geographic reasons why the plot, even with planning permission, is not viable. It may be too far from a good road or on a steep slope. As not all land can hold buildings equally well, the plot may require extensive foundations to support the structure you have in mind. It is always a good idea to remember that, one day, you may want to sell this property on, so it has to be both appealing and economically viable to someone who might not be quite so enamoured with it as you are.

Coastal areas, agricultural land and anywhere of potential strategic interest (such land on a border with a neighbouring country) will almost invariably be problematic. Take legal advice from the outset. (See Chapter 15 Finding a Lawyer.)

Preparing a rough costing for building work

Before spending a lot of time on a prospective project, you need to be able to arrive at a rough costing yourself. If you decide to go ahead, your architect and/or builder will produce a more accurate costing which you should have drawn up into a contract.

If you are buying a building plot, the initial outlay will have to come from your own pocket. For a wreck in need of near total renovation, you may persuade a bank to provide some fairly modest mortgage funding but don't budget on getting much more than between a third and a half of your initial outlay. Then you will have the cost of carrying out the building work to consider. This can be almost anywhere between €100 per square metre in a developing country and €1,600 per square metre in popular coastal areas, depending, naturally, on the quality of the materials you choose.

Interior fittings come in an extremely wide range of prices, so to arrive at a realistic budget you need to decide on an overall quality standard that you are aiming for. A sensible approach is to look at the selling price of a new house, broadly similar to the one you plan to build (e.g. three bedrooms (one en-suite); swimming pool; 1-acre garden, in a similar location (e.g. within walking distance of shops); sea view; 30-minutes from an airport). Take that price (say, €250,000) and deduct the cost of the land you are buying (say, €50,000). That leaves you €200,000 to cover all aspects of the building work, including fitting out the house, design work and the legal costs including conveyancing.

Another approach to costing is to assess the hours and materials required to carry out such work as is needed and then apply the prices prevailing in the country in question. For example, if it requires 100 hours to build a bathroom, then in the UK, at £20 per hour this will cost £2,000; whereas in India, at £2 per hour, it will cost £200 – for the labour element, at any rate.

Websites that can help you estimate rough building works cost

What Price (www.whatprice.co.uk)

Founded in 2000 by Alastair Taylor, a graduate engineer from Cambridge University, and Dr Jonathan Pearson, who has a PhD in physics. This is a slightly quirky site, but it has some useful information on the cost of building works in the UK. From the horizontal menu across the top of the page, select the 'Prices' pull-down bar and then click on 'Buildings'. There you can find prices for various repairs, including walls, roofs, electrical and plumbing. If you deflate these prices by the wages prevailing in the country in which you are carrying out house repair work, you can arrive at a very approximate costing. So, in Bulgaria, for example, if average incomes are £3,000 compared with £21,000 in the UK, then a job costing £7,000 in the UK should cost around £1,000 in Bulgaria.

Estek Ltd (www.estek.co.uk)

Estek is a UK-based limited company, formed in 1995, whose vision has always been to develop high-quality estimating solutions for the construction and allied industries, offering effective tools for those at the 'sharp end' of pricing work. Though aimed at builders, its entry-level software product (Fast Estimate 5) costs £445 and a there is a free download version to try out on its website. The software incorporates:Price

- Books utilising industry-standard price books from SPON Press: the most detailed, professionally relevant source of construction price information currently available anywhere.
- Bill of Quantity Preparation: to calculate materials required for any building job.
- Resource Requirements to specify exactly what you need to complete the job.

- Jewson product prices, giving access to the latest prices from the UK's largest builders' merchant, from which you can estimate likely prices prevailing in the country in which you will be doing building works.
- Link to external applications: view, edit or analyse your reports using Excel, Word or other standard applications.

Engaging an architect and a builder

Architects must usually be registered with the local architects' association which also sets the standard fee rates for their work. You should budget for around 10% of the total building costs for your architect. Their work should cover everything from preparing preliminary sketches and drawings to producing the detailed plans and having them approved, as well as supervising the builders' work to ensure that the plans are followed and the workmanship is satisfactory. Do not exclude this last, supervisory aspect of the architect's job – or, if you do, have someone else (such as a surveyor) carry it out. Unsupervised building work never goes to plan.

Checking out architects' qualifications

You need to ask to see the architect's registration certificate and go around to see other similar work that they have carried out. Ideally, you should only deal with an architect who has been recommended by someone whose judgement you respect. If you are new to the area, such people may be thin on the ground. But if you have seen a number of properties and building plots, you may well have formed a view as to the competence of the local estate agents. They have considerable dealings with architects and would be in a good position to give an opinion. The same would be true of the notary, and perhaps your mortgagor, if they too are reasonably local. A further important consideration is language. Architecture is a much more subtle subject than the hard lines on a drawing plan would suggest and you and your architect will have to have a common language if you are to end up achieving exactly what you want. Fortunately, many architects overseas speak some English. This is particularly the case in the more popular tourist areas. If you don't have a common language, once again you will need a translator to hand – ideally, someone with some experience of building work.

Deciding on a builder

Builders also are usually required to be officially registered. Even if the person you are buying the plot from is offering you a package deal, to include building work, you need to check them out thoroughly. While registration details are a comfort, it is only a small one. You also need to be sure that their workmanship will be to the standard you have in mind. This too, will mean asking around for recommendations from local professionals, seeing some of their workmanship and, if at all possible, speaking to some recent clients. Your architect may have a 'tame' builder but having these two working 'in cahoots' may not be optimal. The ideal relationship between these two professions should be that of a game-keeper and a poacher, with a bit of healthy respect thrown in.

As with any major item of expense, you should try to obtain written quotations from a few builders.

Drawing up the building contract

Once you have decided on a builder, you need to draw up the building contract. This will be a lengthy and detailed documented, listing absolutely everything you are having done. It should specify all the materials to be used, down to the exact make and supplier, giving both quantities and costs; and it should state whether items are fixed prices or estimates. Builders like estimates; they also like you to interfere and change the specification as the building work progresses. Resist both of these, as they will inevitably lead to large cost and time overruns. Make sure that the local taxes (such as VAT in the EU or sales tax in the USA) have been included in the figures.

The contract should clearly define each of the separate building stages, when the architect will in effect 'sign off' that work has been satisfactorily carried out and payment is due. The stages might be: laying the foundations; putting on the roof; tiling the floors; putting in the windows; and so forth. The exact stages will vary from project to project. Typically, you will be asked to pay around 20% to get the ball rolling, and a further three to five stage payments as the work progresses.

The contract can specify penalties for non-performance or missing deadlines and should give guidance as to how disputes will be resolved. It should also contain details of the builders' and the architect's professional indemnity insurances, showing how much cover is provided and under what conditions the policies come into effect. One major concern you might have in this respect is what will happen should the builders go bust. As in the UK, builders abroad feature high up on the list of businesses which fail.

Builders are usually legally responsible for any small defects up to a year or two after completion of the whole project, and for structural defects for a further 3–5 years. This will be implicit in your contract, but be prepared for resistance if you actually try to enforce it. Patience, fortitude and preparation are the key to getting a builder to perform remedial work. If the problems are serious then commission a structural surveyor's report, stating what is wrong and who is responsible.

Your builder and architect will have a standard format for contracts. These may well be fine, but ask your lawyer to check it through before you sign it.

Getting the contract right may seem like a waste of time when you could be getting on with the building work itself. Also, having it vetted by your lawyer and paying the architect (or someone else) to project-manage the building work may seem to be pushing up the costs, when that money could have gone towards a new swimming pool or paid for air-conditioning in a couple of bedrooms. Resist the temptation.

Have a project manager and have a lawyer to vet the contract. It will be money well spent.

Organisations and websites for finding architects and builders

The American Institute of Architects
(http://www.aia.org/architect_finder/)

On 23 February 1857, 13 architects met in a colleague's office to form what would become the American Institute of Architects. Until this point, anyone who wished to call him- or herself an architect could do so. This included masons, carpenters, bricklayers and other members of the building trades. The group set out to create an architecture organisation which would 'promote the scientific and practical perfection of its members' and 'elevate the standing of the profession'.

From the bottom of the central menu pane, you can search for an architect by country and by speciality (such as 'recreation', 'retail' or 'residential'). While only one architect was listed for Turkey and Poland, seven were shown in Italy and 17 in China.

Commonwealth Association of Architects (CAA)
(www.comarchitect.org/find_institute.htm)

CAA's constitution sets out the aim of the organisation as 'The advancement of Architecture throughout the Commonwealth, and the acquisition of knowledge of the various arts and sciences connected therewith'. At this link you will find the designation of the relevant professional association in some 45 countries, starting with the Royal Australian Institute of Architects and ending with the Zimbabwe Institute of Architects. Unfortunately, the web addresses are not included, so you have to search for those yourself. As there are just a couple of variations on those last three words, finding the architects' professional body in most other countries should be a relatively simple matter by using a search engine. Simply putting in the country name first is usually effective. The variations include: 'the Architectural Association of Tanzania'; 'the

Brunei Association of Surveyors Engineers & Architects'; and the rather less obvious 'Botswana Institute of Development Professions'.

Royal Institute of British Architects (RIBA) (www.riba.org)

For its 30,000-strong membership in the UK and abroad, the RIBA provides specialist information and advice, practice promotion, professional support and commercial products. From the left-hand vertical menu, select 'Members Directory'. In the search criteria pane, insert what information you either already know (such as the name or the country) to find a list and contact details of all RIBA members. For Vietnam, two members are shown; for Sweden 16; and for Spain 61.

Chartered Institute of Building (CIOB) (www.ciob.org.uk)

With over 42,000 members, the CIOB is the international voice of the building professional. It has developed a number of partnerships with international organisations, such as the Australian Institute of Building, the American Institute of Constructors and the National Board for Construction Management Accreditation, China. From the horizontal menu bar across the top of the home page, select 'Branches', then, from the bottom of the vertical menu which appears on the left, click on the last heading: 'Overseas'. There you will details of the relevant professional contact point for the county in question, for example 'Chartered Institute of Building Malaysia'.

International Federation of Landscape Architects (IFLA)
(www.ifla.net)

IFLA represents the landscape architectural profession globally, providing leadership and networks supporting the development of the profession. Once you have entered the site from the horizontal menu across the top of the page, select 'Members'. From there, you can search, either by name or by country, for a landscape architect. Thirty four countries have members.

International Union of Architects (UIA) (www.uia-architectes.org)

Founded in Lausanne in 1948, the UIA is a world network representing over a million architects throughout the world through national architectural associations. Clicking on the link 'UIA Member Sections' in the centre of the home page will take you to a brief description of the membership and its geographical composition. From there, click on '102 members' where you will be taken to an A–Z directory of national associations of architects. Countries covered start with the Official College of Architects of Andorra (COAA) and then on through the Federacion Argentina de Entidades de Arquitectos (FADEA) to the Ordre des Architectes de Roumanie (OAR), the Union of Architects of the Tadjikistan Republic and finishing with the Association of Architects of Vietnam. Once on the country association page, the route to membership directories varies in the degree of sophistication, but sites are mostly in English and contact e-mail addresses are given.

CHAPTER 23

Going into the Rental Business

In this chapter:

- Deciding whether or not to keep on your home property.
- Checking out furnishing options.
- Deciding on long- or short-term rentals.
- Calculating the rent.
- Considering managing tenants yourself.
- Finding an agent.
- Assessing taxes.
- Keeping the books.

Rental yield, or at least the prospect of such income, is what ultimately drives property values, so the subject of this chapter, next only to getting the price and location of a property right, is vitally important. However, there are a lot of factors to consider. Buying even just one overseas property provides the opportunity to at least consider renting out two properties: your existing home and the one you have bought or are in the process of buying overseas.

You may not need to have the use of both properties all the time, so you could consider letting out, either short- or long-term, for much of the year and so maximise your income and keep your options open.

Such a strategy will require you to consider furnishing and maintenance costs as well as methods of finding tenants. Ultimately, there also will be tax to pay on profits and additional tax implications when it comes assessing any capital gain on sale of rented properties.

Property, as everyone who is in the trade can tell you, is a long-haul business. Everything about it – from finding a place, to purchasing it, to readying it for occupancy – takes time. If you harbour dreams of a fast gain, go to the races or buy a lottery ticket instead because the rental market is not for you. You may wait 3–5 years before you break even on your initial investment in purchase expenses and furnishing. Only property price inflation makes short-term financial gains economically viable.

However, if you are patient and interested in having your home property and/or the one you are buying abroad help generate income, then it is possible to make a perfectly respectable income. At the same time, the underlying asset may be appreciating healthily.

Keeping on and letting out your current home

This is the first and most fundamental decision to make, from which most others will flow. If you decide to keep your house in the UK after you buy a property abroad, you may not need to have it available to you all the time. After all, you can hardly live in two places at once! This simple fact of life presents you with an opportunity to generate an income to contribute something towards the cost of running two homes – no doubt a welcome proposition.

The benefits of letting out your home property

1. **Peace of mind.** While you're abroad, you may have a nagging feeling that you've left a tap on, a pipe has burst or squatters have moved in. You can cure these worries by having a tenant living in your home.
2. **Potential for capital gain.** By letting out your property, you can afford to stay in the UK housing market for longer and enjoy a healthy growth in value. You can, of course, lose money if the property market turns down but at least if you keep your British home, you stay in the property game.

3. **Protection from lock-out.** Imagine a worst-case scenario: you sell up in the UK, move abroad, live happily for 5 years and then decide to return to Britain. (This is not such an unusual event as it sounds and more than 100,000 British citizens return to live in the UK each year.) The property you sold for £300,000 may cost £600,000 to replace, but the overseas property you bought, though it cost only £100,000 to buy, is worth just £200,000, assuming that the markets moved at the same rate. This situation leaves you with a £400,000 shortfall if you move into a similar property or the prospect of downsizing to a much smaller property or a less desirable neighbourhood.
4. **Propsects of income.** You can make some money from renting out, though it may well be rather less than you hoped.

If you can afford to do so, keeping your British home is almost always a strong financial decision in the long term, though not without pain. So, if letting out your home is the only way you can afford to keep it, this may be your best option under most circumstances.

The dangers in letting out your home property

There are, however, some significant reasons for not letting out your home property, including:

1. **The possibility of a quick return home.** If you think that you or anyone in your household may need to stay in or return to the UK at short notice for a period of weeks or months, then letting out your British home may not be a great idea. People with medical conditions or with family commitments such as an ageing or ailing relative could fit into this bracket.
2. **The cost of upgrades.** You may well have to speculate a fair bit on your property before you can hope to accumulate a stream of rental income. Peeling paintwork, tatty fittings and all kinds of repairs waiting to be done create a shabby, run-down appearance. Good tenants

won't trade a low rent for unsatisfactory conditions; only bad tenants think that way. In time, landlords who don't maintain their properties find that they have less and less money to do *essential* maintenance. They then spiral further and further downmarket, with yields dropping fast.

3. **The cost of maintaining your property while you are away.** To ensure that your home remains in top shape while you're away, create a maintenance plan covering all the following areas:
   - **Emergency repairs.** Build a good relationship with some local tradespeople and make sure that they understand that you are in business too. Your tenants do not want to wait days for the air-conditioner's fuse to be replaced or for the fridge or washing machine to be repaired. Paying promptly for work done is one sure-fire way to get to the top of any supplier's work sheet.
   - **Preventive maintenance.** Heating systems, air-conditioning and swimming pools all need regular servicing to keep them in good repair. Carrying out this work extends an item's life and reduces the occurrence of emergency repairs.
   - **Preventive maintenance.** This type of maintenance is about sorting things out *before* they happen. If a refrigerator is more than a few years old, it's a dead cert for going wrong. If the fridge suddenly fails, you may have to take whatever appliance you can find on the day, which can be expensive and even result in your choosing an unsuitable one. The best strategy is to shop around for replacements before disaster strikes and get the right product at a good price. (You then have the bonus of giving your tenant a pleasant surprise when you turn up (announced in advance, of course) with a shiny new appliance.)
   - **Cosmetic maintenance.** This type of service concerns such items as paintwork, woodwork, work surfaces, pathways, curtains, blinds, wallpaper, carpets and flooring. These visible areas hit the eye first and require regular attention and quick touch-ups.
   - **Cleaning maintenance.** This service is absolutely vital for all holiday and short-term lets, as well as between longer-term

tenancies. The person or service you select has to be able to handle the changeover between lets on their own and, if necessary, replace light bulbs, top up the fridge and handle basic problems. Remember that you won't be there; you may not even be in the country. When you find the right cleaning person, pay them 10 per cent over the local rate and give them a paid holiday too. Small presents when you come back and lots of thank-yous and praise are always appreciated too.

1. **The possible implications for capital gains tax.** Your main residence in the UK is exempt from capital gains tax when sold. Once you start renting it out, some of that privileged tax position is eroded. So you need to check out whether renting out makes sound financial sense in your circumstances. In Chapter 9, you will find details of how to find organisations who can help you with this subject.
2. **Administrative chores.** You will need to carry out a full inspection of the property every year and after each change of tenant. In the inventory, note the condition of every item, as well as when you think it will need servicing, painting or replacing. Doing so ensures that short-term tenants don't escape paying for damage and long-term tenants see that you are interested in their well-being.

Fitting out a property

The standard of equipment and decorative condition of properties in the rental markets, both at home and in all but the most underdeveloped parts of the world, has steadily risen over the years. The days when tenants put up with nearly anything just to have a roof over their heads are long gone.

To compete in the market, you need to up your game. While you may be happy to sleep on a sagging mattress, cook on an ancient, temperamental stove, and leave your clothes around in suitcases, paying tenants are rarely so accommodating. Things don't have to be to designer standards, unless you are aiming at the executive end of the market where that is virtually a given. But the property does have to be clean, functional and complete. So, even if you don't personally find a microwave, a satellite television or an in-home washer/dryer appealing, tenants in rental properties almost certainly do.

The standard you set depends on the income yield you are aiming for. Almost any property in a reasonably desirable location can be let in its peak season. The problem comes in the off-season, when supply exceeds demand and tenants of all hues become much more choosy.

The following are some quick fixes to get a property into shape and make it desirable for long- or short-term rental, regardless of season:

- **First impressions count.** Make sure that the garden, path, front door and hallway are all in excellent repair. New plantings and a fresh coat of paint can work wonders.
- **Choose sturdy, basic furniture.** Cupboards, railings, wardrobes and indeed everything should be wobble-free. No piece of furniture should be so fragile or off-putting to a prospective tenant that they think they might be landed with a bill for putting fixtures right.
- **Go for clean and clutter-free.** Windows should be clean, as should all work surfaces. Simplify interiors by removing any surplus furniture and ornaments. Some landlords believe that more is better and store unwanted odds and ends in their rental properties. Tenants want both the essentials and the space.
- **Include high-quality electrical appliances.** Countertop appliances are relatively inexpensive, and you can make a big impression with a small sum of money. For example, top-of-the-range branded microwaves, food mixers, music centres or DVD players cost little more than basic items, but each can make a big impression, even if tenants don't actually use them.

All essential furnishing should be in place before prospective tenants view the property. Tenants can only buy into what they can see, unlike prospective owners who can indulge their imagination and see how things could be.

If you are marketing through a holiday company, it probably has written specifications of everything you need to include in your property, from eggcups through to bedding and linen, to the number of wardrobes and bedside lights. Brokers too have ideas of what kit should be in your property, though they are unlikely to have a written document on the subject.

Furniture 4 Flats (www.furniture4flats.co.uk)

Founded in 199,7 this organisation starts from the premise that a furniture pack is the next big expense once you have completed the purchase of your investment property, so it aims to gets the best quality for the best price, without compromising on the 'wow' factor; while making sure that properties it furnishes stand out from the rest in a competitive market. Its furnishings are co-ordinated right down to the arrangement, the, blinds, appliances, flooring and even the small things like kettles and toasters. Its furniture packages start from £1,000 and go up to £3,000 for a basic fit-out.

Channel 4
(www.channel4.com/4homes/profitfromproperty/index.html)

This is the TV network Channel 4's section on profiting from property. From the home page, scroll down the central menu to 'Developing to let' where you will find a subsection 'How to furnish rental properties'. This section is itself divided into two parts: 'Minimal furnishing' and 'The whole package'. 'Rental décor', 'How clean is your house?' and 'Making use of a spare room' are all worth a look too.

LandlordZONE (www.landlordzone.co.uk)

This is an on-line community, a portal for landlords involved in letting property – novice and experienced alike. Published by Parkmatic Publications Ltd since 1999, it provides free access to information, resources and contacts of value to residential and commercial landlords, tenants, letting agents, property managers and other property professionals. Access to the whole of LandlordZONE® and the Question and Answer Forum is currently free, though you may in future be required to register in order to gain access to some resources. From the A–Z vertical menu on the left of the screen you can select from over 60 topics ranging from 'Accountants and Tax' to 'Bailiffs' Investigations', 'Emergency Boarding', 'Leases', 'Letting Agents', 'Safety and Security', through to 'Surveyors and Utilities'. While aimed primarily at the UK market, the topics apply in a general sense anywhere. From the directory listing, select 'Furniture and Furnishings for Rental Property' where you will find brief descriptions and links to the websites for around 50 businesses operating in the furnishing field. Companies operating in Spain, Portugal, France and Dubai are among those listed.

Blueprint (`www.bluprint-uk.com/packages.pdf`)

This company specialises in providing furniture packages in the north of England. This link leads directly to an inventory of items required to furnish a property to both basic and complete standards.

Business Rooms-direct (`www.businessrooms-direct.co.uk`)

This company, based in Chester in the north of England, offers the complete interior solution for property developers and landlords, covering everything from soft furnishings to living room furniture, dining room furniture, bedroom furniture and kitchens and bathrooms. From the vertical menu on the left of the screen, select any of these three: 'Standard Package', 'Premier Package' or 'Show Room Package'. From there you will see a sample inventory of all items required for rental properties to progressively superior standards.

jml Property Services (www.jmlproperty.co.uk)

This site offers information on the rental market in the UK and Ireland and other parts of Europe. Topical news items can be found in the left-hand menu, including a Property News section which is updated regularly. Jml are members of the Southern Private Landlords Association, National Landlords Association in the UK and British Chamber of Commerce Côte d'Azur, France. From the left-hand vertical menu, select 'Buy to let in Europe' where you will find in summary form the key issues concerning a range of topics from furnishing to finding a rental agent and dealing with local taxes.

Balkan Ski Chalets
(www.balkanskichalets.com/index.php?menu5furnishing)

This link will take you directly to a comprehensive inventory of the furnishing recommendations of the leading tour companies operating in the holiday market. Don't be put off by the name: the inventory is not restricted in any way to geography. Everything you would expect is listed, but adding a corkscrew, mop and bucket and potato peeler to the list of suggestions gives a flavour of the attention to detail.

Longer-term rentals

The big attraction to letting in the long term is that there is much less to do once your tenant is installed. Unlike holiday and short-term lets, where people come and go virtually every week, here you may not have any change for one or more years.

True, the weekly rent for long-term properties is lower than for short-term ones, but this will almost certainly be compensated for by a higher occupancy rate. The big drawback is that with long-term rentals you won't be able to carve out a few weeks in which to enjoy the property yourself. So mostly, though not exclusively, those going into the long-term market are investing in property rather than buying a home.

Renting long-term overseas

In most developing countries overseas there are really only two prospective sources of longer-term rental clients. The first is incoming business executives whose numbers and quality are closely linked to the amount of inward investment that a country receives. The second is members of the diplomatic community. Numbers in both these groups increase as trade and wealth expand in the recipient country. The local population in these countries is rarely able, at present at any rate, to pay an economic rent for a property sufficiently desirable to have good investment prospects.

When a company chooses to set up operations, facilities or a factory in another country, usually employing local labour, initially it usually sends over a senior skilled team to get the activity underway. These 'executives' in the case of inward investment in Eastern and Central Europe usually come from countries such as the USA, Germany, Austria, Italy, France and the UK. They expect to live in accommodation of at least the same standard as they enjoyed at home. For the most part, there is a shortage of property of that quality in the region – consequently, it is desirable and expensive. These executives usually stay only a year or two in the recipient country before moving on, as their primary role is to establish the venture and train the locals to run it to the standards laid down by the parent business. Consequently, these incoming executives rarely buy property in the local country as, first, they don't know for how long they will be staying and, second, their company often pays or contributes to the cost of rent, while they would not be equally willing to help purchase. A further reason these executives are discouraged from buying is that doing so would eat into valuable time that should be directed to seeing that their businesses succeed.

Organisations to help with finding long-term tenants overseas

Crown Relocations (www.crownrelo.com)

This company is part of the Crown Worldwide group established in 1965 by Jim Thompson, an American, who found out the hard way – when he was transferred to Japan – that relocating executives was a difficult process. The company started its expansion programme in Hong Kong, moving on to Singapore, Indonesia, Malaysia and other Asia–Pacific locations. It now has offices across America and Australasia, as well as in Europe.

Embassy World (www.embassyworld.com)

Embassies are always looking for places for their staff to stay for a year or two while working abroad. This is a directory and search engine of the world's embassies and consulates. It has operated since 1996, providing a comprehensive list of contact resources for all of the world's diplomatic offices. The directory is easy to navigate and is clearly laid out and fully cross-indexed.

Expatriates.com (www.expatriates.com/directory/ps/relocation)

This link is to the relocation services database of this online community for expats. There are details of over 40 companies in the relocation database, many of whom are offering very specific services such as relocating to Cyprus or Denmark. This link (www.expatriates.com/html/poststep1.html) is to a free small ads page where you can advertise property to rent.

Going There (www.going-there.com)

This is a global relocation company established in 2000 to help companies to deploy international assignees around the world. It offers a number of services including a web-based intelligence tool providing practical, city-specific information available anywhere, with over 3,000 answers and solutions for each city: a squad of in-city 'Your Guides' who search out local properties.

Matrix Relocation (www.matrix-relo.com)

This is a division of Matrix International, an executive relocation company working with Fortune 1000 clients, government agencies and NGOs. It helps over 15,000 key employees to relocate around the world each year. Through its property network it can arrange temporary housing in 400 cities worldwide and so is always in the market for quality properties.

Saunders 1865 (`www.saunders1865.com`)

This is a London (Kensington)-based international executive relocation company which specialises in finding temporary accommodation for executives on short-term secondment abroad. This link (`www.saunders1865.com/shorttermaccom.shtml`) takes you to its temporary accommodation database.

Also consider advertising in the relevant local media. (See Chapter 24 on online newspapers or the papers and magazines offering property for sale mentioned in Chapter 14). You should also contact the Human Resources departments of international companies who are sending staff into the country in which you have bought or are buying a property. You can identify such companies from the information provided in Chapter 6. Finally, you can use the estate agent–broker–realtor web sites listed in Chapter 11.

Renting long-term in the UK

In the UK and other developed property markets you can draw on the general population at large for tenants. In the UK, the long-term option paradoxically is to use an assured shorthold tenancy (AST) agreement. Unless you plan to charge an annual rent of less than £250 (£1,000 in London) or more than £25,000, or will be letting to a company or other corporate body, then an AST is the safest legal agreement, from a landlord's perspective. The Housing Act 1988 introduced this new class of tenancies and, with effect from 28 February 1997, the AST is the default or automatic tenancy. The purpose of this new tenancy agreement was to return sufficient power to landlords to make it worth their while renting out their empty properties, keeping them in good repair and investing in bringing new properties onto the market. The £5 billion or so invested in the 'buy-to-let' market is proof of the success of the AST.

The initial period for an AST is 6 months. So, unless the tenant breaks the terms of the agreement (for example by not paying rent, causing damage or some other disturbance), you can't get your property back for that period. As long as you don't need to get back into your home for that period, this is an option worth exploring. After the initial 6 months the AST can be renewed for another fixed period or be allowed to continue on a month-by-month basis indefinitely. The agreement will also stipulate that you, the landlord, need to give 2 months' notice and the tenant 1 month's notice to end the tenancy. You don't have to give any reason for wanting to repossess your property – and you have an absolute right to do so.

You can't occupy a part of your property while an AST tenancy is in force, unless you have a self-contained area with its own entrance.

You don't need a solicitor to draw up an AST; you can buy a form off the shelf for a few pounds from a stationer's or from one of the many websites advertising that service, such as those listed below.

Organisations to help with legal aspects of UK rentals

Oyez Forms Link(www.oyezformslink.co.uk)

This is part of the OyezStraker group, formed in 1997 when Oyez Stationery Group and Straker Office Supplies merged. Both businesses have long, successful histories, with over 300 years' experience in office supplies. For landlords, they offer a comprehensive range of professionally drafted, legally compliant AST forms to help ensure that your lettings fall under the full protection of established law. From the 'Quick start' section of the left-hand vertical menu, scroll down to 'Small Landlord'. From there you can download leases for furnished or unfurnished properties and forms for giving notice of your intention to repossess.

Law Pack (`www.lawpack.co.uk`)

Lawpack is a major UK self-help legal publisher, offering an extensive range of do-it-yourself books, kits, form packs and software. From the left-hand vertical menu, select 'Property letting'. From there, you can download a standard AST form for £4.99 and rent books for £1.99, as well as read a number of free related articles on a range of current topics including information on the mandatory tenancy deposit scheme that all landlords of ASTs in England and Wales were required to join from 6 April 2007.

Finding long-term tenants at home

About two-thirds of all long-term rentals are arranged by estate agents. You will already be aware of the agents in your area who deal in the type of property you are planning to let out. Agents take a hefty commission and often don't do all that much to earn their keep, beyond an introduction. The leases and other legal safeguards can be arranged for a few tens of pounds at the most, rather than the thousands that agents often charge.

After agents come local papers and their websites. Once again, these are very visible. You are left with much of the work in getting a lease organised: showing the property and checking out the prospective tenants. But all you pay is the cost of the advertisement: usually around £10–£20.

Increasingly, the Internet is being used to marry up owners and tenants. The advantages are the Internet classics of richness and reach. While an estate agent can reach hundreds and a local paper perhaps a hundred thousand, some dedicated property rental sites reach a million or more users. Add to this the fact that a vast wealth of data on the property, its location and the neighbouring facilities and amenities can be shown on a selective basis to searchers. The following are some of the players in this market who appear in the listing.

Organisations and websites for finding long-term tenants in the UK

House Ladder (www.houseladder.co.uk)

This site was founded in 2003 and now has over 300,000 visitors a month. For a fee from £69.99 your home will be advertised to 2 million people, using the same 150 property sites as the estate agents and letting agents use. From the left-hand vertical menu, select 'Online Guide' from the 'Landlord' subsection. That contains six links to information of use to prospective landlords in writing up their advertisements: 'Preparation'; 'Gathering information on Your Property'; 'Legal'; 'Marketing'; 'Viewings'; and 'Found a Tenant'. There is also a link to a tenants' guide which also contains useful information on their rights

Fish 4 Homes (www.fish4.co.uk)

This site has been developed by two-thirds of the UK's regional press: a combined 300 daily and weekly regional newspapers. Check out your local newspapers, including the free ones, and the chances are you will see the 'Fish4' logo. The site attracts around 1.5 million visitors a month and carried 72,378 lettings advertisements at the time of writing. Select 'Letting' from the horizontal menu at the top of the page, followed by 'Landlord's centre'. There you will find guidance on placing your advertisement.

OnOneMap (http://ononemap.com)

This site claims to list over two-thirds of all properties for sale or rent in England, Scotland and Wales. It uses an interactive map to show the location of properties.

You can list properties for rent which meet key search criteria and follow links to websites where full property details can be found. Property listed can then be searched by location; by number of bedrooms; by minimum and maximum prices; by distance from tube and train stations; and by distance from motorways and schools.

Paragon Advance (www.paragonadvance.com)

Paragon provides a comprehensive range of products and services to the lettings industry and has been established in tenant referencing companies for over 13 years. For £30 plus VAT it will: carry out a credit history check on prospective tenants; take up a landlord's reference and an employer's reference; and check on the tenants database to ensure that there are no adverse comments from previous landlords.

It also offers a 24-hour service for an additional cost of £5 but must have the application before 12:00pm for this next-day service.

Holiday lets

Being a successful landlord is much like running any business well: find out what your customers want and give it to them at a reasonable price. Good marketing and tenant selection go some way towards achieving this goal, but the safest way is to have satisfied tenants rather than disgruntled ones.

The surest way to make a decent return on your property is to have it occupied for every available day – and that's where the holiday market comes into play.

People coming on holiday have much the same expectations the world over: They hope to find something closely resembling the advertised description when they turn up at the door. A glowing description that is miles from the reality may lure a few customers, but is unlikely to foster much repeat business, either from them or from the agents they came through. Overpromised accomodation also hurts your reputation when word spreads throughout a client's network of friends and contacts.

Fortunately, working out what tenants want is not too difficult because they are all looking for much the same payback. As a landlord, try to:

- **Offer reasonable value for the money paid.** Of course, this seems logical but some landlords believe – incorrectly – that they can trade off bad service or poor conditions in return for a lower rent.
- **Respect your tenants' privacy.** While you have the right to visit or inspect a property, giving tenants plenty of warning and making sure that the time of your visit suits them are common courtesies. You need to create the illusion that a property is your tenants' home, so that they, in turn, treat it with respect and feel at ease.
- **Communicate all vital information all the time.** For holiday and short-term rentals, people don't have long to get to know the property and the area. Provide a property handbook (a few pages will do) explaining how everything inside the property works; who to contact if anything goes wrong; and what the house rules are. Also give details of doctors, good restaurants, supermarkets, taxi services and any other useful tips that can make their stay better. Longer-term tenants need to be kept informed about anything which might affect their stay, such as the common parts being painted or seasonal changes in utilities.
- **Respond quickly to complaints, enquiries or requests from your tenants.** You don't have to give in to unreasonable wishes, but you do have to acknowledge all requests, explain what you can do to resolve the problem and do whatever is needed quickly.
- **Go the extra mile.** This may be as minor as including a welcoming bottle of wine or bunch of flowers on arrival. Or you can upgrade some aspect of the property that was not included in the original contract, for example adding an espresso coffee maker, a second television or some new linen. Tenants' number-one complaint is that landlords don't show they care, and these are all ways to show that you do.

- **Keep everything up to scratch.** Have a maintenance plan to make sure that both the inside and outside of the property meet the best standards.

Finding holiday-let tenants at home

If you want to have the use of your home for any part of the year, you can consider opening your home to holiday renters (as well as students – covered – in the following section).

Most second homers utilise holiday rentals to in order to generate extra cash to cover some of the costs of having a holiday home abroad. Holiday lettings can range in type and duration, from as short as a weekend to as long as several months. A holiday-letting agreement operates fundamentally under contract law and so the tenant in such a letting has few rights of tenure and the repossession procedure is much simpler than for a standard residential tenancy. All that is necessary for the law to apply is that the landlord is satisfied that the purpose of the letting is genuinely for the purpose of a holiday.

You can find holiday-let tenants yourself, by advertising in the press or on the Internet. Alternatively, you can use one of the many companies specialising in holiday lets. As well as taking most of the workload off your shoulders, these services confirm that the tenant is coming on holiday only, has the appropriate agreement in place and is able to deal with problems in your absence.

You still need to arrange for someone local to clean the property between lets and to deal with emergencies. Plan to leave a list with details of the plumber, electrician and any other tradespeople you usually use if things go wrong.

Holiday rents in the United Kingdom typically vary from around £100 per week in low season for a studio, up to £3,000 a week or more for a six- or seven-bedroom property in a prime location in high season. Seasons, of course, vary somewhat. High season in a seaside location is the summer months; in Edinburgh it may be during the annual arts festival; and in Stratford-upon-Avon it can be just about anytime.

Some British holiday rental websites

Country Holidays (`www.country-holidays.co.uk`)

This organisation has been offering cottages and holiday homes for rent throughout the British Isles since 1978. It has a network of regional managers throughout Britain whose responsibilities include making regular checks to ensure that properties are maintaining the appropriate standards. Every property is inspected and graded with one of five grades, depending on property quality. Select 'Letting Your Property' from the horizontal menu at the top of the screen.

English Country Cottages (`www.english-country-cottages.co.uk`)

This site claims to offer landlords exposure and promotion to a database of over 8 million holidaymakers, as well as massive advertising and promotional campaigns in all the major national newspapers and key premium magazine titles. Select 'Letting your property' from the right-hand side of the horizontal menu at the top of the screen'. It also offers a comprehensive range of additional services to relieve landlords of the headache of running a holiday-letting business.

Enjoy England (`www.enjoyengland.com/book/accommodation`)

This is the official tourist board for England which has over 15,000 properties for short-term rental on its books. You can get a feel for the level of rent you might be able to charge by searching its on-line database. You need to register your property with your local tourist board, who will come to inspect and give a star rating. You can find web links to every local tourist board office at this link: `www.enjoyengland.com/home/tic/index.aspx`

Students in the UK home market

Students can also serve as convenient shorter-term renters. In general, students rent properties for the academic year and may or may not be staying over the vacations. In practice and in law, you are safest to insist that student renters take a long-term lease (shorthold), with the rent guaranteed by one or more of their parents.

If you are leasing to multiple students, have the lease signed by all the parties, pointing out to them that they are jointly and severally liable for the rent and any repairs. That means that if one defaults, the others have to cough up. This usually focuses the mind wonderfully, with a resultant quick reshuffle of prospective tenants.

Students are by nature prone to be noisy, accident-prone when it comes to furniture and dilatory with the rent. Take 2 months' rent as deposit, insist on setting up direct debits for rent and make the students sign a copy of the house rules. Draw their attention to the clause in the lease saying that they can be evicted if they cause a nuisance to the neighbours.

Organisations who can assist with letting UK property to students

Letting Property to Students

(www.accommodationforstudents.com)

Co-founded by William Berry (who appeared on the BBC's *Dragon's Den*, only to turn down an offer of funding), this site claims to host more content than any other student accommodation website and to attract more traffic. It is partnered with many other sites (including Funky student; MSN Student; and LandlordZONE) and was a finalist at the New Media Age Awards for Best Use of Web Category in 2005. There is a fully searchable database so that students can retrieve detailed descriptions of properties matching their exact requirements. One-click contact e-mail facilities enable students to contact landlords/agents at the touch of a button; there are also message boards where students can post their accommodation requirements. These requirements are then displayed to relevant landlords and letting agents in the area. The site also provides student reviews (students are asked to rate their last student digs town/city). This enables students to get a feel for a place (very useful for students new to an area and keeps landlords on their toes).

Student Accommodation (www.accommodationforstudents.com)

This site claims to have 200,000 visitors every month and it costs only £10 per month for landlords to advertise a single property. At the time of writing, 2,187 properties were listed, from Aberdeen to Plymouth.

Finding tenants for holiday lets overseas

You have two principal options when it comes to finding holiday-let clients for overseas properties – and there are pros and cons for both. If you do it yourself, you have the potential for greater profit, as you cut out an agent's commission, but if you are not as successful as they might be then this could prove to be an illusory gain. You also have some say over which tenants to take. However, it can prove to be a time-consuming path. Unless you have several properties (in which case it is worth investing time in systematising the process), the amount of effort involved will not be worthwhile.

Using an agent

Rather than doing everything yourself when renting out your property overseas, another option is to use the management services of a local broker, or a tour operator specialising in your particular country. Until you have some experience in letting properties in your new country, working with a professional is almost always your best option. An agent can help you gain a thorough grounding in the intricacies of the rental market and the surrounding bureaucracy. Having a professional barrier between landlord and tenant can also help defuse potentially contentious situations.

You can expect the local managing agent to market your property. You can also expect them to arrange (or at least advise on appropriate sources for) a cleaning service and repairs; reporting breakages and damage; making sure that services and rent are paid for; and depositing your rental income (less the agent's commission) into your bank.

If you own a property with reasonable letting prospects, you may have several managing agencies to choose from. As with nearly everything, a personal recommendation from an informed and unbiased person is the most desirable way forward. If, after those discussions, you still need help with selecting an agent, start with an agency you believe is trustworthy, check out other properties it handles and ask to speak to two or three other clients.

Agents typically charge between 15 and 30% for their services. However, by keeping your property fully occupied, handling bureaucracy and dealing with problem tenants, a good agent is often worth the considerable cost involved.

Confirm exactly what your managing agency does and does not do in terms of marketing and managing the property for you. Be sure that you completely understand all charges, how long the agreement between you and the agent lasts, and what notice is required to terminate the agreement. Keep a close watch on how the agency performs and, if you can, drop into the area unannounced to see how the property looks. See Chapter 13 for details as to how to locate and contact appropriate letting agents in your chosen country.

Doing it yourself

If you don't use an agent, you will have to find clients yourself; arrange to have the property cleaned and serviced between lettings; and handle any problems arising while the property is let. You must accomplish all these at a distance and in a foreign language.

To find clients, you can:

- Advertise in the appropriate British papers, such as *The Times, The Telegraph,* or the *Daily Mail.* This is an expensive and risky route because you may end up with a large bill and no takers.
- Build or buy a website and promote your property on that. This too can be a costly and uncertain way to attract customers. You must pay for the site up front *and* keep it visible on the Internet.
- Promote the property to your family, friends, and business network via email with an attached brochure file. This can actually be a pretty effective technique, capitalising on the power of viral marketing to spread your message quickly.
- List your property on someone else's holiday-letting website. Posting your home on a site such as World Holiday Rentals or Owners Direct (see below) is paid-for by advertising, but you can at least be reasonably confident that the website is visible and user-friendly and may even have on-line booking systems to clinch the deal on the spot.

After you have a client, you still need to find a cleaner or cleaning service and someone to maintain the property. Probably your best bet is to enlist the services of the broker from whom you bought your property. He or she may even be able to help with finding both short- and long-term tenants.

Organisations who can assist with overseas holiday lets

DaltonsHolidays.com (`www.daltonsholidays.com`)

This is the holiday website of *Daltons Weekly.* By placing an ad on this site you put your property in front of over 70,000 unique users every month, for around £120 for an annual listing. For this price you get a full-page ad, including up to 6 photos (which appear to the user as a slide show); a description of the property and its locality; details of the facilities available; rates and availability tables; and direct access to amend all details whenever necessary. You also get access to Dalton's data to see how many people view your property.

Holiday Café (www.holidaycafe.info/owners.html)

Founded in 1998 by Susanna Tatay and run out of Százhalombatta, Madách in Hungary, this link takes you directly to the property owners section of the website. Here you can advertise a single property free for 3 months. If you are satisfied with the results then you can sign up and pay for further advertsing.

Owners Direct (www.ownersdirect.co.uk)

Select 'Advertise here' to be taken to the 'property owners' section of the website. Owners Direct offers an effective and good-value advertising service to private owners of holiday property worldwide. All enquiries and bookings are made with you as the owner, so you can keep full control of your lettings and avoid paying commission to agents. Full details of how to advertise with Owners Direct and for answers to any questions you may have are answered from links on this page. The cost of advertising a single property is £65, with the first 3 months free. Additional properties are £10 each, up to a maximum of three. After that, you need to negotiate special rates. There is a separate listing, and additional fee, for golf or ski properties and for hotels, guest houses and bed and breakfast accommodation listings.

Holiday Lettings (www.holidaylettings.co.uk)

Established in 1999 by business partners Ross Elder and Andy Firth, this is now one of the fastest-growing rental sites online whose purpose is to promote thousands of properties to the widest possible audience, while also helping holidaymakers find good-value holidays.

From the vertical menu on the left, enter the appropriate section under the sub-heading 'Home owners'. Twelve months' advertising for a single property costs £99. In the section 'Owners area' you will find useful tips and advice on buying, letting and marketing your holiday home. This information is drawn from the site owners' experience in supporting over 8,000 holiday home-owners, as well as from letting their own properties overseas.

Finding students for short-term rentals overseas

This is probably the market of last resort for overseas property investors. Students have proved a very profitable market for landlords in the UK market, and for indigenous landlords in some other developed countries including France, Spain and Germany. Each country will have property brokers specialising in letting to students in university towns.

Organisations who can help with letting accommodation to students overseas

Braintrack.com (www.braintrack.com)

This claims to have details of over 8,000 universities in 192 countries. From the relevant university website, search for the link to 'accommodation', 'administration', 'student service', 'welfare' or any similar term. An e-mail to any contact point given is likely to elicit a response, as universities are always on the look out for accommodation for faculty and students. Almost all the universities have websites in English.

Student Accommodation (www.studentaccommodation.org)

This is a global directory of student accommodation websites and associated links. From the vertical menu on the left, under the heading

'Directories', select from the list the country in which you are interested in letting property.

Accountancy, legal and administrative issues

Letting out a property in either the long or the short term is a business activity, though, to the owner of a single property, letting it out for a few weeks or months of the year may seem little more than an innocent activity to accumulate some 'pin money' or just to 'cover the costs' of keeping the property. However, the following administrative factors in the accountancy and legal areas will certainly need attention.

The rental agreement

Although rental agreements vary, a good contract in any country contains the following elements:

- The landlord's and tenant's names, addresses and other contact details.
- A description of the property, including an inventory of contents.
- Length of term, including start and finish dates.
- The amount of rent, payment terms, and whether, when and how the rent can be increased.
- Details of who is responsible for local taxes and utility bills.
- Any other legal provisions to which the parties agree, such as subletting, access and so on.
- A landlord can usually rescind a rental contract if the tenant:
  - Fails to pay the rent or deposit.
  - Sublets without the landlord's consent.
  - Causes damage to the property.
  - Alters the property in any way without the landlord's consent.
  - Causes serious nuisance to neighbours.
- A tenant can usually rescind a rental contract if the landlord:
  - Fails to keep the property in a habitable condition.

- Fails to repair or remedy defects.
- Does anything that makes it difficult for the tenant to enjoy the property, including using all the normal facilities.

Help with preparing leases

Law Pack (www.lawpack.co.uk/faq_landlord_and_tenant.asp)

Lawpack is a major UK self-help legal publisher, offering an extensive range of do-it-yourself books, kits, form packs and software which help you to resolve your legal issues without paying costly solicitors' fees. This link takes you direct to the landlord and tenant section where you will find information on topics as diverse as 'What can I do to improve the chances of letting a property?' to 'What sort of return can I expect from a buy to let property?'. Its publication *Residential Lettings* contains agreements, notices and background information for creating your own residential letting agreement without a solicitor (priced at £14.99).

Insurance

You will need to review your insurance requirements, as the property you rent out – and probably its contents too – will be your responsibility to keep covered. You are not liable for the tenant's personal effects: that is their lookout. You will also need cover for 'public liability'. This is built into your house insurance and covers you if anything happens on or around your property which causes injury or expense to anyone. Public liability insurance is rarely invoked, but it can be disastrously expensive if something goes seriously wrong.

If you have a mortgage on the property involved, you will have to obtain the mortgagor's permission before renting it out. You should clear this up before you take the mortgage, as some providers don't allow letting.

Some organisations specialising in insuring overseas properties

Schofields (www.schofields.ltd.uk)

For over 21 years, Schofields have specialised in holiday home insurance for UK and overseas property, arranged with certain underwriters at Lloyd's of London. Their policies are tailored to the special requirements of holiday home and second home owners, giving you the peace of mind so that you do not have to worry about your property in your absence or while it is being let out.

Somerville
(www.somerville.co.uk/portfolio-overseashomes.htm)

This is a corporate insurance broker based in the city of London and East Anglia. As a Lloyd's broker, it has access to the world's most versatile and advanced insurance market. One interesting twist to its overseas insurance provisions is that should your property be in need of renovating then they can help with cover while this is being done.

Rent and security deposits

The two financial levers you have in this business are the rent (which should be sufficient to make you a profit, if all goes to plan) and deposits from tenants (to cover you against damage if things go awry).

Rent

Deciding on the level of rent is perhaps the most important decision a landlord has to make. Set it too high and you may find it nearly impossible to attract tenants; too low and you won't make a decent profit. You will need to do your research thoroughly in order to get the price right. Just looking at the adverts in the press or on websites will not be enough: you will have to get out and about to see comparable properties in your area and check out their facilities. You can be sure that your prospective clients will have done so.

The main mistakes new landlords make are setting the rental price too high and overestimating the number of weeks each year for the property will be let. Typically, they set the rent 20% above what the market will bear and expect an occupancy rate of 90% of the available weeks, when 75% is a more likely figure. The result is that they actually end up with a third less rent than they expected – and perhaps no profit at all.

Deposits

The deposit is normally about a month's rent and is intended to protect the landlord in case of damage or loss over the period of the tenancy. The law is a bit vague as to how large the deposit should be and when it should be returned. Irrespective of this lack of clarity, the market expects deposits to be equivalent to a month's rent and to be returned within 2–3 weeks of the expiry of the lease.

Deductions from the deposit should be made only against specific items listed in the inventory.

The deposit is not intended to cover any third party (such as an electricity or telephone company) for its services. It has to look after its own interests separately.

Taking the inventory

Whether swapping, sitting or renting, take a full inventory of the property and all its fixtures and furnishings, noting the condition of key items. Renters are typically expected to put up a deposit as a guarantee against damages, so taking a thorough inventory is in the interests of both landlord and tenant. Have the inventory signed and dated by both parties and keep it safely along with the rental contract.

Most estate agents involved in a rental transaction are responsible for taking the inventory as part of their usual services. They often make a small charge for the work (usually between around €40 and €60 (£28 and £41)), both on tenants moving in and on moving out.

Organisations who can help with taking inventories

Lawpack (www.lawpack.co.uk/household_inventory_form.asp)

This site's mission statement is: 'If, with guidance from one of our legal self-help products, you can solve it for yourself, that's great. If you can't, at least we should be able to help you define what the issue really is and put it concisely to a professional. That saves time which means it saves you money.' From this link you can access details on the site's Household Inventory Form Pack (which costs £4.99). Also, from the home page select 'Property buying and selling' from the left-hand vertical menu bar to see details on the site's complete range of products.

MacLeod-Lorway (www.macleod-lorway.com/inventory.asp)

The MacLeod-Lorway Financial Group Ltd has been providing insurance and investment products since 1976 and is now run by second and third generations of insurance families who have been operating in Sydney, Australia since the beginning of the last century. On this link there is a brief guidance note on taking inventories and, towards the bottom of the page, a link to a pdf download 'Free Inventory List', which is an 18-page template of a full room-by-room inventory checklist.

Book keeping and handling taxes

You will be liable for tax on any profit made from rental income in the country in which the profit is made. This is not quite as simple as it sounds, as exactly how much tax you end up paying, to whom you pay it and when will be influenced by your residency and domicile (see Chapter 9).

You will need to keep full accounts of income and expenditure and retain all the relevant paperwork. In practice, property rentals should require no more than a dozen or so entry lines, from rental income down to profit before tax (see Table 23.1).

If you are reasonably proficient with Excel spreadsheets you could put together your own programme to run your property business accounts. Alternatively, you could buy a professionally written property management accounting package from one of the suppliers described below.

Table 23.1 Calculating rental profit and loss

	Optimistic Landlord	**Realistic Landlord**
Weekly rent	€350	€300
Weeks let in year	46	38
Annual rent	€16,100	€11,400
Expenses		
Agency commission (30%)	€4,830	€3,420
Insurance	€700	€700
Service/Community of owners charges	€500	€500
Local rates/IBI	€700	€700
Wear and tear allowance (10%)	€1,610	€1,140
Total expenses	€8,340	€6,460
Profit before tax	€7,760	€4,940
Mortgage (50% of €200,000 at 5%)	€5,000	€5,000
Profit before tax	€2,750	(€60)

Note: These are very approximate figures. The expenses and rental yields will vary from country to country and area to area.

Help with keeping the books

Estate Computers (ECS) (www.estatecomputers.co.uk)

Established for over 25 years, ECS has grown to be one of the largest software houses in the property marketplace, employing around 85 staff. Major clients include Grosvenor Estates, Workspace, Peverel, CIM Management, the Duchy of Cornwall and Ladbrokes. However, its software applications are designed to meet the business needs of every company with an interest in property, whether it be commercial or residential, investor, occupier or managing agent. Products feature not only the standard property management database and accounting functionality, but can also easily cater for client-specific property information requirements.

EZPZ Software (www.ezpzsoftware.co.uk)

EZPZ Landlord is a computerised property management system for landlords who manage their own properties. The software enables you to keep details of your properties and tenants and the links between them and has all the standard accounting features you would expect from a computerised book keeping system, such as: 'Sales ledger'; 'Purchase ledger'; 'Nominal ledger'; 'Bank reconciliation'; 'VAT analysis'; 'Automated entries'; 'Prepayments'; and 'Accruals', together with additional features such as the calculation of rents and automated credit control for tenants. Prices start from £99 for a package suitable for a single owner, up to £450 for one to handle multiple properties with different owners and with a year's technical support.

Worldwide-Tax (www.worldwide-tax.com)

This site is a very comprehensive one dealing with a host of taxation and financial subjects for some 70 countries. Each country includes general and economic surveys. The site includes tips for investors (including those buying properties) who are not residents of that country and lists any investment benefits available. The site has around 3,000 links to providers of supporting services such as accountants, lawyers and government sites, as well as a complete and comprehensive section on the embassies in that country.

From the home page, select 'World Tax and Revenue Administrations' from the central menu option. There you will find web links to the tax authorities in each country where, with varying degrees of difficulty, you can find out about the tax rules. Most of the countries have tax pages in English and there are sections specifically dealing with property rental issues that can be found with a little perseverance.

PriceWaterhouseCoopers (PWC)
(`www.pwc.com/uk/eng/main/home/index.html`)

This is the website of the firm of accountants who employ more than 130,000 people in 148 countries and cover every aspect of tax and business affairs in each of them. From this page, select 'Tax' from the left-hand vertical menu bar in the centre of the page. You will be asked to register on the site before you can uncover much useful information from this section, but that takes no more than 5 minutes and is free. The tax site contains up-to-the minute breaking tax news and a range of publications including Worldwide Tax Summaries. Select 'Worldwide Tax Summaries Online' from the menu box centre right and you will be taken to an up-to-date overview of the corporate and individual tax rates and rules in operation in over 109 countries worldwide, as well as important aspects of the relevant laws shaping taxation in the countries covered.

Dealing with problem tenants

If you are careful in choosing tenants or if you use a professional letting agency, you should have few problems. Table 23.2 shows the most usual problems landlords might have to deal with.

Table 23.2 Dealing with problem tenants

Problem	Solution
Late payment of rent	Inform tenant that they are in breach of the tenancy agreement. If persistent, pursue other tenant(s) who is/are jointly liable. Finally, evict.
Additional occupants	First, gather the facts. If it warrants it, draw tenant's attention to guest policy in rental agreement and insist additional occupant leaves as soon as possible otherwise lease will be terminated.
Nuisance and noise	Difficult to observe at first hand, as often happens late at night. Get complainant to put complaint in writing and, if possible, record and independently verify. Give tenant written warning and, if serious and repeated, advise that they are in breach of their lease.
Unsupervised children	What goes on behind closed doors is rarely a landlord's concern unless it causes actual disturbance to neighbours. Children marauding around common parts are a different matter. Deal with as for 'Nuisance and noise'.
Subletting	Tenants, particularly students, often ask to sublet part of a property. Treat any such proposal using the same criteria you would use for a new tenant.
Sharers split up	Where you are letting to more than one person, one may well leave earlier than the rest. The ideal solution is for a new tenancy agreement to be drawn up, with the deposit being refunded to the outgoing tenant.
Sitting tenants	If a tenant fails to vacate at the end of their lease, either evict or sign a new agreement. Accepting rent at the end of the lease period could create a continuation of the tenant's occupancy.
Broken tenancy agreements	If a tenant leaves before the term of the lease expires, they are technically liable to honour the agreement. However, they will expect the landlord to make reasonable efforts to re-let the property promptly.
Tenant goes bankrupt	You must stop any proceedings against the tenant and deal through the bankruptcy court.

Table 23.2 *(Continued)*

Death	If a tenant dies in your property, the coroner must deal with the body. You must take reasonable steps to secure the deceased's property, ideally having an inventory prepared by an outside professional. Contact your lawyer for advice on how to proceed.

Help in dealing with tenancy problems (UK only)

LandlordZONE (www.landlordzone.co.uk)

This is an on-line community: a portal for landlords involved in letting property – novice and experienced alike. Published by Parkmatic Publications Ltd since 1999, it provides free access to information, resources and contacts of value to residential and commercial landlords, tenants, letting agents, property managers and other property professionals. Access to the whole site and the 'Question and Answer Forum' is currently free, though you may in future be required to register in order to gain access to some resources. From the A–Z vertical menu on the left of the screen you can select from over 60 topics, ranging from 'Accountants and tax', through 'Bailiffs' Investigations', 'Emergency Boarding', 'Leases', 'Letting Agents', 'Safety and Security' through to 'Surveyors' and 'Utilities'. Select 'Eviction', where you will find the web links to around a dozen organisations who can advise, help or execute actions such as serving eviction notices.

Landlord Action (www.landlordaction.co.uk)

Landlord Action recovers rent and property from bad tenants. Started by landlords, for the benefit of landlords, this is a simple, cost-effective and fast service. The people involved are not solicitors and work for both corporate and private landlords. They are fast and their fixed fees include everything courts, solicitors, advocates, bailiffs and VAT. Fees range from £115 for all that is usually needed to evict a troublesome tenant, up to £800 in the most difficult cases.

Easy Landlords (www.easylandlords.co.uk)

Easy Landlords specialise in helping landlords with tenant eviction and rent arrears. They have fixed fees to include everything – courts, solicitors, barristers and bailiffs – ranging between £90 and £700. They have three stated aims for all their cases:

1. To get your property back fast, cost-effectively and without hassle.
2. When your case has concluded, to teach you the most effective method of renting your property again.
3. To ensure that you reduce the risk of any future financial losses.

CHAPTER 24

Staying in Touch with Home

In this chapter:

- Keeping down phone costs.
- Finding a local Internet café.
- Plugging into local networks.
- Tuning the airwaves.
- Reading online.

However much you immerse yourself in a new country, it is useful – and socially probably essential – to maintain ways both to keep in contact and to keep up to date on events 'back home'. The Internet has opened up many more possibilities for keeping in touch. Some aspects of communications are still frustrating, usually because of the revenue-generating model of the relevant service provider. Subscribing to Sky's English-language channels is nearly impossible once abroad, for example, so you need to sign up in the UK and take your Videocrypt decoder box and card with you. When it comes to renewal time you will need to 'borrow' a family member's UK address, as Sky will have you registered as a UK subscriber.

Mobile phone roaming costs are generally so prohibitive as to make it essential to get a local phone network too. But Skype and other Internet telephony companies are moving in on the market, introducing products and service that will make it possible to have a single world telephone number from which you can receive and make calls at competitive rates.

Organisations that make staying in touch both possible and affordable

OO44 UK (www.0044.co.uk)

You can buy a pay-as-you-go SIM card from countries around the world from this company and avoid all mobile roaming charges. By switching your SIM card for a foreign SIM or a global SIM while abroad, you can save up to 90%, receive calls for free and make outgoing calls at local rates. Another great advantage in using this service rather than buying a card abroad is that the on-phone instructions (on such subjects as checking how much credit you still have) will be in English, together with English-language back-up. The disadvantages are that you need a new phone number and you pay credit on the card in advance, so 'use it or lose it'.

BBC World Service (www.bbc.co.uk/worldservice)

The BBC broadcasts around the globe, covering local, British and international topics. You can find the frequency being used for its broadcast in each country by selecting 'Radio schedules' from the left-hand vertical menu. Alternatively, you can listen online via the Internet, or download a podcast.

Beeline (http://wwitv.com)

Here you will find links to 154 TV stations from 30 countries, direct from the home page. There are a number of mainstream programmes but many are fairly esoteric, such as Hotspot TV from Hungary (playing dance music) and another channel dealing with medical matters.

The British Corner Shop (www.britishcornershop.co.uk)

This company supplies an extensive range of products such as you would expect to find in your local corner shop back home. You don't have to survive abroad without porridge oats, English marmalade, Colman's Mustard or Christmas puddings and mince pies. Orders are despatched within 48 hours and delivered to most European destinations within 2–5 working days. Deliveries to other destinations are delivered within 4–10 working days, depending on how long the local customs authorities take to clear the goods. For the USA, this usually means 5 working days: Russia usually 10 working days.

Expatica (`www.expatica.com`)

This is the English-language news and information source for expatriates living in, working in or moving to the Netherlands, Germany, France, Belgium or Spain. Expatica publishes eight websites and five country-oriented survival guides.

Expats Radio (`www.expatsradio.com`)

This is a free online information resource for expats. You can listen to any one of its audio programmes either from the 'listen now' section or from its 'library'.

It currently has correspondents in Spain, Bahrain, France, Denmark, Portugal, Madeira, Singapore, Canada, Belgium, Italy, Turkey, Australia/New Zealand and the Netherlands.

Expats Shopping Index (`www.expats.org.uk/shopping/index.html`)

This service is provided by Expats.org.uk, a free source of information for British expatriates, contracting or living overseas; a sort of *Yellow Pages* for UK expats.

Insat International (`www.insatinternational.com`)

This provides British ex-pats and other European customers with the means to watch British Sky Television abroad, from Albania to Turkey and every country in between.

Live Radio Net (www.live-radio.net)

There are links to thousands of radio stations via this site, together with helpful advice on how to set up your computer to enable listening. Free software is on offer, which is required for some stations, while others have embedded players on their websites. The stations are listed geographically rather than alphabetically, so the Canary Islands come under the African section!

Net Cafes (www.netcafes.com)

This site is run by CyberLeader Systems, founded in 2000 and specialising in serving Internet and gaming cafés, libraries, hotels, schools and other institutions providing computers for public use. The site contains a database of 4,207 Internet cafés in 140 countries. To search for a cyber café near you, either click on the map on the home page to search by continent or type a city into the search box.

Online Newspapers (www.onlinenewspapers.com)

Virtually every online newspaper in the world is listed here. You can search straight from the home page, either by continent or by county. You can also find the 50 most popular online newspapers from a link in the top centre of the home page. There is also a separate site for online magazines (www.onlinenewspapers.com/SiteMap/magazines-sitemap.htm) that, for some reason, is difficult to locate except by going through the site map link.

Radio Locator (www.radio-locator.com)

This claims to be the most comprehensive radio station search engine on the Internet. It has links to over 10,000 radio station web pages and over 2,500 audio streams from radio stations in the US and around the world. As well as being able to search for a station by country, you can also search by format to locate those specialising in business news, dance, easy listening, sports, general news, politics, religion and a hundred other formats.

World Radio Network (WRN) (www.wrn.org)

Founded in 1992, WRN (based in London) aims to enable broadcasters – large and small, long-established and new – to reach new audiences in new markets. From the home page, select 'Listeners' Area' from the horizontal menu bar. Then click on 'Stations' for an alphabetical list of radio broadcasters or 'Languages' to see the same stations listed by language of broadcast. Follow the link to the relevant broadcaster's website and from there select a phrase such as 'Listen to live broadcast'.

World Wide Internet TV (http://wwitv.com)

Here you will find links to 1,718 TV stations around the globe – from Albania to Zimbabwe. You will need either Real Player, Windows Media Player or Apple Quicktime Player software to be able to see the programmes.

Appendix: Overseas Property Visit Checklist

(To be used in conjunction with the country appraisal checklist in Chapter 12)

PROPERTY	1	2	3	4
Score each property being considered against each of the following factors, rating it between 0 and 4: the higher the score, the better. You can, of course, add to or vary these criteria to meet your own particular needs.				
Town/Area				
1. **Proximity to international airport** (Over 2 hours is average; less than 1 hour is good; over 3 hours is poor.)				
2. **Tourist appeal** (At least some attractions beyond its main one of, say, ski-ing or beaches: none is poor,;1 or 2 is average; 5 or more is good.)				
3. **Proximity to business and commercial centre** (Within daily commuting is average; impossible to reach daily is poor; access to a range of urban transport services is good.)				
4. **Roads, infrastructure and utilities** (Town roads, water supply, electricity, drainage, gas and telephone lines are all connected and functioning.)				

5. **Schools, colleges and universities** (To what extent is there local access to such facilities?: none is poor; a wide choice is good.)				
6. **Take-up rate** (How many other foreign buyers have taken up properties in the area?: none warrants a low score from an investment perspective, though you may have an alternative personal preference.)				
Property features				
7. **Unique features** (Property has same features, say balconies, swimming pool etc., as most others in the area: this is average.)				
8. **Habitable status** (Can at least live in now is average; will take over 6 months to knock into shape is poor; can rent out immediately is good.)				
9. **Common community services** (Property is connected to water, electricity, gas, telephone; refuse collection is organised; and access roads are made up and are a town responsibility rather than that of owners: all connected now is good; mostly connected now is average; none connected yet is poor.)				
10. **Management company arrangements** (Is there is a functioning arrangement for managing any common parts to the building, such as lifts, swimming pools, reception areas?)				
11. **Resale prospects** (Have many similar properties been sold?: none warrants a low score; dozens a high score.)				
Developer status				
12. **Previous experience** (Has the developer a successful track record of building properties in this area?)				

13. **Financial status** (Is the developer backed by a substantial financial institution underwriting progress payments?)				
14. **Build quality** (Are the developers other projects of an acceptable standard?)				
15. **Referrals** (Can the developer provide several references from satisfied overseas buyers?: no references would be poor; 3 or more good)				
Rental prospects				
16. **Holiday market** (Is there an established market for ski-ing, beach holidays or some other unique attraction that appeals to international visitors?: market undeveloped would be poor; well established market with tour operators in place would be good.)				
17. **All-season appeal** (Does the area have attractions that cover more than one season?: 1 season would be poor; 2 average; and all-year appeal good.)				
18. **Business and other longer-term rental markets** (What are the prospects for renting to business people, diplomats, executives on secondment?: no embassies or international businesses in the area would warrant a poor score; a substantial population of such bodies a high score.)				
19. **Students** (Are there universities, language schools or other substantial student bodies in need of accommodation in the immediate neighbourhood?: none would be poor; 1 average and several would warrant a high score.)				
20. **Occupation rate** (Overall, what is your realistic estimate of for how many weeks of the year this property could be let?: under 16 weeks a year would be poor; over 36 exceptional.)				

Purchase costs and related financial matters				
21. Initial price (Is the purchase price within your budget?: 10% above is poor; 10% below merits a good score.)				
22. Essential repairs, renovations and additions (How much will it cost to bring the property up to the desired standard to meet the demands of the local rental markets?: a sum that will put you over your purchase price budget is poor; one that leaves a surplus for dealing with contingencies is good.)				
23. Availability of local skilled workmen (Serious labour shortage warrants a low score; a wide choice of reputable experienced tradespeople a high one.)				
24. Legal and transaction costs (Are these average for the country?: below average is good; above average poor.)				
25. Mortgage finance (What proportion of the capital cost can be supported by a mortgage?: less than 70% is poor; over 95% is good. Even if you don't require finance, your buyer may.)				
Score				
(Maximum score is 4 x 25 = 100; less than 70 is unlikely to prove to be a profitable investment.)				

Index

Printed in the United States
By Bookmasters